Transport Services in the Law of the Sea and the World Trade Organization

Studies in Global Economic Law
Studien zum globalen Wirtschaftsrecht
Études en droit économique mondial

edited by Thomas Cottier

Volume 14

PETER LANG
Bern · Berlin · Bruxelles · Frankfurt am Main · New York · Oxford · Wien

Chuyang Liu

Maritime Transport Services in the Law of the Sea and the World Trade Organization

PETER LANG
Bern · Berlin · Bruxelles · Frankfurt am Main · New York · Oxford · Wien

Bibliographic information published by Die Deutsche Nationalbibliothek
Die Deutsche Nationalbibliothek lists this publication in the Deutsche Nationalbibliografie; detailed bibliographic data is available on the Internet at ‹http://dnb.d-nb.de›.

British Library and Library of Congress Cataloguing-in-Publication Data:
A catalogue record for this book is available from *The British Library*, Great Britain.

Library of Congress Cataloging-in-Publication Data

Liu, Chuyang.
Maritime transport services in the law of the sea and the World Trade Organization / Chuyang Liu.
p. cm. – (Studies in global economic law = Studien zum globalen wirtschaftsrecht = Etudes en droit économique mondial, 1423-9531 ; v. 14)
Includes bibliographical references.
ISBN 978-3-0343-0099-5 (alk. paper)
1. Maritime law. 2. Foreign trade regulation. 3. Law of the sea. I. Title.
K4150.L58 2009
343.09'6–dc22

2009036745

ISSN 1423-9531
ISBN 978-3-0343-0099-5

Hochfeldstrasse 32, CH-3012 Bern, Switzerland
info@peterlang.com, www.peterlang.com, www.peterlang.net

Printed in Germany

Acknowledgement

Sponsored by the Swiss Government, I began my research work as a visiting scholar in the World Trade Institute from September 2000. My supervisor was Professor Thomas Cottier, the Managing Director of the Institute. He is also Professor of European and International Economic Law at the University of Bern. With a long-standing involvement in GATT/WTO activities, not only did Professor Cottier serve on the Swiss negotiating team of the Uruguay Round from 1986 to 1993, he has also served as a member or chair of several GATT or WTO panels.

During one of our early discussions in late 2000, Professor Cottier advised that I consider a doctoral project on the relationship between the law of the sea and the WTO. Little research having previously been done in this area, under his guidance, I immediately started with the preparatory work. This was the beginning of my research journey. In early 2001, I was granted a two-year doctoral funding from the Swiss National Foundation. I would like to express my appreciation to this Foundation for its sponsorship of my work. My thanks also go to the World Trade Institute, where I spent most of my research time.

Giving the law of the sea elements of this work, in 2002, Professor Cottier sent me to the Lauterpacht Centre for International Law, Cambridge University of the UK as visiting fellow. I worked there under the supervision of Professor James Crawford, who was the Director of the Centre and a member of the United Nations International Law Commission. I would like to thank Professor Crawford for his advice on my thesis.

During the years working with Professor Cottier, he had given me many opportunities to participate in high level academic activities in Switzerland and other European countries. Without his guidance, support and encouragement, I would not be able to finish this rewarding intellectual voyage. I am most grateful to Professor Cottier for what he did for me over many years.

I also owe special thanks to Professor Ichiro Araki from Yokohama University, Japan, for his External Examiner's Evaluation Report on my thesis.

The other person I am indebted to for the completion of this work, is my mentor and friend, Mr Mark Brownell from the Western Australia Government. Mark works as the key policy advisor in the State Department of Transport. From late 2008 to early 2009, Mark spent a lot of time giving an overhaul review to the language and style of my thesis. His advice is indispensable to the appropriate presentation of this work. I express my heartfelt gratitude to Mark for his invaluable help.

Chuyang Liu
2009, Melbourne

Table of Contents

Part Two
Analysis of Selected Issues

Part Three
Jurisdiction and Dispute Settlement

Part Four
Conclusions

Preface

Ever since the beginnings of international law, the law of the sea has been of paramount importance for international trade. The regime of the high seas and access to ports was an issue of prime importance, shaping international trade relations over time. Yet, the law of the sea and international trade regulation, in particular under GATT since World War II, emerged as two very distinct areas of law, hardly interfacing with each other. The same holds true for maritime law, entailing regulation of commerce. The WTO emerged in parallel to the LOS Convention, both areas each amounting to perhaps the broadest efforts in international treaty making since the 1970s. Both areas, moreover, are accompanied by additional instruments under the auspices of the International Maritime Organization. The relationship of trade regulation and the law of the sea has hardly been explored. The same is true for trade regulation and commercial, maritime law. Unlike environmental law, or human rights, the triangular linkage still waited to be explored in greater depth. This is what this is book is all about.

Dr. Chuyang Liu, former lecturer in maritime law in the People's Republic of China and current senior adviser in a global professional services company, undertakes to explore this relationship in her doctoral dissertation, based upon a project supported by the Swiss National Research Foundation and the World Trade Institute at the University of Bern, Switzerland. The book essentially focuses on the general relationship of the WTO law and the law of the seas. It then turns to selected and specific issues, in particular access to ports, access to cargo in coastal shipping (cabotage) and access to cargo in international shipping. The book deals with the problem of choice of law and competing jurisdiction between trade law and maritime law. The inclusion of services in WTO law will render the relationship of great importance in the future as the agreement basically covers maritime transportation. It is a matter of time until the current exclusion of it under special exemptions will be reviewed in future negotiations. The book provides the background and a normative basis for approaching some the problems which Members of the WTO will have to address in coming years. Many other pertinent facets, in particular subsidies to shipbuilding, TBT and SPS measures restricting landing of goods and other types of controls, labour standards for sailors and port workers, access to auxiliary port services await for further work. The present book offers a most valuable foundation for further efforts in the field, which should be encouraged.

The work of Dr. Chuyang Liu is the fruit of a long and impressing working process. The author undertook extensive studies in WTO law which, at the time, was new to Chinese scholars upon the entry of China into the WTO in 2001. I sincerely wish to congratulate the author to her effort of venturing into this truly new triangular relation of areas of international law.

Bern, July 2009 Prof. Thomas Cottier

Abbreviations

AB	Appellate Body (WTO)
ABR	Appellate Body Report (WTO)
ADA	Anti-Dumping Agreement (WTO)
AJIL	American Journal of International Law
APEC	Asia Pacific Economic Cooperation
Art.	Article
ASEAN	Association of South East Asian Nations
ASIL	American Society of International Law
B. C.	Before Christ
BIMCO	Baltic and International Maritime Conference
BISD	(WTO) Basic Instruments and Selected Documents
BOP	Balance of Payments
BPM5	Fifth edition of the IMF *Balance of Payments Manual*
CEWAL	Associated Central West Africa Lines
c. i. f.	cost, insurance and freight
CIRM	International Radio-Maritime Committee
CITES	Convention on International Trade in Endangered Species of Wild Flora and Fauna
CMI	Comite Maritime International
COLREG	Convention on the International Regulations for Preventing Collision at Sea
COSCO	China Ocean Shipping Company
CPC	the Central Product Classification (UN)
CRF	Clean Report of Finding (preshipment inspection)
CTE	Committee on Trade and Environment (WTO)
DG	Director General (WTO); Direction Generale (EC)
DSB	Dispute Settlement Body (WTO)
DSU	Dispute Settlement Understanding (WTO)
EC	European Community; European Communities
ECJ	European Court of Justice
ed., eds.	editor, editors
EEC	European Economic Community

EEZ	Exclusive Economic Zone
EFTA	European Fair Trade Association
e.g.	exempli gratia (for example)
EJIL	European Journal of International Law
ELJ	European Law Journal
EU	European Union
FAO	UN Food and Agriculture Organization
FATSFCN	Foreign affiliates trade in services statistics (UN)treaty of Friendship, Commerce and Navigation
FCN	(treaty on) friendship, commerce and navigation
FDI	foreign direct investment
FIATA	the International Association of Freight Forwarders' Associations
FMC	Federal Maritime Commission (US)
FOB, f.o.b.	free on board
FONASBA	the Federation of National Associations of Ship Brokers and Agents
FTAA	Free Trade Area for the Americas
g	gram
GATS	General Agreement on Trade in Services (WTO)
GATT	General Agreement on Tariff and Trade (WTO)
GDP	Gross Domestic Product
Harv. Int'l L.J.	Harvard International Law Journal
Harv. L. Rev.	Harvard Law Review
IACS	the International Association of Classification Societies
IALA	International Association of Lighthouse Authorities
IAPH	International Association of Ports and Harbors
ICAO	International Civil Aviation Organization
ICC	International Chamber of Commerce
ICFTU	International Confederation of Free Trade Unions
ICJ	International Court of Justice
ICS	International Chamber of Shipping
ICTSD	International Centre for Trade and Sustainable Development
i.e.	id est (that is)
IFIA	International Federation of Inventors' Associations
IICL	the Institute of International Container Lessors
ILC	International Law Commission
ILM	International Legal Materials

ILO	International Labor Organization
ILU	Institute of London Underwriters
IMCO	Inter-governmental Maritime Consultative Organization
IMF	International Monetary Fund
IMLI	International Maritime Law Institute (IMO)
IMO	International Maritime Organization
IMPA	International Maritime Pilots' Association
INTERTANKO	the International Association of Independent Tanker Owners
IP	intellectual property
ISF	the International Shipping Federation Ltd.
ISIC	the International Standard Industrial Classification
ISO	International Organization for Standardization
ISSA	the International Ship Suppliers Agency
IT	Information Technology
ITLOS	International Tribunal for the Law of the Sea
ITO	International Trade Organization
IUMI	International Union of Marine Insurance
JIEL	Journal of International Economic Law
JWT	Journal of World Trade
LDCs	least developed countries
LIRMA	the London Insurance and Reinsurance Market Association
LNTS	League of Nations Treaty Series
LOS Convention	UN Convention on the Law of the Sea 1982
MARPOL	International Convention for the Prevention of Pollution from Ships
MEA	Multilateral Environmental Agreement
MFN	most favored nation (clause, principle or treatment)
MIT	Massachusetts Institute of Technology
MLAANZ	Maritime Law Association of Australia and New Zealand
MOC	Ministry of Communications (P.R. China)
MOFTEC	Ministry of Foreign Trade and Economic Cooperation (P.R. China)
MOU	memorandum of understanding
MTCNAFTA	Maritime Transport Committee (OECD)North America Free Trade Agreement
MTS	Maritime Transport Services
NAFTA	North American Free Trade Agreement
NGMTS	Negotiating Group on Maritime Transport Services (WTO)

NGO	non-governmental organizations
N., No., Nr.	Number
NT	national treatment (principle or clause)
NVCBO	Non-vessel Carriage Business Operator
NVOCC	Non-vessel Operating Common Carrier
OECD	Organization of Economic Cooperation and Development
OJ	Official Journal (EC)
OSRA	Ocean Shipping Reform Act (US)
OTC	Organization for Trade Cooperation
OTIs	ocean transportation intermediaries
p./pp.	page/pages
para./paras.	Paragraph, paragraphs
p.a.	per annum
PCIJ	Permanent Court of International Justice
PRC	People's Republic of China
PSI	Preshipment Inspection
QRs	quantitative restrictions
RBPs	restrictive business practices
RTA	Regional trade agreement
S. s.	section
S & D	special and differential treatment
1993SNA	System of National Accounts, 1993
SOLAS	International Convention for the Safety of Life at Sea
SPS	Sanitary and Phytosanitory Agreement (WTO)
STCW	(international convention on) Standards of Training, Certification and Watchkeeping
STEs	state trading enterprises
TACA	Trans-Atlantic Conference Agreement
TBR	Trade Barriers Regulation (EC)
TBT	Technical Barrier to Trade Agreement (WTO)
TEU	Twenty-foot Equivalent Units
TIR	Transports Internationaux Routiers (international Customs transit system)
TPR	trade policy review (WTO)
TPRM	trade policy review mechanism (WTO)
TRIMs	(Agreement on) Trade-related Investment Measures (WTO)
TRIPs	(Agreement on) Trade-related Intellectual Property (WTO)
TSA	Transpacific Stabilization Agreement

TSS	traffic separation scheme
UCC	the Uniform Commercial Code
UK	United Kingdom
UKTS	United Kingdom Treaty Series
UN	United Nations
UNCED	UN Conference on Environment and Development
UNCITRAL	UN Centre for International Trade Law
UNCLOS I, II & III	the 1st, 2nd and 3rd UN Conferences on the Law of the sea
UNCTAD	UN Conference on Trade and Development
UNDP	UN Development Programme
UNECE	UN Economic Commission for Europe
UNEP	UN Environment Programme
UNESCAP	UN Economic and Social Commission for Asia and the Pacific
UNIDROIT	International Institute for the Unification of Private Law
UNITAR	UN Institutes for Training and Research
UNSITC	UN Standard International Trade Classification
UNTS	UN Treaty Series
UPU	Universal Postal Union
UR	Uruguay Round
U.S., US(A)	United States (of America)
USD	US dollar
USSR	The Union of Socialist Soviet Republics
WCO	World Customs Organization
WIPO	World Intellectual Property Organization
WPDR	Working Party on Domestic Regulation (WTO)
WTO	World Trade Organization
Yale J. Int'l Law	Yale Journal of International Law

Part One
Foundations

1 Introduction

Prior to the advent of the United Nations Convention on the Law of the Sea in 1982 (the LOS Convention), the focus of the law of the sea was on navigation and shipping. With the coming of the LOS Convention, the utility of the sea, in particular the continental shelf and exclusive economic zone, has been greatly expanded. This is also the case with the regulation of marine natural resources, which were brought under more uniform, strict and transparent disciplines on an international scale and had exerted crucial influences on maritime transport and trade. On the one hand, with more demanding requirements imposed on maritime transport, relating to, for example, seaworthiness, due diligence, tort, privity, and maritime liens, the safety of maritime transport and the more reliable and efficient operation of international trade have therefore been noticeably assured. On the other hand, some relevant rules and regulations may at the same time constitute technical barriers to trade and restrict access to free trade and market. Such regulations are mainly based on the conditions for the right of passage in certain maritime zones, shipping safety, prevention and control of pollution, and the right of access of land-locked states.

Before the establishment of the WTO in 1995, the GATT 1947 was a relatively self-contained legal regime which was limited to disciplines on goods. With the expansion of trade rules to services and intellectual property under the new WTO framework, and foremost the reinforcement of dispute settlement mechanism, the WTO has been integrated as a part of international law which can no longer be isolated. This has been mainly experienced in the field of trade and environment, where rules sometimes are mutually supportive and sometimes cause considerable tensions[1]. The

1 The relationship between trade and environment in the WTO is mainly worked out in two ways: the Committee on Trade and Environment, and the Environment-Related Provisions in WTO Agreements. For further read-

case law of the WTO has made considerable progress in interfacing the two areas, yet the matter is far from being solved and settled[2].

This work explores another issue critical to international trade – the impact of the interface relationship of the WTO trade law and the law of the sea on maritime transport services. The inclusion of services in the WTO system under the GATS has broadened the relevance of the WTO law for maritime transport and navigation, which have essentially come under the umbrella of the trading system, albeit still operating under basic exemptions for maritime transport services at this stage. Theoretically, the rules under the GATT 1994 in respect of goods already fully apply to maritime transport, and the principles of the WTO law in respect of securing market access rights and non-discrimination have been of increasing relevance to this field. Although no substantive agreement was reached on this issue in the Uruguay Round, there are ongoing discussions on achieving a more open shipping market and further liberalization of maritime transport services.

The hypothesis of this work is based on the feasibility of mutual integration of these two international systems and the potential for commonalties. These systems to date have still operated in different and independent regimes with different constituencies, and suffer from lack of co-ordination and interaction. Through analysis of certain issues that are likely to overlap and create tensions in both forums, the research offers an insight into how the two systems may

ing: Gary P. Sampson & W. Bradnee Chambers: *Trade, Environment, and the Millennium*, UN University Press, Tokyo, 1999; Horst Siebert: *Economics of the Environment Theory and Policy*, Springer-Verlag, Heidelberg, 1998 (5th edition); Caroline London, Michael Llamas: *EC Law on Protection of the Environment and the Free Movement of goods*, Butterworths, 1995.

2 Cases in the WTO dealing with fisheries and the protection of marine environment include: US-Shrimp Case, the Tuna-dolphin Cases, and the Shrimp-Turtles Case; for further readings on the Shrimp Case, see Dukgeun Ahn: "Environmental Disputes in the GATT/WTO: before and after US-SHRIMP Case", Michigan Journal of International Law, Vol. 20. No. 4, 1999; Rebecca DeWinter: "Issues of Fairness in the Tuna-Dolphin Cases", available at the website of International Economics Study Centre: http://internationalecon.com revisited in February 2006.

achieve further harmonization and mutual integration. It also examines the issue of international organizations and international dispute settlement, including the improvement of the WTO case law, the overlapping jurisdictions between panels and the Appellate Body of the WTO and other pertinent international courts/tribunals such as the ICJ and the ITLOS. The research will be of interest in respect of further study on the relationship of public international law and the WTO trade law.

This work assesses the convergence and divergence of maritime transport services in respect of the law of the sea and the WTO in some of their most important aspects. Particular emphasis is laid on the substantive integration of the law of the sea regulations with disciplines under the WTO. After a brief exploration of the evolving process of maritime transport in the law of the sea and the WTO, the study shifts to the analysis of selected related issues. Three areas that may constitute non-tariff barriers to trade in maritime transport services are examined: the right of access to port, maritime cabotage and international liner shipping. Corresponding discussion is then undertaken, especially in respect of the possibility of integrating these issues into the framework of international regulatory regimes, in particular that of the WTO. The study concludes with a systematic analysis of relevant dispute settlement forums under the LOS Convention and the WTO. Recommendations are then made in respect of assessing jurisdiction and the choice of forum, including an analogy to private international law.

To the present, the WTO regulatory system has dealt with a number of issues relating to the law of the sea, focusing essentially on fisheries and the protection of the marine environment. These cases, however, addressed either anti-dumping, subsidies or environment-related issues, rather than the law of the sea as such. Moreover, there has been considerable discussion on the relationship of fishing subsidies and the environment, as a case of whether further the WTO disciplines may bring about improvements in the conservation of marine resources. However, there has been little further systematic research on the interface between these two major areas of international law, which have to date been developing separately as two succinct systems and operating in different forums.

This work provides an innovative discussion of the complex subject of maritime transport services. However, significant challenges are imposed on research in this area because of the sensitivity of the topics in political and international trade terms, together with the depth and breadth of the field. This situation also partially explains why negotiations on maritime transport services within the WTO have encountered serious controversy over the years, and failed to produce the anticipated breakthrough despite the efforts of the member countries.

In addressing these issues, the study is divided into four parts.

Part I makes a survey of maritime transport services in the law of the sea and the WTO. Part II turns to selected issues. It discusses port access both in the law of the sea and the WTO law. It deals with the problem of coastal shipping (cabotage) and with access to cargo in international liner shipping. Part III turns to issue of jurisdiction and dispute settlement under the law of the sea and WTO law. The work concludes with brief reflection and policy recommendations in Part IV.

Part I: Chapter 1 provides a snapshot of the state of research, dissertation objects and summary of the work. Chapter 2 explores the evolution of the issues and points out that while the law of the sea has been serving international trade over centuries, it has been entrusted with new meanings and new fulfillments in today's new era. Although maritime transport is still at the heart of major law of the sea conventions such as the LOS Convention, it is no longer the sole focus of the law of the sea. The key task is to achieve a "co-regulation" of maritime transport between the LOS Convention and other international organizations (in particular the WTO), that have different, but sometimes overlapping jurisdictions. This situation is made more complex by the fact that, with the transforming of the self-contained legal regime of the GATT to the comprehensive WTO law, maritime transport has been essentially included under the umbrella of the international trading system. Many of the WTO disciplines fully apply to this area of service, but at the same time, there is no clear delineation of the jurisdictional relationships between international institutions.

Chapter 3 explores the relevance of the WTO principles to the operation of maritime transport services. It starts with a brief introduction to the GATT/GATS and the related liberalization of trade in services, it then discusses some important issues and principles as well as the main impediments on maritime transport services. The discussion ends up by putting forward the recommendation that instead of the three-pillar approach, an integrated model schedule may help to facilitate the WTO negotiations in this field.

Part II: Chapter 4 introduces port access issue in the law of the sea, which includes the port state's jurisdiction over its ports in customary international law, key international conventions and treaties on this issue, as well as relevant work under international organizations. It then studies principles concerning port access and use of port facilities in the GATT/GATS provisions and agreements. GATT Article V is the main provision for the study. The Chapter addresses the question of whether this provision implies a right to port. The conclusion it draws is that Article V does not imply such a right although it does contribute to the facilitation of transit for international trade. The proposals of this Chapter include options to further strengthen the WTO principles in order to facilitate the access to port. Besides enhancing transparency in the relevant procedures and requirements for port access, it also makes recommendation on the strengthening of bilateral and regional consultation and cooperation on this issue. Furthermore, the work recommends that GATT Article VIII on fees and formalities should also be clarified in order to make it more operational. GATT Articles XX and XXI could be used by port states to hinder the access right of other countries' vessels under the guise of safety or security considerations. Countries should be cautious when interpreting these articles and try to distinguish between justified protection and disguised protectionism.

Coastal shipping is one of the most controversial areas in maritime transport where no consensus has been reached as to whether or not it shall be deregulated. Chapter 5 discusses the economic issues and legal framework for cabotage. It then studies the current regulatory mechanisms on cabotage under both international institutions and domestic legislations. The cabotage policy of a number of countries is discussed, from which the work identifies little evidence that the deregulation initiatives in countries such as New Zealand have adversely affected the domestic economy or national defence. This work recommends that cabotage protection should be phased out, but on a gradual basis due to its complex nature. At the same time, more domestic and international cooperation and consultation should be conducted for the benefit for international trade.

Moreover, this work suggests that the WTO principles on security exceptions should be clarified. These are reflected in GATT Article XXI, GATS Article XIVbis, Article 2.2 of TBT Agreement, and Article XXII of the Government Procurement Agreement.

There have been substantial debates over a long period of time as to whether or not the anti-competition exemption system for liner shipping should be repealed. Chapter 6 argues that under current global market circumstances it is still premature to replace the present regulatory instrument with some sort of new system. Instead, this work takes the position that regulation of liner shipping in different countries and regions should be brought into a more harmonized monitoring mechanism under a WTO framework. Against a background of the existing GATS provisions on restrictive business practices being merely for information exchange and consultation, this work puts forward suggestions on ways to establish pro-competitive principles and strengthen the enforcement capability of developing countries.

Part III: Chapter 7 deals with jurisdiction and dispute settlement. Based on earlier discussions, this Part examines the convergence and divergence among the various jurisdictions of international institutions. It introduces the dispute settlement systems under the WTO and the LOS Convention, on basis of which it assesses the jurisdictional similarities and differences among the WTO, the International Court of Justice and the International Tribunal for the Law of the Sea.

This work then draws an analogy to private international law in assisting the determination of jurisdiction and the choice of legal forums. The EU-Chilean Swordfish case, in which the dispute settlement mechanisms of both the WTO and the LOS Convention was invoked, illustrates how disputes may end up in two jurisdictional forums coming to contradictory or at least incompatible decisions. This case is discussed as an example of how to determine the most substantive links in a dispute.

Part IV: This part summarizes the whole work and elaborates on a number of recommendations on the three selected issues in Part II.

2 Maritime Transport Services in the Law of the Sea

2.1 General Background

2.1.1 Industry Structures and Regulatory Regimes

The term "services" represents a wide range of products whose common characteristic is their intangibility. Allan Fisher and Colin Clark in the 1930's and 1940's were among the first to propose a breakdown of the economy into three sectors: primary, secondary and tertiary[3]. Clark described the tertiary sector as "all forms of economic activity not included under primary and secondary". This description reflects that for a long time the tertiary sector of services were considered as residuals, whereas manufacturing was understood to be a solid structural basis on which the rest of the economy would lie[4].

T.P. Hill is regarded as the first scholar to define services as opposed to simply categorizing them as residuals. He defined services as "a change in the condition of a person, or a good belonging to some economic unit, with the prior agreement of the former person or economic unit"[5]. Although the definition of services has

3 Angus Maddison, "Quantifying and interpreting world development: macro-measurement before and after Colin Clark", Australian Economic History Review, Volume 44, Issue 1, March 2004, Blackwell Publishing.

4 Id.

5 T.P. Hill, "On goods and services", in the Review of Income and Wealth, Number 4, December 1977, pp. 315–338. For analysis on services and alternative definitions, see also Dorothy I. Riddle, *Service-Led Growth: The Role of the Service Sector in World Development*, New York, Praeger, 1986; Jadish N. Bhagwati, "Splintering and disembodiment of services and developing nations", The World Economy, 7, June 1984, pp. 133–143.

evolved over time, no consensus has been reached and the economic literature uses the term in many different ways. This definitional problem reflects the difficulty of adopting a standard definition that will meet all the different characteristics of services[6].

Maritime transport services can be classified into several types of services, from shipping and navigation to the access and use of sea port facilities[7]. Each of these services is organized in different and complex ways[8]. Some of them such as bulk shipping are strongly competitive while others such as liner shipping had been dominated by rate-setting conferences for decades. Some services are operated by state enterprises, while others are privately run but highly protected with strong domestic political lobbies and long-established labour union practices.

Apart from international shipping, port and auxiliary services are also integrated parts of the maritime transport system which provides the interface between land and sea transport. Key services in these areas include cargo handling, storage and warehousing, maintenance and repair of vessels, as well as customs clearance, quarantine inspection and documentation processing. Maritime cabotage which offers preference to domestic shipping is also an important maritime transport service. Although some economists argue that the costs of cabotage protection is very high[9], countries

6 The definitional difficulty of services has been discussed by many scholars. See for example Peter Walters Daniels, *Service Industries: A Geographical Appraisal*, Routledge 1985, Chapter 1 of which focuses on the identity and delimitation of service industries.

7 For basic terminology applicable to maritime transport services see OECD "Information related to WTO and Maritime Transport Services", at: http://www.oecd.org/document revisited in July 2006; see also Benjamin Parameswaran, *The Liberalization of Maritime Transport Services, With Special Reference to the WTO/GATS Framework*, Springer, September 2004, p. 217.

8 The description of these services is made in the WTO paper: WTO Council for Trade in Services, "Maritime Transport Services, Background Note by the Secretariat", S/C/W/62, 16 November 1998, p. 2.

9 See for example, Nancy Ruth Fox, Lawrence J. White, "U.S. Ocean Shipping Policy: Going against the Tide", *Annals of the American Academy of Political and Social Science*, Vol. 553, Transport at the Millennium (Sep., 1997), pp. 75–86.

still essentially reserve domestic sea carriage for national-flag ships, for reasons of national security and the preservation of maritime skills. During the WTO negotiation on maritime transport services, it has also been proposed that multi-modal transport, which involves the use of one or more modes in addition to shipping by sea, should be incorporated into the negotiation. However, no consensus has been reached on this issue to date[10].

The focus of this work is on the general relationship of the law of the sea and the WTO together with a number of select issues, including access to ports, access to domestic sea freight (cabotage) and access to cargo in international shipping. However, it should be noted that many other facets not covered in this work, for example maritime-related labour law and standards, subsidies to shipbuilding, and access to auxiliary port services, are of equal importance to the relationship between the WTO and the law of the sea.

Maritime transport services are regulated under both domestic and international regulations[11]. Broadly speaking, these regulations and practices can be classified into two groups, the first being the rights and obligations of states, and the safety and protection of the environment; the second focuses on commercial activities in international shipping[12].

The regulations in the first group are based on international conventions under the authority of the UN (such as the LOS Convention and the IMO conventions), which reflect the opinions of the international community and put emphasis on public interest and social benefits[13]. The regulations in the second group fall more within the regime of national laws that aim to achieve economic

10 WTO Council for Trade in Services, "Maritime Transport Services, Background Note by the Secretariat", S/CSS/W/106, 4 October 2001, pp. 25–26.

11 For a detailed analysis of the regulatory framework of international maritime transport, see OECD Division of Transport, "Regulatory Issues in International Maritime Transport", 1999, Part II. The paper is available at OECD website: http://www.oecd.org/dataoecd revisited in July 2006.

12 Id. p. 26.

13 Id. p. 26.

or national objectives, together with ensuring national participation in commercial activities. The nature of the regulations in the latter group is rather mixed. Some of them, like competition or anti-trust laws, have the objective of freeing up the market, while others like cargo reservation schemes encourage market intervention. The value of these regulations should reflect their overall social and economic benefits, however the management of them remains problematic[14].

The rationale for safety and environmental regulations is that market intervention is necessary because of market failure to ensure ship safety and environmental protection in accordance with the accepted international standards. Market failure can be attributed to the following several reasons[15]: Firstly, from the point of view of the ship-owner, the ultimate goal of shipping is to maximize profits. There may not be a commercial benefit for the ship-owners in regards to the safety and environment issues. However, without the mandatory safety and environment regulations, there is a strong risk that low quality ship-owners and substandard ships will increase in numbers[16].

Secondly, the nature of international shipping gives rise to difficulty in assessing the responsibilities of accidents and incidents, a situation more complicated if ships are registered in flag states which have little interest in the management of these ships[17]. Besides, maritime insurance also means that those responsible for the operation and use of substandard ships do not have to bear any direct cost by themselves. Thirdly, the enormous costs related to oil spill suggest another powerful argument for providing internationally enforceable ways of effectively and adequately compensating for such loss or damage[18].

14 Id. p. 26.
15 Id. p. 27.
16 Id. p. 27. See also Alan TAN Khee Jin, "The Sea Transport Industry and the Challenge of State Regulations", UNITAR Conference on the Seas and Security, 6–8 March 2002, Hiroshima, Japan.
17 Id. p. 27.
18 Id. p. 27.

In respect of competition, the capital intensive nature of international liner shipping has brought entry barriers to shipping operators, which is particularly the case in long distance routes with limited cargo volumes. In order to avoid any related service unreliability which may affect shippers and trade flows, governments have often allowed liner shipping conferences, which, through co-operative arrangements, offered more reliable and frequent services as well as better equipment and greater price stability[19].

2.1.2 *Further Liberalization Initiatives*

Services represent the fastest growing sector of the global economy, and trade in services has grown faster than trade in goods over the past decade[20]. Statistics show that the performance of the services sectors can make the difference between rapid and sluggish growth[21]. Developing countries, in particular, are likely to benefit from further domestic liberalization and the elimination of barriers to their exports. The income gains from a reduction in protection to services are estimated to be multiples of those from trade liberalization in goods. Liberalization of trade in services, accompanied by the reform of complementary policies, may lead to improvements in performance in substantial ways[22].

Safe, reliable and competitive maritime transport services benefit the economy as a whole and are key factors in efficient production of both goods and services. The WTO observed that ship-

19 Id. p. 28.

20 For more elaboration on the growth of services and their impacts on global economy, see for example Hoekman, B. and Sauvé, P., "Liberalizing Trade in Services" Discussion Paper No. 243. Washington D. C.: The World Bank, 1994.

21 See for example, Hoekman, Bernard and Braga Carlos A. Primo, "Protection and trade in services: a survey", Policy Research Working Paper, No. 1747, April 1997.

22 Sherry M. Stephenson, "Approaches to Services Liberalization by Developing Countries", Publication of the Organization of American States Trade Unit, February 1999. The paper is available at: http://www.sice.oas.org/tunit/studies revisited in July 2006.

ping remains by far the main mode of international transport of goods and maritime transport is still an expanding activity[23]. Maritime transport is thus an important facilitator of world trade, and this role becomes even more apparent and crucial in an expanded and diversified world trade system[24]. A proper treatment of this sector in the world trade system through the GATS Agreement is thus essential.

Maritime transport provides services to other sectors, notably agricultural, resources and manufacturing. An efficient and competitive maritime transport network is crucial to the sustained competitiveness of these sectors. Taken as a whole, the international maritime transport sector is regarded as liberal and competitive, especially when compared with other services sectors and other transport sub-sectors[25]. The international bulk services which serve agricultural and resource sectors operate largely without unnecessary regulatory restriction, with price and contracts being set in highly-competitive, price-sensitive markets. On the other hand, the international liner services which serve the manufacturing sectors operate mainly within a framework of liner shipping conferences, which are industry self-regulated arrangements operating in a competitive market-place[26].

However, there still exist restrictive policies and practices that limit market access, such as numerical quotas for shipping providers on given routes, exclusive service agreements and economic needs tests[27]. Further market-opening reforms will be worthwhile and can be achieved through bilateral, regional and multilateral forums and mechanisms. Under the framework of the GATS, liberalization promoting more liberal market access should be pursued, building upon the core principles of MFN and national treatment.

There are substantial experiences illustrating that restrictions on trade in services and investment incur high cost and liberaliza-

23 Supra note 8, p. 3.
24 Supra note 8, pp. 2–3.
25 Id. p. 2.
26 Id. p. 2.
27 Id. p. 8.

tion can lead to efficiency and welfare gains[28]. For example, this is demonstrated by the case of the US Merchant Marine Act of 1920 – the Jones Act[29], where foreign shipping firms are prohibited from transporting goods or people from one US location to another[30]. The Jones Act and its impact on coastal shipping will be further discussed in Chapter 5 of this work. The purported rationale for this restriction is the need to maintain an adequate marine capacity to meet defence needs, which is, however, proved not effective during the 1990 Gulf War, where American subsidized merchant fleet directly distributed only 6 ships to the more than 460 ships that transported military materials into the Saudi ports. Yet studies have indicated that the cost of this protection is at least $3 billion annually[31]. It is also shown that prohibition of this restriction would increase cabotage traffic and demand for services incidental to water transport, while the decline in domestic employment in cabotage sector could be more than compensated by the increased employment in other sectors[32].

28 Hoekman, B. and Braga Carlos A. Primo, supra note 21, p. 12.

29 The elaboration of the nature and definition of Jones Act is available at the US Department of Transportation: http://www.dot.gov revisited in July 2006. According to Jones Act, foreign-built (or rebuilt) vessels are prohibited from engaging in coastwise trade either directly between two points of the US or via a foreign port. Trade with US island territories and possessions are included in the definition of coastwise trade (Merchant Marine Act of 1920 – the Jones Act, which requires that vessels used to transport cargo and passengers between US ports be owned by US citizens, built in US shipyards, and manned by US citizen crews. The Jones Act and related statutes are known as cabotage laws). Moreover, the definition of vessels has been interpreted by the US Administration to cover hover-craft and inflatable rafts. In addition, no foreign-built vessels can be documented and registered for dredging, towing or salvaging in the US. Third countries are thus not able to have access to the US market at a time when part of the ageing US fleet needs to be renewed and many US ports are in need of dredging.

30 Hoekman, B. and Braga Carlos A. Primo, supra note 21, p. 13.

31 Id., p. 13. See also Cato Handbook for Congress, Policy Recommendations for the 108th Congress, Cato Institute, Washington D.C., US: http://www.cato.org revisited in July 2006, p. 12.

32 Id. 12.

Moreover, a study on the effects on flag discrimination and cargo preference policies maintained by Chile until the late 1970s serves as an example of the qualitative effects of these restrictions[33]. Although the cargo preference policies expanded the size of the Chilean flag fleet, it was not only inefficient but also imposed higher costs on shippers than would have been available in a competitive environment. The restrictions also restricted the availability of efficient/specialized ships required to transport new products developed by Chilean industries during the 1970s, such as fresh fruits and fish[34]. Subsequent liberalization of flag discrimination has led to great diversification of Chilean exporters away from domestic shipping lines, allowing products to be shipped at significantly lower cost[35].

2.1.3 Evolution of Maritime Jurisprudence

It is recorded that around 1500 B.C., the Phoenicians founded several colonies in the Mediterranean, amongst which was the island of Rhodes, located at the crossroads of traffic in the eastern Mediterranean[36]. Because of its strategic position between Egypt, Cyprus, the Syrian, Phoenician coasts and the Greek cities, Rhode emerged as an important intermediary point between Greece and the Orient, and also the foremost commercial centre in the Mediterranean. The Rhodes believed in the philosophy of the freedom of the seas and acted as the protector of those who followed the sea[37].

33 Hoekman, B. and Braga Carlos A. Primo, supra note 21, p. 13.

34 Id. p. 14.

35 Id. p. 14.

36 Jean-Paul Rodrigue, Claude Comtois, Brian Slack, *The Geography of Transport Systems*, Part I, Routledge, 2006.

37 John Wilkinson, "The First Declaration of the Freedom of the Seas: The Rhodian Sea Laws", Appendix to Chapter XIX of John Wilkinson's paper "A Tentative Program for Simulation of Historical Ecology of the Mediterranean", The Mediterranean Marine Environment and Development of Region, Pacem in Maribus, pp. 391–92.

Between the 3rd and 2nd century B.C., the Rhodes codified the commercial practices of the time in the form of Rhodian sea law (the Rhodian Code) which was regarded as the foundation of modern maritime jurisprudence, that later influenced the Byzantine Empire and the Roman law[38]. The Rhodes Code was probably a codification of various ancient legal principles regarding navigation and commerce, which set up exclusive jurisdiction over its own and adjacent seas, and provided freedom for its own maritime commerce and trade. It included regulations regarding the partnership, joint ventures, charter parties and bills of lading, as well as established standards of behaviour of passengers on ship and the liability of commander or seaman in cases of carelessness or dereliction of duty.

The Digest of Justinian[39] recorded the earliest maritime codification by the Romans. It incorporated concepts from Rhodian maritime law from around 800 B.C. During the Middle Ages, several maritime codes emerged in the Mediterranean, the Atlantic and the Baltic Sea, which had much in common and borrowed from the Rhodian law and also from each other. Among them, the one with special significance was the maritime laws of the city Oleron, which were codified in 15th century into a famous manuscript known as "the Black Book of Admiralty"[40]. The laws and customs of Oleron contained in the Black Book were among the oldest law of the sea documents that survived. It was a compilation

38 It may be noted that the Rhodes was annexed by Rome in 164 B.C., and the rise of Rome in the Mediterranean put an end to the Rhodian ascendancy. When the Roman Empire was divided in 395 A.D., the Rhodes was assigned to the Eastern Roman (Byzantine) Empire. See John Wilkinson, id.

39 Alan Watson, "Revised English-language Edition of the Digest of Justinian", University of Pennsylvania Press, 1997. The Digest of Justinian was one of the four books of the Corpus Juris Civilis, drafted in Constantinople between 528 and 534 A.D., by a committee of 10 scholars under the Minister of Justice, Tribonian, at the order of Emperor Justinian I (483–565 A.D.). The other three books are the Institutes, the Code and the Novels.

40 Cambridge Journal Online, Volume 36, Issue 01 Mar.2000, available at: http://journals.cambridge.org revisited in April 2006.

of rules and precedents affecting the administration of maritime law and the functions of the Lord High Admiral of England and the officers of the Court, after Oleron was passed into the possession of England during the reign of King Henry II. The 15th century saw the birth of Maritime Code of Barcelona, which was considered to hold the same position as the Rhodian law in its day, and which was composed of around 300 chapters with detailed answers to many practical and legal problems in maritime commercial and trading affairs. The same period also saw the emergence of the Visby Sea laws[41], as well as the Hansa Towns Shipping Ordinance of the Hanseatic League[42], which was a comprehensive code covering essentially private law relationships.

The evolution of the law of the sea in its modern sense is an integral part of the growth of international law[43], which has strong relevance with the European countries' conflicts inside and outside Europe during the post-medieval time. An early example was Grotius's work titled "Mare Liberum", which was published in 1609 with the purpose of justifying the claims of the Dutch East India Company to trade in the Far East. This was in the context that the Portuguese claimed monopoly on trade in the area at that time[44].

The English navigation acts dating back to the 17th century had major impacts on the evolution of maritime transport and the development of international trade. The Navigation Acts were certain parliamentary legislation, more often addressed as the British

41 Visby is an island off Gothand in the Baltic and in the 20th century its name has been commemorated through the Visby amendments to the 1921 Hague Rules which governs the conditions for the carriage of goods by sea.

42 The Hanseatic League was a strong multinational alliance in Europe in the 15th and 16th century, which was composed of many cities (nearly 80 at the most) who banded together for the purpose of trade and commerce, and to control and suppress piracy and other harmful activities on the sea.

43 See for example, Charles Pergler, "Constitutional Recognition of International Law", Virginia Law Review, Vol. 30, No. 2 (March 1944), pp. 318–330.

44 Vieira, Monica Brito, "Mare Liberum vs. Mare Clausum: Grotius, Freitas, and Selden's Debate on Dominion over the Seas", Journal of the History of Ideas – Volume 64, Number 3, July 2003, pp. 361–377.

Acts of Trade[45]. The Acts were a product of the philosophy of mercantilism common at that time, whose purpose was to expand English trade and the establishment of colonial markets for English manufacturers. The rise of Dutch overseas trading, which threatened to drive English shipping from the seas, was the immediate cause of the Navigation Act of 1651, and it in turn was a major cause of the First Dutch War (1652–1654). This Act was expanded and amended by the successive Navigation Acts of 1662, 1663, 1670 and 1673, together with the Act to Prevent Frauds and Abuses of 1696. Mercantilism and associated trade legislation were drawn into question by the American Revolution, and the acts were finally repealed in 1849[46]. The impact of the Navigation Act 1651 on maritime cabotage will be further discussed in Chapter 5 of this work.

The development of modern maritime legislation has reflected both social and technological changes, including the defining and distinguishing of new types of vessels[47], as well as the stricter liability for pollution damages[48]. As an international industry, maritime transport requires the monitoring and supervision at an international level. Created in 1873, the International Law Association set up the Maritime Law Committee in 1897, which was among the earliest of the international organizations in the shipping field[49]. The 1924 York/Antwerp Rules and the 1924 Convention for the Unification of Certain Rules Relating to Bill of Lading are regarded

45 William Freeman Galpin, *A History of England,* Prentice-Hall, inc., New York, US, 1938, p. 540.

46 Robert L. Schuyler, *The Making of English History,* Dryden Press, 1952, pp. 638–639.

47 For example, see Canada Shipping Act s. 673; Federal Court Act s. 2 (1), United Kingdom, Hovercraft Act 1968; Supreme Court Act 1981 s. 24 (1); Merchant Shipping Act 1995 s. 170 (1).

48 See for example, Swedish Act on liability in case of oil pollution at sea; Merchant Shipping Act 1995 of UK, s. 153, 154, 155; Oil Pollution Act 1990 of the US, § 2702 (a).

49 Lawrence Juda, *International Law and Ocean Use Management,* Routledge UK, 1996, p. 17.

as the best accomplishments of the Maritime Law Committee of the International Law Association[50].

Created after World War I, the League of Nations Communications and Transit Organization adopted the Convention on the International Regime of Maritime Ports in 1923[51], which will be discussed in Chapter 4 of this work. With the winding-up of the League of Nations[52], this inter-governmental organization on shipping also came to an end. In 1946, the Temporary Transport and Communications Commission were set up by the Economic and Social Council in accordance with the recommendations of the UN Preparatory Commission, which recommended the establishment of an international organization to deal with technical matters concerning shipping, and coordinating and promoting further broader issues on a continuing basis. This development led to the adoption of the Convention on the International Maritime Organization (IMO)[53] by the UN Maritime Conference in 1948, which came into force on March 17, 1958.

Currently, there are a number of inter-governmental organizations concerned with maritime industry in one way or another. Some major ones such as the IMO and the UNCTAD-Shipping Committee will be discussed in the following Chapters of this work[54].

50 The legal texts of the two Rules are available from the website of Comite Maritime International at: http://www.comitemaritime.org/ revisited in June 2006.

51 "Research Guide to League of Nations Document and Publications", Northwestern University Library, US.

52 Amry Vandenbosch, Willard Newton Hogan, *The United Nations: Background, Organization, Functions, Activities*, McGraw-Hill, New York, US, 1952, p. 154.

53 The IMO was known until May 22, 1982, as the Inter-governmental Maritime Consultative Organization (IMCO).

54 Some other inter-governmental bodies or groups concerned with matters relating to shipping include: the International Oil Pollution Fund, the International Maritime Satellite Organization, the International Telecommunication Union, International Atomic Energy Agency, the UN Development Program, the UN Environment Program, the International Hydrographic Organization, the Organization for Economic Co-operation and Development, the EC, Organization of American States, the League of Arab States,

2.1.4 Evolution of Maritime Treaties and Conventions

While discussing the relationship between maritime law and trade law, it is interesting to note that several fundamental principles in modern international trade, such as the principles of national treatment and most-favoured-nation treatment, have their origin in maritime law and maritime treaties.

Granting other countries favourable treatment in commercial transactions is one of the most important principles in international trade. The first "favoured-nation" arrangement was granted by the kingdom of the Bosporus to Athens in the 4th century B.C. As the centre for the distribution of south Russian grains to Greece at that time, the kingdom of the Bosporus which was located in the Crimea granted ships destined for Athens loading priority and reduced harbour taxes. In return, the city Athens repaid the royal family with honorary citizenship.

The conception of bilateral treaties on friendship, commerce and navigation (FCN) emerged from as early as 12th and 13th centuries and were fully developed during the 17th and 18th centuries. They marked an important step in regulating economic relations among the emerging nation-states[55]. These treaties involved clauses dealing with most-favoured-nation status and national treatment, which later became pillars of the GATT/WTO frameworks.

During the 12th and 13th centuries, non-discrimination clauses between nations came into being in treaties on FCN, which was the earliest form of national treatment. One example was the Hanseatic League, in whose treaties non-discriminatory treatment among city-states concerning trade and navigation was stipulated.

---

and the Caribbean Community Secretariat. At the regional level, the United Nations Regional Commissions for Africa, Asia and the Pacific, Europe, Latin America, and Western Asia endeavour to achieve co-ordination in the development of maritime activities in the respective regions. Information source: the Maritime Law Association of the United States, http://www.mlaus.org revisited in June 2006.

55 George Schwarzenberger, *The Principles and Standards of International Economic Law*, Recueil des Cours – Academie de Droit International (1965/1), 1.

By the first half of the 20th century, the US had made a series of FCN treaties with several European countries[56].

The first MFN treatment appeared in provisions on commerce and navigation in the 1778 Treaty of Amity and Commerce between the US and France, Articles 2 and 3 of which set for the first time, clauses on conditional MFN treatment. The 1800 Convention between France and the US strengthened this relationship by establishing an unconditional MFN clause for trade and navigation. Furthermore, this Convention set up an article (Art. X) on the freedom to appoint commercial agents in both countries for the protection of trade. This seems to be the first time the concept of "agency service" was mentioned in a bilateral agreement.

One of the most important bilateral treaties containing provisions on navigation and commerce was the Treaties of Utrecht of 1713[57]. It was composed of a series of bilateral treaties between eight European countries: the Netherlands, Great Britain, Holy Roman Empire, Prussia, France, Portugal, Savoy and Spain. These Treaties put an end to the War of Spanish Succession (1701–13). Together with their numerous modifications later, they served as the basis for European diplomacy for the next 80 years. The Treaties of Utrecht have been cited by many scholars as the forerunner of the GATT[58].

In 1921, the International Law Association adopted a body of rules known as the Hague Rule in order to avoid differences in the use of bills of lading between countries and to achieve uniformity.

56 For example, Treaty of Friendship, Commerce and Consular Rights with Germany, 1923, http://usa.usembassy.de/garelations0139.htm revisited in July 2006.

57 The full text of the treaties can be found in "Major Peace Treaties of Modern History, 1648–1967", edited by Fred L. Israel (New York: Chelsea House, 1967), pp. 177–239.

58 See for example, John H. Jackson, *the World Trading System, Law and Policy of International Economic Relations*, 2nd edition (The MIT Press, 1997) Also see Pieter Verloren van Themaat, "Restructuring the International Economic Order: Some Keynotes", in *Restructuring the International Economic Order: The Role of Law and Lawyers*, Peter van Dijk, Fried van Hoof, Alfred Koers, and Kamiel Mortelmans, eds. (Deventer: Kluwer, 1987), 1.

It was originally meant to be incorporated by the parties in bills of lading, however later it was decided to make the rules compulsory[59], which were adopted in 1924 in the International Convention for the Unification of Certain Rules Relating to Bills of Lading (the Convention)[60].

The Hague Rules are seen as the first international attempt to harmonize international cargo liability rules, by establishing the minimum standards of legal responsibility for carriers concerning cargo loss or damage[61]. The Rules were amended by the Visby Protocol of 1968 (the Hague-visby Rules). These included certain technical amendments to the provisions of law in the Convention, including periods of limitation in which action must be brought, defences and limits of liability in actions founded in contracts or in tort, and the subrogation of servants or agents in the limits of liability of the carrier when they are sued directly. Any dispute between two or more Contracting Parties concerning the interpretation or application of the Convention which cannot be settled through negotiation is submitted to arbitration at the request of one party[62].

With the development of containerized cargoes from the 1970s, it became evident that further work was required in respect of granting more rights in favour of the shippers. Besides, there were also political changes since the introduction of the Hague Rules, when maritime powers generated overwhelming international political power that led to a pro-carrier approach. In 1971, through the auspices of the UNCITRAL, a new attempt was made to further harmonize international cargo liability rules. In 1976, a Draft Convention completed by the UNCITRAL was submitted to a diplomatic conference at Hamburg and resulted in the adoption of

59 C.R. Dunlop, "The Hague Rules, 1921", Journal of Comparative Legislation and International Law, Vol. 4, No. 1 (1922), pp. 24–34.

60 120 LNTS (League of Nations Treaty Series) 155.

61 Francis Reynolds, "The Hague Rules, The Hague-Visby Rules, and the Hamburg Rules", (1990) 7 MLAANZ Journal, pp. 16–34.

62 The Hague-Visby Rules, the Hague Rules as Amended by the Brussels Protocol 1968. Full text is available at Lex Mercatoria: http://www.jus.uio.no revisited in July 2006.

the UN Convention on the Carriage of Goods by Sea 1978 (the Hamburg Rules)[63]. These came into force in November 1992 and are seen as favouring shippers to the detriment of ship-owners and their liability insurers.

Besides the Hague, Hague-visby and the Hamburg Rules, important maritime conventions concerning carriage of goods and passengers include[64]:

- the UN Convention on International Multi-modal transport of Goods (Geneva 1980);
- Convention on the Contract for the International Carriage of Goods by Road (Geneva 1956);
- UN Convention on Contracts for the International Sale of Goods (Vienna 1980);
- UN Convention on the Liability of Operators of Transport Terminals in International Trade (Vienna 1991);
- UNCTAD Minimum Standards for Shipping Agents (1988);
- Convention on a Code of Conduct for Liner Conferences (Geneva 1974);
- International Convention on Safe Containers (Geneva 1972);
- Convention relating to Civil Liability in the Field of Maritime Carriage of Nuclear Material (Brussels 1971);
- CMI Rules for Electronic Bills of Lading;
- CMI Uniform Rules for Sea-waybills;
- International Commercial Terms 1990 (INCOTERMS);
- Convention Relating to the Carriage of Passengers and their Luggage by Sea (Athens 1974);
- UNCITRAL Model Law on Electronic Commerce; and
- The EC Convention on the Law Applicable to Contractual Obligations (Rome 1980)

63 Full text of the Rules is available from the website of Comite Maritime International at: http://www.comitemaritime.org/ revisited in June 2006.

64 For a comprehensive list of international conventions on admiralty and maritime law, see the website of supra note 63.

2.2 Maritime Transport in the 1982 LOS Convention

2.2.1 Codification of the Law of the Sea before the 1982 LOS Convention

Before the establishment of the UN, there had been considerable but unsuccessful efforts to codify the rules of customary international law applicable to the seas. When the League of Nations was replaced by the UN in 1945, a specific body, the International Law Commission (ILC), was founded with the aim of establishing progressive codification of international law. During the early years of its work, the ILC prepared articles on the high seas and territorial seas. By 1956, at the request of the UN General Assembly, the ILC produced a report covering most aspects of the law of the sea of contemporary importance. This paved the way for later codification work under the auspices of the UN[65].

The first United Nations conference on the law of the sea was convened in 1958, which produced four conventions dealing with the territorial sea and the contiguous zone, the high seas, fishing and conservation of the living resources of the high seas, and the continental shelf. This first UN Conference on the Law of the Sea (UNCLOS I), together with the 1958 Conventions on the Law of the Sea (the Geneva Conventions), represented the first effort to progress the newly emerging doctrine of the continental shelf in treaty law[66]. However, the conference did not make breakthrough on the contro-

65 For the work of ILC on the development and codification of international law, see ILC website: http://untreaty.un.org/ilc/ilcintro.htm revisited in July 2006.

66 "Convention on the Continental Shelf", drafted 29 April 1958, entered into force on 10 June 1964; "Convention on the High Seas", drafted 29 April 1958, entered into force on 30 Sept. 1962; "Convention on the Territorial Sea and the Contiguous Zone", drafted 29 April, entered into force on 10 Sept. 1964. The 1958 Geneva Conventions established the first successful and negotiated development of the law of the seas. The Conventions and more information are available at the website of UN Environment Program: www.unep.org visited in July 2004.

versial issues of the breadth of the territorial sea and of limits on fisheries, and the resultant agreements never achieved the status of a universally accepted body of law.

UNCLOS II in 1960 was to discuss the unresolved problems from the original conference. But this second attempt failed by one vote to adopt a compromise formula providing for a six-mile territorial sea plus a six-mile fishery zone. Agreements on these issues had to wait for the UNCLOS III[67]. While the earlier LOS Conferences solved a number of questions concerning international ocean affairs, the majority of problems remained unresolved. The task of creating a comprehensive international convention was left with UNCLOS III.

2.2.2 UNCLOS III and the 1982 LOS Convention

The 1982 UN Convention of the Law of the Sea (the LOS Convention)[68] is one of the most fundamental legal instruments for

67 Agustín Blanco-Bazán, "IMO Interface with the Law of the Sea Convention", January 2000, available at the website of IMO: http://www.imo.org/ Circulars revisited in July 2006.

68 The full text of the LOS Convention is available on the website of the United Nations, under: www.un.org revisited in June 2006, UN Pub. Sales No E. 83, V. 5, 1983.
For important works on the law of the sea, see for example Jonathan I. Charney, "Introduction" 1 ASIL, International Maritime Boundaries xxiii (J. Charney & L. Alexander eds., 1993); Ian Brownlie, "Principles of Public International Law" 177–254 Clarendon Press, Oxford, 1979; Akl, Joseph. The legal status, privileges and immunities of the International Tribunal for the Law of the Sea, 2 Max Planck Yearbook of United Nations Law (1998), pp. 341–364; Churchill R. & Lowe A. V., *the Law of the Sea*, 3rd ed., Manchester University Press, 1999; Eiriksson, Gudmundur. *The International Tribunal for the Law of the Sea* (The Hague, Martinus Nijhoff Publishers, 2000); Kolodkin, Anatoly L. "National legislation in the light of UNCLOS and the practice of the International Tribunal for the Law of the Sea", *in* Current Marine Environmental Issues and the International Tribunal for the Law of the Sea (Myron H. Nordquist and John Norton Moore, eds., The Hague, Martinus Nijhoff Publishers, 2001), pp. 239–242; Carstensen, Nils Christian. [Comment] A re-internationalization of dispute settlement

the law of the sea. It establishes a comprehensive set of regulations governing seas and oceans, and the rights and obligations of states over vessels flying their flags. The objective of this Convention is to serve as an umbrella treaty providing a legal and institutional framework for the equitable use of the oceans and their resources. As the oldest and key maritime activity, navigation enjoys a prominent place in the Convention, with around one third of its articles containing provisions dealing with different issues of navigation and shipping, particularly Part II (territorial sea and contiguous zone); part III (straits used for international navigation); Part IV (archipelagic states); Part V (Exclusive Economic Zone); Part VII (high seas) and Part XII (protection and preservation of the marine environment). The introduction of various functional zones processing different legal regimes for navigation has helped to ensure the achievement of a compromise that led to the ultimate acceptance of the Convention by the member States[69].

The Convention allows coastal states to exercise sovereignty over their territorial sea of up to twelve nautical miles in breadth. However foreign vessels are allowed peaceful "innocent passage" through those waters[70]. Ships and aircraft of all countries are allowed "transit passage" through straits used for international navigation; states alongside the straits are able to regulate navigational and other aspects of passage, but passage cannot be suspended; passage includes aircraft overflight and submerged transit of sub-

---

in the law of the sea, 62 (1/2) *Zeitschrift für ausländisches öffentliches Recht und Völkerrecht* (2002), pp. 73–76; Churchill, Robin, The International Tribunal for the Law of the Sea: Survey for 2003, 19 (4) International Journal of Marine and Coastal Law (2004), pp. 369–382; Boyle, Alan E., "Further development of the Law of the sea convention: mechanisms for change", 54 (3) International and Comparative Law Quarterly (2005), pp. 563–584; Churchill R., Dispute settlement under UN Convention on the Law of the Sea: survey for 2004 International Journal of Marine & Coastal Law, 21 (1) (2006) 1–14.

69 For a classification of the key features of the LOS Convention, see for example George Galdorisi, "the United States and the Law of the Sea, Changing Interests and New Imperatives", US Navy, Naval War College Review, autumn 1996, Vol. LXIX, No. 4.

70 Part II.

marines[71]. Archipelagic states have sovereignty over a sea area enclosed by straight lines drawn between the outermost points of the islands; all other states enjoy the right of archipelagic passage (similar to transit passage) through designated sea lanes[72].

The LOS Convention grants coastal states exclusive resource exploitation rights within a two-hundred-nautical-mile exclusive economic zone (EEZ). Coastal states may also exercise jurisdiction over marine science research and environmental protection[73]. In addition, landlocked and geographically disadvantaged states have the opportunity to participate in exploiting part of the EEZ's fisheries on an equitable basis[74].

Coastal states have exclusive rights out to at least two hundred nautical miles offshore (and possibly more under specified conditions) to explore and exploit the resources of the continental shelf[75]. Coastal states must also share with the international community part of the revenue they derive from exploiting resources from the continental shelf beyond two hundred miles. A Commission on the Limits of the Continental Shelf makes recommendations to states on the shelf's outer boundaries beyond two hundred miles[76].

All nations are endorsed with the traditional freedoms of navigation, overflight, scientific research and fishing on the high seas[77]. States bordering enclosed or semi-enclosed seas are required to cooperate in managing living resources and environmental research policies and activities[78]. Landlocked states have the right of access to and from the sea and enjoy freedom of transit through the territory of applicable coastal states[79]. The Convention establishes that States are bound to prevent and control marine pollution and are liable for damage caused by violation of their international

71 Part III.
72 Part IV.
73 Part V.
74 Part V.
75 Part VI.
76 Part VI.
77 Part VII.
78 Part IX.
79 Part X.

obligations to combat such pollution[80]. All marine scientific research in the EEZ and on the continental shelf is subject to the consent of the coastal states, but they are generally obliged to grant consent when the research is to be conducted for peaceful purposes and fulfills specified criteria[81]. States are also bound to promote the development and transfer of marine technology "on fair and reasonable terms and conditions" with proper regard for all legitimate interests[82], as well as to settle by peaceful means any disputes concerning the interpretation or application of the Convention[83].

The LOS Convention entered into force on 16 November 1994, and as at September 2008, there were 157 countries ratified or acceded to it[84]. Although there were some dissatisfactions upon the form of declarations made by states on signature, ratification or accession to the LOS Convention[85], the extraordinary achievement of this complicated regulatory mechanism is universally recognized.

One of the most important contributions of this Convention is that it established a balance between the interests of the international maritime community in maintaining freedom of navigation and of coastal states in preserving their national jurisdiction[86]. This balance is under constant pressure from various players and forces, such as the jurisdictional conflicts between the flag

80 Part XII.
81 Part XIII.
82 Part XIV.
83 Part XV.
84 Source of information: UN website, Division for Ocean Affairs and the Law of the Sea, at: http://www.un.org visited in April 2006 and revisited in August 2007.
85 The Declarations are reprinted in The Law of the Sea: Declarations and Statements with respect to the United Nations Convention on the Law of the Sea and to the Agreement relating to the Implementation of Part XI of the United Nations Convention on the Law of the Sea (New York, United Nations), 1997. The updated list is available at UN website: www.un.org revisited in August 2005.
86 Myron H. Nordquist, *United Nations Convention on the Law of the Sea, 1982*, Martinus Nijhoff Publishers, 1985, p. 38.

states and the coastal and port states. However, this balance is guaranteed by several important requirements, such as the 12-nautical-mile limit of the territorial sea; the protection for navigational rights through internal waters, the territorial sea, international straits and archipelagic waters, including innocent passage and transit passage; the confirmation of the traditional freedom of navigation on the high seas; and the establishment of dispute settlement mechanism including adjudication and arbitration[87].

2.2.2.1 *Territorial Sea, Contiguous Zone and Straits for International Navigation*

Prior to the LOS Convention, the basic rules of international law on passage through the territorial sea were embedded in the Geneva Convention on the Territorial Sea and the Contiguous Zone of 1958 (the Geneva Convention). Article 17 (Right of innocent passage) of the LOS Convention follows closely the language of Article 14 of the Geneva Convention in providing the right of passage: "Subject to this Convention, ships of all States, whether coastal or land-locked, enjoy the right of innocent passage through the territorial sea."

Innocent passage is defined in the LOS Convention as navigation through the territorial sea whether or not actually entering

87 The 1982 LOS Convention has a single system of rules on the settlement of disputes between states parties concerning the interpretation or application of the Convention (which is different from the 1958 Convention). The backbone of this system is Part XV of the Convention on Settlement of Disputes, as well as Annexes V–VIII to the Convention, which cover Conciliation, Statute of the International Tribunal for the Law of the Sea, Arbitration, Special Arbitration, respectively. In other parts and annexes of the Convention there are also provisions on the settlement of disputes, one of a particular important places is in Section 5 of Part XI, handling with the settlement of disputes and advisory opinions with respect to activities in the Area. State parties to a dispute are free to agree to settle the dispute by any peaceful means of their own choice. A dispute where no settlement has been reached by recourse to negotiation or other peaceful means may be submitted at the request of any party to a court of tribunal. For more elaboration on jurisdiction and dispute settlement under the LOS Convention, see Part III of this work.

internal waters or calling at a roadstead or port facility. To be innocent, a ship's passage must not be prejudicial to the peace, good order or security of the coastal state. Activities that may render a passage to be other than innocent include the threat or use of force, use of weapons, spying or propaganda dissemination affecting the defence or security of coastal state, launching or landing any aircraft, loading or unloading of anything that may contravene fiscal, immigration or sanitary laws of the coastal state, willful and serious pollution, fishing, research and survey activities, and any other activities not having a direct bearing on passage.

Article 18 (Meaning of Passage) of the LOS Convention follows the same pattern as the Geneva Convention:

> 1. Passage means navigation through the territorial sea for the purpose of: (a) traversing that sea without entering internal waters or calling at a roadstead or port facility outside internal water, or (b) proceeding to or from internal waters or a call at such roadstead or port facility.
> 2. Passage shall be continuous and expeditious. However, passage includes stopping and anchoring, but only in so far as the same are incidental to ordinary navigation or are rendered necessary by force majeure or distress or for the purpose of rendering assistance to persons, ships or aircraft in danger or distress.

It then gives the meaning of innocent passage in Article 19, in which it defines that the passage shall be deemed to be innocent as long as it is not prejudicial to the peace, good order or security of the coastal State. The meaning of prejudicial is specified in Article 19 (2) by listing out 12 activities. Article 20 (2) provides that in the territorial sea, submarines and other underwater vehicles are required to navigate on the surface and to show their flag, which are assumed to be a condition of innocence.

The right of innocent passage through the territorial sea is limited in Article 21[88] by allowing states specific powers to adopt laws and regulations in conformity with pertinent international law. Coastal states may regulate maritime traffic; protect navigational

88 Article 21 "Laws and regulations of the coastal State relating to innocent passage".

aids, cables and pipelines; conserve living resources and protect the environment generally; prevent, reduce or control pollution; and prevent the infringement of customs, fiscal, immigration or sanitary laws. At the same time, coastal states may not impose conditions relating to the design, construction, manning or equipment of foreign ships unless they are giving effect to internationally accepted rules or standards and they must give due publicity to measures being taken by them to enable foreign ships to comply.

In addition to the rights and obligations of the coastal State, the LOS Convention also sets up the obligations of the coastal state to practice its right in good faith. Article 24 (1) provides that:

> The coastal State shall not hamper the innocent passage of foreign ships through the territorial sea except in accordance with this Convention. In particular, in the application of this Convention or of any laws or regulations adopted in conformity with this Convention, the coastal State shall not: a) Impose requirements on foreign ships which have the practical effect of denying or impairing the right of innocent passage; or b) Discriminate in form or in fact against the ships of any State or against ships carrying cargoes to, from or on behalf of any State.

Part III of the LOS Convention addresses a wide range of issues relating to navigation regimes in different types of straits used for international navigation. This establishes a solid foundation for the effective exercise of the general freedom of navigation. The fundamental principle of the navigation regime in the straits shall be the complete freedom of transit and navigation enjoyed by merchant vessels, in time of peace, which may not be subject to any formalities other than those agreed.

One issue is the prevention of collisions at sea and the routeing of ships. Articles 39 and 54 of the LOS Convention stipulate that, ships exercising the right of transit passage in straits used for international navigation or the right of the archipelagic sea lanes passage are obliged to comply with pertinent IMO safety regulations, particularly the COLREG 72, including provisions on traffic separation schemes. The IMO General Provisions on Ships' Routeing also apply to straits used for international navigation and to the archipelagic waters, as well as to the territorial sea and the EEZ[89]. A fundamental requirement with respect to the designation of sea-lanes and the prescription of TSS is that they must conform to "generally accepted international regulations"[90]. Coastal states are expected to enact and enforce regulations establishing sea-lanes and TSS after they have been formally adopted by the IMO.

Another issue relating to the safety of navigation through straits concerning cost sharing. Article 26 of the Convention[91] prohibits any charges being levied on foreign ships for their passage through the territorial sea. Charges are only allowed on specific services provided to foreign vessels, such as towage and pilotage. This requirement is equally applicable to straits used for international navigation.

2.2.2.2 *The Archipelagic Waters, the Exclusive Economic Zone and the High Seas*

Neither the 1930 Hague Conference nor the 1958 Conference agreed on any provisions dealing specifically and comprehensively with the issue of archipelagos[92]. The legal regime of archipelagos was finally settled by the LOS Convention, which regulates two types of passage, namely, innocent passage and archipelagic sea lanes passage. For innocent passage, Article 52 (1) (Right of Innocent Passage) provides that:

> Subject to Article 53 (on the right of archipelagic sea lanes passage) and without prejudice to Article 50 (on delimitation of internal waters), ships of all States enjoy the right of innocent passage through archipelagic waters, in accordance with Part II, section 3.

89 IMO regulations on ship routeing are available at IMO website: http://www.imo.org revisited in February 2006.

90 Art. 41 (3).

91 Art. 26.

92 On the 1958 Convention, J. Evensen from Norway contributed an article on the issue under the title of: "Certain legal aspects concerning the delimitation of the territorial waters of archipelagos", First UN Conference on the Law of the Sea, Official Records, vol. I. pp. 289–302.

Article 54[93] confirms the commonality between the regimes of transit passage through straits and through archipelagic sea lanes, by stating that the following provisions on transit passage through straits are made applicable, *mutatis mutandis*, to archipelagic sea lanes passage:

- Article 39: Duties of ships and aircraft during transit passage;
- Article 40: Research and survey activities;
- Article 42: Laws and regulations of States bordering straits relating to transit passage;
- Article 44: Duties of States bordering straits.

Articles 58 (rights and duties of other States in the exclusive economic zone) and 87 (freedom of the high seas) respectively grants all States, whether coastal or landlocked, the freedom of navigation in exclusive economic zone and on the high seas[94]. The Convention stipulates at the same time the duties of other States who enjoy this freedom. Paragraph 3 of Article 58 further stipulates that, in exercising their rights and performing their duties under this Convention in the exclusive economic zone, States shall have due regard to the rights and duties of the coastal state and shall comply with the laws and regulations adopted by the coastal state in accordance with the provisions of this Convention and other rules of international law, in so far as they are not incompatible with this Part.

The freedom of navigation in the EEZ is subject to a number of limitations: Firstly, the general limitation governing all freedom of the high seas as set out in Article 87 (2)[95], which means this freedom must be exercised "with due regard for the interests of other States in the exercise of the freedom of the high seas". Secondly,

93 Article 54 "Duties of ships and aircraft during their passage, research and survey activities, duties of the archipelagic State and laws and regulations of the archipelagic State relating to archipelagic sea lanes passage".

94 Freedom of navigation on the high seas is reiterated in Article 90 under the title of "Right of Navigation", which stipulates that every State, whether coastal or land-locked, has the right to sail ships flying its flag on the high seas.

95 Article 87 "the Freedom of the High Seas".

under Article 58 (2), the freedom of navigation in the EEZ is subject to the provisions of Articles 88 to 115 and the other relevant rules of international law that deal with navigation on the high seas, in so far as they are not incompatible with the Convention's provisions on the EEZ[96].

Moreover, in respect of the presence of artificial islands and installations, Article 211 (Pollution from vessels) of the Convention confirms that mandatory sea-lanes may be established in the EEZ. Paragraph 1 provides that States, acting through the competent international organization or general diplomatic conference, shall promote the adoption whenever appropriate, of routeing systems designed to minimize the threat of accidents that might cause pollution. However, States wishing to proceed under this provision would clearly be required to do so either through IMO or diplomatic conferences and could not simply act unilaterally.

Due to the fact that it is very difficult for individual states to control the activities of other states on the high seas, the use of the high seas has remained essentially free except for a few restrictive rules. In addition, the constant development of new ocean technology makes it impossible to give an exhaustive list of the freedom of the high seas. This was recognized by the 1958 High Seas Convention and claimed to be "generally declaratory of established principles of international law".

Article 87 lists out the various freedoms of the high seas. The first on the list is the freedom of navigation, which, like other freedoms of the high seas, is subject to a wide range of international and municipal rules. This Article also states in paragraph (1) that freedom of the high seas is to be exercised under the conditions laid down in the LOS Convention and by other rules of international law. Compliance by ships with such conditions is undertaken in two ways. Firstly, limitation through flag state's jurisdiction: Article 94 states in its first paragraph that the duties of flag states cover administrative, technical and social matters.

96 For further explanation of the effects of this qualifying phrase on the provisions contained in Articles 88 to 115, see F. Orrego Vicuna, *The Exclusive Economic Zone* (Cambridge, Cambridge University Press), 1989.

The range of subjects on which the flag state is required to exercise such jurisdiction and control is indicated in several articles of the Convention, which include specific duties of the flag state (Art. 94); marine casualties (Art. 94 & Art. 97); the duty to render assistance (Art. 98); the prohibition of the transport of slaves (Art. 99); and laws and regulations on submarine cables and pipeline (Art. 113 & Art. 115). Secondly, limitation through extraordinary jurisdiction: The Convention empowers states other than the flag state to exercise extraordinary jurisdiction in relation to a certain range of abuses of the freedom of the high seas, which include: right of hot pursuit (Art. 111); piracy and suppression of unlawful acts (Arts. 100–107); the transport of slaves (Art. 110); unauthorized broadcasting from the high seas (Art. 109); the right of visit and other rights over foreign ships (Art. 110).

3 Maritime Transport Services in the WTO

3.1 General Background

3.1.1 The WTO/GATS and Process of Negotiation

The WTO is a global umbrella organization responsible for the surveillance of the multilateral and plurilateral agreements negotiated in the Uruguay Round, including the GATT, the GATS, the TRIPs and other associate agreements. It provides a forum for continuous negotiations among its member countries for the further liberalization of the trade in goods and services and for discussions on other trade-related issues that may be selected for the development of rules and regulations[97].

The WTO Agreement serves as a constitution for setting out the fundamental rights and duties of its member countries and laying the legal framework for international economic order. It provides broader and more integrated legal guarantees for market access, non-discrimination and rule of law. It also provides a system of rules and procedures applicable to dispute arising under its legal instruments for the proper functioning of its multilateral trading system[98].

97 Id.

98 Id. Some general works on WTO include: *The GATT Uruguay Round: A Negotiating History (1986–1992)*. Vols. I and II *Commentary*; vol. III *Documents*; vol. IV *The End Game*. Deventer; Boston: Kluwer Law and Taxation Publishers, 1993–99; *Guide to the Uruguay Round Agreements*. WTO Secretariat. The Hague; Boston: Kluwer Law International, 1999; Christopher Arup, *The New World Trade Organization Agreements: Globalizing Law Through Services and Intellectual Property*, Cambridge Studies in Law and Society. New York: Cambridge University Press, 2000; Richard Senti and Patricia Conlan: *WTO Regulation of World Trade after the Uruguay Round*, *Schulthess*, Zurich, 1997; John H. Jackson and Alan O. Sykes, *Implement-*

As one of the three international trade agreements under the WTO, the GATS puts in place a framework of rules governing international services trade and creating a more open and transparent trading system. It also provides a forum for settling trade disputes and for eliminating trade barriers progressively through negotiations.

---

ing the Uruguay Round. Oxford: Oxford University Press, 1997; John H. Jackson, *The Jurisprudence of GATT & the WTO*, Cambridge University Press, 2000; Ernst-Ulrich Petersmann: *International Trade Law and the GATT/WTO*, Martinus Nijhoff Publisher, 1997; Thomas C. Fischer: *The United States, the European Union, and the Globalization of World Trade*, Quorum/Greenwood, London, 2000; Sauvé, Pierre and Robert M. Stern, eds., *GATS 2000: New Directions in Services Trade Liberalization*, Washington, D. C.: Centre for Business and Government, Harvard University and the Brookings Institution Press, 2000.
Writings of Thomas Cottier on general topics of WTO include: "The Relationship between World Trade Organization Law, National and Regional Law", in: Journal of International Economic Law, Vol. 1 (1998), No. 1, pp. 83–122; "Conflict Resolution in the World Trade Organization. Assessing the story so far: hope on the horizon?", in: Halina Ward/Duncan Brack (eds.). *Trade, Investment and the Environment Proceedings of the Royal Institute of International Affairs Conference,* Chatham House, London, October 1998. London 2000, pp. 187–202 (with Krista N. Schefer); "Good Faith and the Protection of Legitimate Expectations in the WTO", in: Marco Bronckers/Reinhard Quick (eds.). *New Directions in International Economic Law: Essays in Honour of John H. Jackson*. The Hague/London/Boston 2000, pp. 47–68 (with Krista N. Schefer); "WTO Law, Precedents and Legal Change", in: Turku Law Journal, Vol. 3 (2001), No. 1, pp. 27–41 (with Matthias Oesch); "The WTO Permanent Panel Body: A Bridge Too Far?" in: Journal of International Economic Law, Vol. 6 (2003), No. 1 (March), pp. 187–202; "The Legal Framework for Free Trade Areas & Customs Unions in WTO Law", in: Martin Godel/Jonathan Gage (eds.). *Multilateralism and Bilateralism After Cancún. Challenges and Opportunities of Regionalism*. Bern 2004, pp. 107–119; *International Trade Regulation, Law and Policy in the WTO, the EU and Switzerland. Cases, Materials and Comments*. Bern/London 2004, (with Matthias Oesch/Thomas Fischer); "From Progressive Liberalization to Progressive Regulation in WTO Law", Journal of International Economic Law 2006 9: 779–821.

Coverage and Structure of the GATS

The coverage of the GATS is very extensive, which encompasses practically all government measures, including laws, regulations, guidelines and even unwritten practices for example subsidies and grants, licensing standards and qualifications, limitations on access to markets, economic needs to test and local content provisions. No government measure "affecting trade in services", is, in principle, beyond GATS scrutiny[99]. It covers all service sectors and all modes of supply. The agreement covers not only cross-border trade, but every possible means of supplying a service, including through electronic commerce, international travel and foreign investment.

The GATS approach is a hybrid one which combines features of both a "top-down" agreement (which covers all sectors and measures unless they are explicitly excluded) and a "bottom-up" agreement (which covers only sectors and measures that are specifically identified)[100]. It is designed to embrace all governmental measures that affect the supply of services with some international elements. The agreement prohibits discrimination in sectors specified by individual members. Its most significant constraints apply only to sectors covered by member governments. The most powerful GATS provisions, such as national treatment and market access, currently apply only to those sectors that are specifically listed in a member government's country schedule. However, the coverage of these provisions is intended to become increasingly comprehensive through successive rounds of future negotiations[101].

99 Department of Foreign Affairs and Trade, Australia, "Discussion Paper on the General Agreement on Trade in Services (GATS)", 2003, p. 8.

100 Mina Mashayekhi, "GATS 2000 Negotiations: Options for Developing Countries", South Centre, December 2000, this paper is available at: http://www.southcentre.org revisited in July 2006.

101 Id.

Modes of Supply

The GATS recognizes four service delivery models, namely[102]:

Cross Border Supply:	Services flow from one territory of one Member to the territory of another.
Consumption Abroad:	Consumers travel to another Member's territory to obtain a service.
Commercial Presence:	A service supplier from one Member establishes a physical presence (e.g. office, branch) in the territory of another to deliver services to consumers in that territory.
Presence of Natural Persons	Temporary movement of people to deliver a service in the territory of another Member.

The GATS Obligations

The GATS sets out the basic rules that apply to all Members and, for the most part, to all services. These can be categorized into two main elements, firstly, a set of general concepts, principles and rules that apply to all measures affecting trade in services (general obligations) and secondly, specific commitments that apply to the services sector and sub-sectors listed in each Member's schedule[103].

Broadly speaking, the services package under the GATS resembles that for goods. The GATS, which is directly modeled on the GATT, relies on many similar principles. However, some major differences do exist between them. For example, although the principle of national treatment is fundamental to both the GATT and the GATS, it is applied in very different ways. It is a general, non-negotiable obligation under the GATT, while under the GATS it is only applied to specific commitments subject to negotiation and scheduling.

102 WTO, "The General Agreement on Trade in Services (GATS): objectives, coverage and disciplines", available at WTO website at: www.wto.org visited in August 2006.

103 Mina Mashayekhi, supra note 100, p. 10.

General Obligations under the GATS

Most Favoured Nation Treatment

Under Article II of the GATS, Members are held to extend immediately and unconditionally to services and service suppliers of all other Members "treatment no less favourable than it accords to like services and service suppliers of any other country". However, the MFN principle in GATS is qualified. Members were allowed to list MFN exemptions on entry into force of the agreement. MFN exemptions are, in principle, to last no longer than 10 years and are subject to negotiation in the current and future trade rounds.

Transparency

Transparency is the other key principle designed to achieve multilateral liberalization. The GATS requires each Member to publish promptly "all relevant measures of general application" that affect operation of the agreement. Members must also notify the Council of Trade in Services of new or changed laws, regulations or administrative guidelines that affect trade in services covered by their specific commitments under the agreement.

Specific Commitments under the GATS

National Treatment

Article XVII.1 contains the basic national treatment obligation, which is a so-called specific commitment.

> In the sectors inscribed in its Schedule, and subject to any conditions and qualifications set out therein, each Member shall accord to services and service suppliers of any other Member, in respect of all measures affecting the supply of services, treatment no less favourable than that it accords to its own like services and service suppliers.

Therefore, national treatment applies only to those services inscribed in a Member's schedule, and then only to the extent that no qualifications or conditions are listed on the schedule[104].

104 Id. p. 11.

Market Access

Market access is a negotiated commitment to guarantee a certain level of access in specified sectors. Article XVI also defines a set of policies that may only be used to restrict Market access for a scheduled sector if they are listed in a Member's specific commitments. For instance, limitations may be imposed on the number of service suppliers, total value of services transactions, total quantity of service output, the number of persons that may be employed in a particular sector, the specific types of legal entity or joint venture for supply of services and the participation of foreign capital[105].

The Uruguay round and post-Uruguay round negotiations on maritime transport services have gone through several stages[106].

The first stage was from 1986 to 1993, during which time member countries could not reach an agreement on maritime transport services due to the lack of consensus among principal member countries. Consequently it was decided to continue the discussion on this issue at the Uruguay Round of negotiations in December 1993. However, this meeting concluded without general agreement on maritime transport services. As a result, a decision was taken to continue the maritime negotiations in a special Negotiating Group on Maritime Transport Services (NGMTS)[107], which aimed to achieve commitments in international shipping, port services and auxiliary services by June 1996. The NGMTS also considered the possibility of including multimodal transport services as part of a Maritime Transport Services (MTS) agreement[108].

The second stage ran between 1993 and 1996, with the establishment of Negotiating Group on Maritime Transport Services[109]. At the Council for Trade in Services in June 1996, it was decided that the next negotiation would be resumed with the beginning of

105 Id. p. 11.

106 A detailed description of the negotiation process on maritime transport services is available at the website of the Japanese Ministry of Foreign Affairs: www.mofa.go.jp/policy/economy/wto revisited in August 2005.

107 More information on the negotiating Group is available on WTO website at: http://www.wto.org revisited in April 2006.

108 Id.

109 Id.

the comprehensive negotiating round including items such as agricultural service and financial service. It was also agreed that MFN for the maritime transport services would not apply until an agreement was reached.

From the beginning of 2000, negotiation on maritime transport services entered the third phase leading up to the Doha Conference in 2001[110]. Article XIX of GATS states that the next negotiating round would begin no later than 5 years from the date of entry into force of the WTO agreement. The negotiation on the maritime transport sector was resumed as Built-in-Agenda at Special Session of Council for Trade in Services. The 4th Ministerial Conference in Doha in November 2001 marked the latest stage of the negotiation and adopted the Ministerial Declaration to launch a new round of the WTO negotiations.

The Doha Ministerial Declaration reaffirmed the negotiating guidelines and established some key elements of the timetable including the deadline of 1 January 2005 for concluding the negotiations as part of a single undertaking[111]. It recognized the work already undertaken in the negotiations, initiated in January 2000 under Article XIX of the GATS, and the large number of proposals submitted by Members on a wider range of sectors and several horizontal issues, as well as on movement of natural persons. It reaffirmed the Guidelines and Procedures for the Negotiations adopted by the Council for Trade in Services on 28 March 2001 as the basis for continuing the negotiations, with a view to achieving the objectives of the GATS, as stipulated in the Preamble, Article IV and Article XIX of that Agreement[112].

Following the Doha Conference, negotiators continued discussing members' proposals to liberalize a wide range of sectors as well as the movement of natural persons. More than 150 proposals have been submitted covering sectors such as professional services, telecommunications, tourism, financial services, distribution

110 Id.

111 Doha WTO Ministerial 2001: Ministerial Declaration, WT/MIN (01)/DEC/1, 20 November 2001.

112 Id.

services, construction services, energy services, maritime transport, postal services and environmental services[113].

3.1.2 *Some Important Issues in the Negotiations*

3.1.2.1 *Negotiating Modality*

Trade agreements on international and regional levels which include national treatment and liberalization provisions have generally adopted lists and schedules, indicating specific reservations and commitments related to the fulfillment of agreement obligations, as appendixes to the agreement[114]. This is also the case with the GATT/GATS. The modalities adopted for these reservations and commitments can be broadly divided into two types: positive list approach and negative list approach. These approaches and their application are elaborated in an OECD paper on the relationship between regional trade agreement and multilateral trading system (the OECD Paper)[115].

Under a positive approach to scheduling liberalization commitments, countries agree to meet national treatment and market access commitments specifying the nature of treatment or access offered to foreign services or foreign service-suppliers through reservations in scheduled areas. Under such an approach, countries retain the full right to not to meet any commitments. In such in-

113 Bernard Hoekman, "Strengthening the global trade architecture for development: the post Doha agenda", World Trade Review, Volume 1, Issue 01, March 2002, Cambridge University Press, pp. 23–45; see also: Rudolf Adlung, "Services Negotiations in the Doha Round: Lost in Flexibility?", Journal of International Economic Law 2006 9: 865–893; Sauvé Pierre (1996), "Services and the International Contestability of Markets", in Transnational Corporations, Vol. 5, No. 1, (April), pp. 37–55.

114 WTO, Working Group on the Relationship between Trade and Investment-Communication from Japan, WT/WGTI/W/125, 28th June 2002, p. 2.

115 OECD, "The Relationship between Regional Trade Agreement and the Multilateral Trading System", Working Party of the Trade Committee, TD/TC/WP(2002)27/FINAL, 09-Oct-2002.

stances, they are under no legal obligation to supply information to their trading partners on the nature of discriminatory or access-impeding regulations maintained at the domestic level. The alternative – negative "top-down" approach to services trade and investment liberalization is based upon the concept of negative listing, whereby all sectors and non-conforming measures are to be liberalized unless otherwise specified in a transparent manner in reservation lists appended to an agreement. Non-conforming measures contained in reservation lists are then usually liberalized through consultations or, as in the GATS, periodic negotiations[116].

It is noted that an important governance-enhancing feature arising from the adoption of a negative list approach is the greater level of transparency it generates. The information contained in reservation lists will be important to prospective investors, who value the one-stop shopping attributes of a comprehensive inventory of potential restrictions in foreign markets. They are also likely to benefit home country negotiators, assisting them in establishing a hierarchy of impediments to tackle in future negotiations. Moreover, the production of a negative list may also help to generate a useful domestic policy dialogue between the trade negotiating and regulatory communities, thus encouraging countries to perform a comprehensive audit of existing trade-restrictive measures, benchmark domestic regulatory regimes against best international practices, and revisit the rationale for domestic policy objectives[117].

There may be two potential pitfalls arising from the use of negative listing[118]. Firstly, that such an approach may be administratively burdensome, particularly for developing countries, although the costs of compliance should be judged against the resultant benefits in governance and regulatory practices. Secondly, the adoption of a negative list implies that governments ultimately forgo the right to introduce discriminatory or access-impairing measures in future, including in sectors that do not exist or are not regulated at the time of an agreement's entry into force.

116 Id. p. 16.
117 Id. p. 19.
118 Id. p. 20.

The choice between these two approaches is generally made on the basis of factors such as the member countries, the objectives of the agreement, and the rights and obligations under the agreement[119]. As the positive list approach of the GATS allows the registration of national treatment and market access commitments only in those areas where countries are prepared to guarantee these, it seems to be a flexible approach making it easier to accept for developing countries concerned about maintaining a balance with their development policies.

Positive list approach for national treatment and market access: Article XVII of national treatment has adopted a positive list approach. The GATS obligates members to refrain from not only formal discrimination, but also effective discrimination. In other words, the issue is not formal non-discrimination in terms of member countries' measures influencing the supply of services, but rather the need to provide competitive conditions whereby suppliers of services from other state parties will not be less favourably treated than domestic service suppliers. In terms of provisions concerning investment entry restrictions, a market access obligation is prescribed in Article XVI. Like national treatment, members' commitments are made based on a positive list basis[120].

Negative list approach for MFN treatment: Under Article II of the GATS, member countries take on the general obligation of extending MFN treatment to measures having an impact on trade in services in all service areas. In other words, this is a negative list approach. However, member countries could register measures to be exempted from MFN treatment when the GATS was established with an exemption period of up to 10 years. A right is also extended to new members at the time of WTO accession[121].

As far as the negative list/positive list approach to market access and national treatment is concerned, some confusion has resulted from the scheduling convention in Article XX.2. It provides that

119 WTO, supra note 114, p. 3.
120 Id. p. 5.
121 Id. p. 5.

where restrictive measures fall within the scope of both market access and national treatment, the measures then should be inscribed in the market access column and be understood to provide a condition or qualification to Article XVII as well[122]. As there is no indication as to whether the measures scheduled under Article XVI are discriminatory or non-discriminatory, the scope of national treatment commitments remains unclear. Low and Mattoo have suggested several possibilities in relation to the scope of national treatment in these circumstances[123]: (i) national treatment would apply to all present and future market access commitments with respect to entry and post entry operations; (ii) national treatment applies to market access commitments entered into at the time the national treatment commitment itself was made, but not to subsequent entry beyond scheduled commitments. This would need clarification particularly in respect to mode 3.

3.1.2.2 Schedule of Commitments

A specific commitment in a services schedule is interpreted as "an undertaking to provide market access and national treatment for the service activity in question on the terms and conditions specified in the schedule"[124]. Governments of member countries are expected to refrain from imposing new measures that may run contrary to the commitments in market access or national treatment. No withdrawals or modifications can be made until three years after the Agreement enters into force.

The schedule of commitments follows a standard format which is divided into limitations on market access, national treatment and additional commitments. In each of these sections, the schedule is supposed to indicate whether or not limitation exists with

122 Patrick Low and Aaditya Mattoo, "Is There a Better Way? Alternative Approaches to Liberalization under the GATS" presented at the Conference on Services 2000 – New Directions In Services Liberalization, 1999, p. 3.

123 Id. p. 4.

124 WTO trade topics on schedules: "Guide to reading the GATS Schedules of Specific Commitments and the list of Article II (MFN) exemptions", available at WTO website: www.wto.org revisited in July 2006.

respect to each of the four modes of supply, namely, cross border supply, consumption abroad, commercial presence and presence of natural persons.

In nearly all schedules, commitments are split into two sections. In the first section, "horizontal" commitments stipulate limitations that apply to all of the sectors included in the schedule; and often refer to a particular mode of supply, notably commercial presence and the presence of natural persons. Any evaluation of sector-specific commitments must therefore take the horizontal entries into account.

In the second section of the schedule, commitments which apply to trade in services in a particular sector or sub-sector are listed[125]. "Sector or sub-sector" column: this column contains a clear definition of the sector, sub-sector or activity that is the subject of the specific commitment. In most cases, the sectoral entries are accompanied by numerical references to the Central Product Classification system of the United Nations which gives a detailed explanation of the services activities covered by each listed sector or sub-sector, and on which the secretariat list is based[126].

"Limitation on market access" column: When a Member undertakes a commitment in a sector or sub-sector it must indicate for each mode of supply what limitations, if any, it maintains on market access. Article XVI:2 of the GATS lists six categories of restriction which may not be adopted or maintained unless they are specified in the schedule. All limitations in schedules therefore fall into one of these categories. They comprise four types of quantitative restriction plus limitations on types of legal entity and on foreign equity participation[127].

"Limitation on national treatment" column: The national treatment obligation under Article XVII of the GATS is to accord to the services and service suppliers of any other Member treatment no less favourable than is accorded to domestic services and service suppliers. A Member wishing to maintain any limitations on na-

125 Id.
126 Id.
127 Id.

tional treatment – that is any measures which result in less-favourable treatment of foreign services or service suppliers – must indicate these limitations in the third column of its schedule[128]

"Additional commitments" column: Entries in this column are not obligatory but a Member may decide in a given sector to make additional commitments relating to measures other than those subject to scheduling under Articles XVI and XVII, for example qualifications, standards and licensing matters. This column is to be used to indicate positive undertakings, not the listing of additional limitations or restrictions[129].

In essence, the entries which constitute a legally binding commitment in a Member's schedule indicate the presence or absence of limitations on market access and national treatment in relation to each of the four modes of supply for a listed sector, sub-sector or activity. In the following cases, the entries use uniform terminology[130]:

- Where there are no limitations on market access or national treatment in a given sector and mode of supply, the entry reads NONE. However, it should be noted that when the term NONE is used in the second or sector-specific part of the schedule, it means that there are no limitations specific to this sector: it must be borne in mind that, as noted above, there may be relevant horizontal limitations in the first part of the schedule.
- All commitments in a schedule are bound unless otherwise specified. In such a case, where a Member wishes to remain free in a given sector and mode of supply to introduce or maintain measures inconsistent with market access or national treatment, the entry reads UNBOUND.
- In some situations a particular mode of supply may not be technically possible or feasible. In such cases, the term UNBOUND has been used, usually in conjunction with an explanatory footnote stating "Unbound due to lack of technical feasibility".

128 Id.
129 Id.
130 Id.

The rest of this section refers to part of the Schedule of Specific Commitments of China[131] as an example of how to read the specific commitments. On top of the schedule table are the four modes of supply. The commitments are split into two sections: the horizontal commitments and specific commitments in transport services. In the horizontal commitments which apply to all sectors included in the schedule, China has listed out limitations in mode 3 of commercial presence in certain service fields for market access. In the limitation on national treatment, the horizontal commitments do not apply to all the existing subsidies to domestic services suppliers in the sectors of audio-visual, aviation and medical services, which are termed as "UNBOUND". There is no additional commitment under the horizontal commitment schedule.

In specific commitments, Sub-section A of maritime transport under Section 11 of transport services is taken as an example. For market access, there is no limitation on modes 1 and 2, which reads "NONE". Mode 3 is divided into two sub-sections. In sub-section One, China makes commitment on the establishment of registered companies for the purpose of operating a fleet under the national flag of the People's Republic of China. There are certain limitations such as the ceiling percentage of foreign investment in the total registered capital of joint ventures. In sub-section Two, China makes no commitment in "other forms of commercial presence for the supply of international maritime transport services", which reads "UNBOUND". For mode 4, China makes no specific commitments in ship's crew and key personnel except as indicated in horizontal commitments.

For national treatment, there is no limitation on modes 1 and 2, which read "NONE". In mode 3, there is no limitation on the establishment of registered companies for the purpose of operating a fleet under the national flag of the People's Republic of China, which read "NONE"; similarly in market access, China makes no commitment in "other forms of commercial presence for the sup-

131 WTO, Trade in Services, The People's Republic of China, Schedule of Specific Commitments, GATS/SC/135, 14th February 2002.

ply of international maritime transport services", which reads "UNBOUND". For mode 4, China makes no specific commitments in ship's crew and key personnel except as indicated in horizontal commitments. In addition, China makes additional commitments in a number of services at the port to international maritime transport suppliers on reasonable and non-discriminatory terms and conditions.

Modes of supply: (1) Cross-border supply (2) Consumption abroad
(3) Commercial presence (4) Presence of natural persons

Sector or sub-sector	Limitation on market access	Limitation on national treatment	Additional commitments
I. HORIZONTAL COMMITMENTS			
ALL SECTORS INCLUDED IN THIS SCHEDULE	(3) In China, foreign invested enterprises include foreign capital enterprises (also referred to as wholly foreign-owned enterprises) and joint venture enterprises and there are two types of joint venture enterprises: equity joint ventures and contractual joint ventures. The proportion of foreign investment in an equity joint venture shall be no less than 25 per cent of the registered capital of the joint venture. The establishment of branches by foreign enterprises is unbound, unless otherwise indicated in specific sub-sectors, as the laws and regulations on branches of foreign enterprises are under formulation.	(3) Unbound for all the existing subsidies to domestic services suppliers in the sectors of audio-visual, aviation and medical services.	
II. SPECIFIC COMMITMENTS			
11. TRANSPORT SERVICES			

Modes of supply: (1) Cross-border supply (2) Consumption abroad
(3) Commercial presence (4) Presence of natural persons

Sector or sub-sector	Limitation on market access	Limitation on national treatment	Additional commitments
A. Maritime Transport Services – International transport (freight and passengers) (CPC 7211 and 7212 less cabotage transport services)	(1) (a) Liner shipping (including passenger transportation): None (b) Bulk, tramp and other international shipping (including passenger transportation): None (2) None (3) (a) Establishment of registered companies for the purpose of operating a fleet under the national flag of the People's Republic of China: – Foreign service suppliers are permitted to establish joint venture shipping companies. – Foreign investment shall not exceed 49 per cent of the total registered capital of the joint venture. – The chairman of board of directors and the general manager of the joint venture shall be appointed by the Chinese side. (b) Other forms of commercial presence for the supply of international maritime transport services: Unbound (4) (a) Ship's crew: Unbound except as indicated in horizontal commitments. (b) Key personnel employed by Commercial Presence as defined under mode (3) (b) above: Unbound except as indicated in horizontal commitments.	(1) (a) None (b) None (2) None (3) (a) None (b) Unbound (4) (a) Unbound except as indicated in horizontal commitments. (b) Unbound except as indicated in horizontal commitments.	The following services at the port are made available to international maritime transport suppliers on reasonable and non-discriminatory terms and conditions: 1. Pilotage 2. Towing and tug assistance 3. Provisioning, fuelling and watering 4. Garbage collecting and ballast waste disposal 5. Port Captain's services 6. Navigation aids 7. Shore-based operational services essential to ship operations, including communications, water and electrical supplies 8. Emergency repair facilities 9. Anchorage, berth and berthing services.

3.1.2.3 Three-pillar Schedule

The schedules of maritime transport services that formed the basis of negotiations in the Uruguay Round comprised three pillars: international maritime transport, maritime auxiliary services and access to and use of port services[132].

132 For a comprehensive analysis of coverage of maritime transport services under the GATS, see WTO Secretariat, *Guide to the GATS, an Overview of*

Apart from issues such as national cargo reservation, the first pillar, international maritime transport is relatively liberal. As discussed in Chapter 2 of this work, international maritime freight transport has developed in two specialized activities based on the differences in commodity types and technological requirements, liner shipping and tramp shipping. According to WTO documents[133], tramp shipping is a highly competitive market and free from most restrictions, while liner shipping is subject to both government restrictions and private arrangements.

With the greater demand for the international freight logistics services, carriers have increased their involvement in landside activities such as cargo handling and storage services. This situation has brought increased focus on the second pillar – maritime auxiliary services, during WTO negotiations, with countries starting to make some commitments in respect of auxiliary services.

The third pillar, access to and use of port services covered all other services provided to ships while accessing and berthing in ports. This represents a fundamental part of international maritime transport services concerned with the smooth and effective transfer of goods and passengers. However, due to the sensitive nature of port access issue, which will be discussed in Chapter 4 of this work, countries are only willing to offer port services on a reciprocal and non-discriminatory basis. Therefore in the schedules, this section was listed under the "Additional Commitments" column.

During the Uruguay Round, it was suggested by some member states that various elements of multimodal transport services should be included in the negotiations. It was pointed out that the suppliers of international maritime transport services should be able to have access to services necessary for providing door-to-door transport services on reasonable and non-discriminatory terms and conditions[134]. In the Doha Round of negotiations, some WTO mem-

---

Issues for Further Liberalization of Trade in Services, Kluwer Law International, 2000. See also the OECD introduction to basic terminology as applicable to maritime transport services schedules, supra footnote 7.

133 WTO Secretariat Background Paper, see supra note 8, p. 3.

134 UNCTAD, "Negotiations on Transport and Logistics Services: Issues to Consider", UNCTAD/SDTE/TLB/2005/3, Geneva, 2006, p. 11.

ber countries continued to stress the importance of multimodal transport and put forward proposals to integrate it into the negotiations. Several proposals were raised to define multimodal transport and its proposed scope in the negotiation[135]. Multimodal transport will be further discussed in the later section of this Chapter.

Besides the GATS, the provisions and associated multilateral agreements under the GATT also relate to maritime transport services from different perspectives. Among them, Article V on Freedom of Transit aims to ensure the smooth movement of goods and vessels in international trade. Moreover, several pertinent multilateral agreements, including Agreements on Preshipment Inspection, Technical Barriers to Trade, and the Application of Sanitary and Phytosanitary Measures, also affect different aspects of maritime transport services. These provisions and agreements will be discussed later in this work.

3.1.2.4 The United Nations Central Product Classification

International classifications refer to statistical standards developed and adopted by international agencies and recommended for use by international, national and regional statistical institutions. They are used directly or as reference classifications for grouping and organizing statistical information relating to a wide range of economic and social issues[136]. The Central Product Classification Version 1.0 (CPC v. 1) is the international classification of all products, both goods and services, developed by the UN[137]. It serves as a statistical reference classification for services, together with product data relating to production, distribution and international trade of goods and services.

135 Id. p. 12.

136 Shaila Nijhowne, "Classification, the Measurement of Production and International Trade in Services and GATS", Statistics Canada and David Usher, Services Trade Policy, Department of Foreign Affairs and International Trade, Canada, p. 2.

137 Id. p. 2. See also United Nations (1998) "Central Product Classification" (CPC), Statistical Papers, Series No. 77, Version 1.0, United Nations, New York, US.

Under the GATS, schedules are based on a service classification table (W/120)[138] drawn from the United Nations CPC. The scheduling guidelines developed during the Uruguay Round indicate "Schedules record, for each sector, the legally enforceable commitments of each Member. It is therefore vital that schedules be clear, precise and based on a common format and terminology."[139] In order to maintain certainty and clarity in the schedules, the sectors and sub-sectors contained in the Secretariat list are identified by the corresponding CPC number. Many WTO member countries use the W/120 list to schedule their commitments. At the same time, many of them also clarify the commitments under CPC.

As discussed earlier in this Chapter, the negotiations on maritime transport services evolved on the three pillars of international shipping, maritime auxiliary services, and access to and use of port facilities. Commitments on the first two pillars are scheduled under Article XVI and Article XVII while commitments on the third pillar are scheduled under Article XVIII on additional commitments. Some countries followed the W/120 classification in their commitments, yet other countries chose to follow the draft schedule classification. According to the WTO Secretariat, these different approaches have created difficulties in comparing the range of commitments undertaken by the Member countries. To be specific[140]:

Differences in coverage: as illustrated in the table below[141], the coverage of maritime transport services in the two classifications is not exactly the same. In the W/120 classification, the second

138 WTO Secretariat, "Uruguay Round – Group of Negotiations on Services – Services Sectoral Classification List – Note by the Secretariat", MTN.GNS/W/120, 10 July 1991.

139 Shaila Nijhowne, supra note 136. See also WTO Secretariat, "Uruguay Round – Group of Negotiations on Services – Scheduling of Initial Commitments in Trade in Services: Explanatory Note", MTN.GNS/W/164, 3 September 1993, p. 6.

140 The following analysis is from WTO Secretariat, supra note 138, pp. 451–453.

141 Source of table: id. p. 453.

pillar of auxiliary services is not part of maritime transport services alone. Instead, it is part of a general category under the title of "services auxiliary to all modes of transport". On the other hand, the draft schedule does not include "rental of vessels with crew (CPC 7213)" as well as "maintenance and repair of vessels (part of CPC 8868)".

Difference in scope of commitments: scheduling commitments are also different under the two classifications in some respects. The WTO Secretariat points out that this issue is particularly serious with regard to port services[142]. A major gap exists between the two classifications, whereby W/120 is concerned only with the rights of suppliers of port services, the draft schedule is concerned only with the rights of consumers of port services. At a time when many countries are in the process of privatizing their port facilities and attracting foreign investment, this problem may lead to serious difficulties when countries choose different classifications[143].

The WTO Secretariat suggests that one solution is that member countries reach an agreement on a composite list combining both the draft schedule and the W/120 at the beginning of the negotiation. Countries who followed the draft schedule before may consider inserting in "rental of vessel with crew" and "maintenance and repair of vessels" into their commitments. Countries who chose W/120 in the previous commitments may explicitly list out in their commitments certain "auxiliary services" such as customs clearance and container station and depot services, and certain "port services"[144]. Whether or not this suggestion will be workable depends on the willingness of member countries to come to such an agreement. Some countries are reluctant to open up markets for various services, especially in areas of port services. This would make it hard for them to accept a combined schedule of commitments.

142 Id. p. 452.
143 Id. p. 452.
144 Id. p. 453.

Table 16.5: Alternative classifications of maritime transport services: draft schedule and W/120

DRAFT SCHEDULE	GNS/W/120	
MARITIME TRANSPORT SERVICES	11A. MARITIME TRANSPORT SERVICES	
International Transport (freight and passengers)	Aa. Passenger transportation	CPC 7211
CPC 7211 end 7212 less cabotage transport	Ab. Freight transportation	CPC 7212
	Ac. Rental of vessels with crew	CPC 7213
MARITIME AUXILIARY SERVICES	11H. SERVICES AUXILIARY TO All MODES OF TRANSPORT	
.. Maritime Cargo Handling Services (not including direct activities of independently organized dockers)	Ha. Cargo-handling services	CPC 741
.. Storage and Warehousing Services CPC 742 (as amended)	Hb. Storage and warehouse services	CPC 742
– Customs Clearance Services		
– Container Station and Depot Services		
Maritime Agency Services		
– Maritime Freight Forwarding Services	Hc. Freight transport agency services	CPC 748
PORT SERVICES	11Af. SUPPORTING SERVICES FOR MARITIME TRANSPORT	CPC 745
1. Pilotage	(Af) Pilotage ond berthing	CPC 7452
2. Towing and tug assistance	Ae. Pushing and towing services	CPC 7214
3. Provisioning, fuelling and watering		
4. Garbage collecting and ballast waste disposal	(Af) Other supporting services for water transport	CPC 7459
5. Port Captains' services		
6. Navigation aids	(Af) Navigation aids	CPC7453
7. Shore-based operational services essential to ship operations, including communications, water and electrical supplies		
8. Emergency repair facilities	Ad. Maintenance and repair of vessels	CPC 8868*
[9. Anchorage, berth and berthing services]	(Af) Pilotage and berthing	CPC 7452
	(Af) Port and waterway operation	CPC 7451
	(Af) Vessel salvage und refloating	CPC 7454

Source of table: WTO Secretariat, "Uruguay Round – Group of Negotiations on Services – Services Sectoral Classification List – Note by the Secretariat", MTN.GNS/W/120, 10 July 1991, p. 453.

3.1.3 Impediments on Maritime Transport Services

Maritime transport is a relatively liberal transport sector. Nevertheless, there remain some impediments to free and open access to maritime transport services in a number of areas in developing and developed countries alike.

Restrictions on trade in maritime transport services are barriers that limit the service suppliers from having access to and entering or operating in a market[145]. These restrictions are usually imposed by governments and in nature they can be either discriminatory or non-discriminatory. Discriminatory regulations treat foreign maritime service suppliers less favourably than domestic maritime service suppliers and often aim to restrict trade. The most obvious example is cabotage. Non-discriminatory regulations, on the other hand, treat domestic and foreign maritime service suppliers equally. However, they still can have restrictive impact by, for example, requiring mandatory use of a designated supply of port services by domestic and foreign shipping service suppliers. In many cases, such restrictions can be more burdensome than necessary for the efficient operation of maritime transport services[146].

Market access restrictions on maritime transport services include restrictions on commercial presence, such as restrictions on entry of foreign capital; requirements for domestic equity participation; requirements for joint venture arrangements; as well as other legislative and regulatory restrictions on foreign presence in the maritime transport industry. Moreover, it may also include restrictions on access to international maritime transport such as restrictions on allocation of cargo on particular routes to bilateral, plurilateral and multilateral agreements (cargo sharing); preferential treatment of shipping service providers from specific economies on the basis of international agreements or for other reasons; restrictions on carrying government cargo to national flag vessels (except defence and other national security-related cargoes); and discriminatory taxation regimes and port dues for foreign companies and foreign flag vessels.

145 Analysis of restrictions on trade in maritime transport services can be found in many writings, such as Greg McGuire, Michele Schuele and Tina Smith, "Restrictiveness of international trade in maritime services", in Christopher Findley and Tony Warren, *Impediments to Trade in Services: Measurement and Policy Implications,* Routledge, London, 2000, pp. 172–189.

146 Id.

The restrictions on maritime transport services have been summarized in various ways, which generally encompass the following points[147]:

- Right to fly the national flag: Requires ships to be registered or licensed to provide maritime services on domestic and international routes. The conditions on registration may include having a commercial presence in the domestic economy, the ship being built and owned domestically, and meeting seaworthiness and safety requirements.
- Cabotage: Restricts shipping services on domestic or coastal routes to licensed vessels that meet certain conditions. Shipping services between domestic ports may be required to be carried out by domestically owned, operated, built and crewed ships.
- Cargo sharing: Stipulates the allocation of cargo on particular routes between parties to bilateral and multilateral agreements.
- Bilateral agreements: Agreements between two economies that primarily restrict the supply of shipping services and the allocation of cargo. Some bilateral agreements also restrict the use of port facilities.
- United Nations Convention on a Code of Conduct for Liner Conferences (UN Liner Code)[148]: it stipulates that conference trade between two countries can allocate cargo according to a 40:40:20 principle, with 40 percent of tonnage reserved for the national flag lines of each economy and the remaining 20 percent to be allocated to liner ships from third countries. The Code also entitles any national flag shipping line to be a member of a conference and to fix freight rates.

Burdensome non-tariff measures and anti-competitive business practices often become barriers to free and efficient trade. Such measures and practices can include, for example, unreasonable

147 Id.

148 A detailed discussion of the UN Liner Code is made in Chapter 6 of this work.

environmental and safety standards, burdensome vessel and cargo examination procedures and cumbersome port access and clearance procedures[149]. Restrictions on maritime transport services not only hinder the efficient and timely operation of transport itself, but also incur high transport cost. Despite efficiencies from the technological revolution in transport, such as containerization, maritime transport costs still have a profound influence on international trade. As pointed out by the World Bank, restrictions such as the UN Liner Code, bilateral agreements with state trading countries, unilateral cargo reservations, and public monopoly of harbour services, have diminished noticeably, but significant obstacles still exist in maritime transport services[150].

The restriction to maritime transport services may also be reflected in the limitation to MFN treatment, government procurement and multi-modal transport. In MFN treatment limitation (which will be further discussed later in this Chapter), reciprocity conditions and counter-measures may be used by governments in the supply of maritime-related services[151]. For government procurement, the so-called "non-commercial" cargoes may be used against the free supply of maritime and related services. In the field of multi-modal transport, which will also be discussed later, any restriction on the access to and use of inland transport could prove to be an impediment directly affecting the whole transport chains including maritime transport services.

149 Department of Foreign Affairs and Trade, Australia, "Negotiating Proposal for Maritime Transport Services", available at the website of the Department: www.dfat.gov.au revisited in June 2007.

150 Fink, C., Matoo, A. & Neagru, C., "Trade in International Maritime Services: How Much Does Policy Matter?" World Bank Development Research Group Working Paper No. 2522, 2000, p. 4.

151 See for example, Mattoo, "MFN and the GATS", infra note 154.

3.2 Key Principles and Issues

Many issues relating to the provisions of maritime transport services come under the WTO general disciplines, which can be classified under the principles of MFN, national treatment and market access respectively. For example:

- Issues under the principle of most-favoured-nation treatment
  - Cargo-sharing mechanism with partner countries
  - Preferential treatment regarding the supply of international transport
  - Unilateral counter-measures against perceived restrictions by partner countries
  - Selective reciprocity and/or selective restrictions
- Issues under the principle of national treatment
  - Direct preferential treatment to national shipping enterprises
  - Indirect preferential treatment to national shipping enterprises
- Issues under the principle of market access
  - Minimum conditions for granting the right to fly national flag
  - The number of maritime transport suppliers in the form of numerical quotas, monopolies, exclusive suppliers, etc.
  - The total value of maritime transport transactions, the total number of maritime transport operation, or the total quantity of maritime transport output
  - The total number of foreign natural persons employed
  - The requirements of economic needs test

The table below shows the regime of maritime transport services under GATS general principles. The GATS recognizes the right of governments to impose minimum standards and conditions such as qualification requirements and procedures, technical standards, licensing and authorization. In maritime services, many of these regulations have been laid down to ensure safe shipping and port operations.

Maritime transport services regime under GATS general principles[152]

	GATS general principles	*Relevance to shipping regime*
MFN/Non-discrimination	Unconditional application	Removal of cargo reservation and other discriminatory measures
Transparency	Prompt (at least by the time of enforcement) announcement of all relevant measures pertaining to/affecting the operation of GATS	Transparency in government practices in cargo preference, private agreement/measures for cargo reservation and subsidies, technical standards, and so on
Increasing participation of developing countries	Promotion of service industries in developing countries	Removal of cargo allocation in developed countries; promotion of technology transfer and application; support for staff training; investment in ships
General exceptions	When related to national security or national interest	For example, transportation of military items

In October 2000, the European Communities; Hong Kong, China; Japan; the Republic of Korea; Norway and Singapore put forward to the WTO Secretariat their joint statement on maritime transport services[153]. This made maritime transport part of the agenda and work program for the Special Session of the Council for Trade in Services. There seems to be a growing need to enhance the position of this sector in the WTO system through real and meaningful liberalization and an increased number of commitments in the course of the negotiations. One of the key issues for many member countries is how to expand the coverage of commitments and create a more transparent and secure trading environment by making more market access commitments. The feasibility of integrating multi-modal transport into the negotiation agenda remains a

152 Source of the table: CHIA Lin Sien, Lloyd C. Onyirimba and George S. Akpan, "Liberalization of Maritime Transport Services: Directions and Options for Asia", in Will Martin and Mari Pangestu (eds.), *Options for Global Trade Reform, A View from the Asia-Pacific*, Cambridge University Press, 2003, pp. 145–173.

153 WTO Council for Trade in Services, "Joint Statement from the European Communities and Their Member States; Hong Kong, China; Japan; Republic of Korea; Norway and Singapore, the Negotiations on Maritime Transport Services", S/CSS/W/8, 6 October 2000.

controversial topic. In addition, it is also a shared concern as to when the MFN clause can come into force and the current MFN exemptions can be reduced or eliminated. Whether the GATS disciplines on market access and national treatment can be effectively strengthened is critical to the success of the coming negotiations on this section of transport.

3.2.1 The Principle of Most-Favoured-Nation Treatment

As reflected in both the GATT (Article I) and the GATS (Article II), the MFN principle is one of the most important pillars for realizing trade liberalization in a multilateral framework[154]. The MFN obligation under the GATT covers not only internal taxes and regulations referred to in the GATT national treatment provision but also relevant border measures[155]. In regard to state enterprises and enterprises enjoying exclusive or special privileges, Article XVII of the GATT requires that such enterprises shall, in their purchases or sales involving imports or exports, act in a manner consistent with the general principles of non-discriminatory treatment described in the GATT for governmental measures affecting imports or exports by private traders.

Under the GATS, whereas the national treatment obligation only applies where a specific commitment has been made, the MFN obligation contained in Article II is a general application subject to an once-off list of exceptions. In respect of monopolies and exclusive service suppliers, the provisions of Article VIII require that any such enterprise, in the supply of a monopoly service in a

154 For elaboration of MFN principle, see for example Mattoo Aaditya, "MFN and the GATS", in: Cottier, Thomas and Petros Mavroidis (eds.), *Regulatory Barriers and the Principle of Non-discrimination in World Trade Law*. Ann Arbour: University of Michigan Press, 2000.

155 "Customs, duties and charges of any kind imposed on or in connection with importation or exportation or imposed on the international transfer of payments for imports or exports, and with respect to the method of levying such duties and charges, and with respect to all rules and formalities in connection with importation and exportation ..." Article I:1 of the GATT.

relevant market, not act in a manner inconsistent with a Member's MFN obligation[156]. In addition, instead of requesting the MFN obligation to be extended "immediately and unconditionally" to all WTO Members, the GATS applies a "treatment no less favourable" standard for expressing its MFN obligation.

There exist a number of important exceptions or qualifications to the application of the MFN principle. In addition, in regard to the GATT, important exceptions to the MFN principle are permitted for customs unions and free-trade area agreements (Article XXIV), and preferences in favour of and between developing countries (the Enabling Clause)[157]. Under the GATS, Members are allowed to register a once-off list of exemptions from the MFN treatment standard. These exemptions are subject to review five years after the entry into force of the WTO and, in principle, should not exceed a period of ten years[158]. The GATS also allows an exception from MFN treatment for economic integration agreements, subject to certain conditions, and exempts from its rules air transport traffic rights and services directly related to their exercise, as well as measures taken for prudential reasons in the financial services sector[159].

Due to the fact that many WTO member countries are not willing to eliminate all the discriminatory measures in the fields of trade in services, the MFN principle has been challenged by departures from its obligations, such as the exceptions for regional integration agreements and the MFN exemptions listed by member countries.

One major departure from MFN obligations are regional integration agreements under GATT Article XXIV (Territorial Appli-

156 WTO, "The Fundamental WTO Principles of National Treatment, Most-Favoured-Nation Treatment and Transparency", WT/WGTCP/W/114, 14 April 1999, p. 12.

157 Id. p. 14. Decision of 28 November 1979 on "Differential and More Favourable Treatment, Reciprocity and Fuller Participation of Developing Countries", GATT, BISD 26S/203.

158 Most of the exemptions listed are in the areas of maritime, transport and audiovisual services.

159 Annexes to the GATS on Air Transport Services and Financial Services.

cation – Frontier Traffic – Customs Unions and Free-trade Areas) and GATS Article V (Economic Integration), which allow the WTO members to liberalize trade in services under certain conditions within their regional scopes. Besides, under Article Vbis of the GATS (Labour Markets Integration Agreements), countries are allowed to take part in agreements which establish full integration of labour markets. In both Article V and Vbis, the parties have to ensure that the agreement in question meets the criteria set out in Article V and Vbis, e.g., substantial sectoral coverage and the absence or elimination of substantially all discrimination[160].

The other departure from MFN obligations is the MFN exemptions listed by members. Member countries can establish a list of Article II Exemptions which is attached to the schedule of commitments. This was considered necessary because when GATS came into force, some countries already had bilateral or regional agreements with trading partners, either bilaterally or in small groups. WTO members felt it was necessary to maintain these preferences temporarily. However, the exemption could only be made once and nothing can be added to the lists. The MFN exemption list contains:

- Description of the sector or sub-sector to which the exemption applies;
- Description of the measure, indicating why it is inconsistent with Article II;
- The country or countries to which the measure applies;
- The intended duration of the exemption;
- The conditions creating the need for the exemption

Annex on Article II Exemptions of the GATS specifies the conditions that are exempt from obligations under paragraph 1 of Article II, such as "in principle, such exemptions should not exceed a period of 10 years", or "in any event, they shall be subject to

160 "Trade in Services: A Roadmap to GATS MFN Exemptions", OECD Working Party of the Trade Committee, TD/TC/WP (2001)25/FINAL, 29-Oct-2001, p. 5.

negotiation in subsequent trade-liberalizing rounds"[161]. Thus, the MFN exemptions are subject to the current services negotiations pursuant to paragraph 6 of the Guidelines and Procedures for the Negotiations (S/L/93), and their elimination and reduction should be one of the most important topics of discussion in progressively achieving a higher level of liberalization. Japan stated in its proposal (S/CS/W/42) submitted in December 2000, that it shares with other Members, for example Hong Kong, China (S/CS/W/6), the idea of eliminating all registered MFN exemptions by the end of 2004, or at the conclusion of the current negotiations, whichever comes earlier[162].

Meetings on the MFN exemption review were held in 2000 as ad hoc sessions of the Council for Trade in Services, which provided background information on the registered measures, including the conditions that created the need for the exemptions at the outset. The results of the MFN exemption review, and the subsequent discussions, should be effectively used during the future negotiations regarding the reduction and elimination of MFN exemptions[163]. Mattoo pointed out that during the negotiations, the possibility of retaining MFN exemptions had been used by some countries as negotiating leverage to obtain additional concessions, rather than for its original purpose of "grandfathering" existing preferential treatment or reciprocity requirements in domestic legislation[164].

The MFN exemption has been widely utilized in maritime transport services. Up to date, however, not many specific commitments have been made and discriminatory practices remain a serious problem. According to Mattoo's argument[165], one major reason for the MFN exempted measures is the existence of sector-specific bilateral,

161 The Ministry of Foreign Affairs of Japan, "MFN exemption: Analysis and Proposal", May 2001, available at the website of the Ministry: http://www.mofa.go.jp revisited in August 2007.

162 Id.

163 Id.

164 Mattoo, supra note 154.

165 Mattoo, supra note 154, p. 18.

regional or plurilateral agreements. In maritime transport services, nearly half of the exemptions are for measures implementing the provisions of the UN Liner Code[166]. Another agreement-related exemption in maritime transport services typically refers to existing or future bilateral or multilateral agreements granting cabotage rights on a reciprocal basis. In addition, many countries have unilaterally imposed reciprocity conditions which specify that they are willing to provide access to their market only to those countries which provide them with access to their own market.

The GATS *Annex on Negotiations on Maritime Transport Services* has special implications for the MFN coverage and listing of the MFN exemptions. It provides for the suspension of Article II until the conclusion of the negotiations in this sector which, in accordance with Article XIX of the GATS, resumed in January 2000. Article 1 of the Annex states that:

> Article II and the Annex on Article II Exemptions, including the requirement to list in the Annex any measure inconsistent with most-favoured-nation treatment that a Member will maintain, shall enter into force for international shipping, auxiliary services and access to and use of port facilities only on:
>
> (a) the implementation date to be determined under paragraph 4 of the Ministerial Decision on Negotiations on Maritime Transport Services; or,
> (b) should the negotiations not succeed, the date of the final report of the Negotiating Group on Maritime Transport Services provided for in that Decision.

At the same time, Article 2 of the Annex also provides that the regulation in Article 1 does not apply to maritime transport activities for which specific commitments have been made in a Member's schedule. These regulations have limited the effectiveness of MFN in maritime transport sectors and given member countries larger flexibility to bypass their MFN obligations.

The exclusion of maritime transport services seriously undermines the operation of GATS principles in the field. Countries like

166 More discussion of this Convention is conducted in Chapter 6 of this work.

the US, who have suspended the MFN obligation from the section, have had a major disruptive effect on the relevant negotiations[167]. In order to gradually diminish the negative effects of the MFN exemptions, liberalization work should start from bilateral and regional agreements on maritime transport services that contain the MFN exemptions. In the communication to the WTO Council for Trade in Service, Norway put forward several principles on the MFN exemption[168], according to which, provisions in bilateral agreements which are entered as the MFN exemptions should only be recognized when both parties to the agreement take equivalent MFN exemptions. The MFN exemption lists in these agreements should not be allowed to contain reservations or measures aiming at securing access to cargo on a basis of reciprocity. The existing reservations or measures with this purpose should be phased out during future negotiations. In addition, such lists should not establish any right to introduce future restrictions beyond what is directly provided for by the GATS agreement. Lastly, the existing MFN exemptions in bilateral and regional agreements should not provide a basis for countermeasures in the future negotiations on maritime transport services[169].

3.2.2 The Principle of National Treatment

Together with MFN, national treatment represents the fundamental principle of non-discrimination in the WTO law. It is also regarded as one of the cornerstones of the WTO system which is applicable throughout WTO agreements.

167 The original US MFN exemption for maritime transport services reserved the "right to investigate and take action against foreign carriers to address adverse or unfavourable actions affecting US shipping or US carriers in US ocean-borne commerce and the cross trades between foreign ports". See supra note 154, p. 20.

168 WTO, Council for Trade in Services, Communication from Norway, S/CSS/W/59.

169 Id.

Under the GATT, national treatment refers to the treatment of foreign products (or suppliers) not with respect to each other but with respect to national products (or suppliers). According to the WTO Secretariat[170], the essence of the principle of national treatment is to require that a WTO Member does not put the goods or services or persons of other WTO Members at a competitive disadvantage *vis-à-vis* its own goods or services or nationals.

Article III of the GATT serves the purpose of ensuring that internal measures are not used to nullify or impair the effect of tariff concessions and other multilateral rules applicable to border measures[171]. It requires that internal taxes, regulations and the like should not be applied to imported or domestic products so as to afford protection to domestic production. The WTO Secretariat points out that the focus of the GATT is on the control and liberalization of border measures restricting international trade. Any border measures designed to give a competitive advantage to domestic products should take the form of customs tariffs imposed at the border. The level of such customs tariffs should be a matter for negotiation and binding in national schedules[172].

The closest applicability of this Article to maritime transport services is in paragraphs (1) and (4), in which the types of measures applies are "all laws, regulations and requirements affecting the internal sale, offering for sale, purchase, ***transportation***, distribution or use" of products of national origin (emphasis added by the author). Thus the laws, regulations and requirements on maritime transportation are within the scope of this Article. Furthermore, the provisions of paragraph (4) are highly relevant to the area of competition law and policy, which significantly influence the further liberalization of maritime transport services, especially on those fields discussed in this work: access to port, cabotage, as well as liner shipping.

170 WTO Secretariat, supra note 156, p. 4.
171 Id. p. 4.
172 Id. p. 4.

In both the GATT and GATS, the scope of the national treatment is limited in one way or another[173]. The GATT requirement is limited to internal measures and the corresponding requirement in the GATS is dependent on specific commitments having been scheduled by the Member concerned. In addition, there are a number of permissible exceptions to the national treatment principle under the two Agreements[174]. Some key exceptions that GATT and GATS share include:

- government procurement of goods and services (Article III:8 (a) of the GATT and Article XIII of the GATS);
- general exceptions covering such matters as measures necessary to protect public morals or maintain public order, to protect human, animal, or plant life or health and to secure compliance with laws and regulations not inconsistent with the provisions of the agreement in question (Article XX of GATT and Article XIV of GATS);
- security exceptions (Article XXI of the GATT and Article XIV*bis* of the GATS).

Moreover, in both GATT and the GATS, the no-less-favourable-treatment standard has to be met in regard, respectively, to "like products" and "like services and service suppliers"[175].

While national treatment applies in general for trade in goods, this principle is relevant to trade in services only to the extent that it is listed in the members' schedules of commitments. Moreover, the principle of national treatment is also incorporated in various other agreements that form part of Annex IA of the WTO Agreement – the part of the WTO that contains multilateral agreements on trade in goods, for example the TBT Agreement and the SPS Agreement.

The WTO has identified some major differences of national treatment in the GATS compared to in the GATT, which include the difference in subject-matter, the scopes of application and the

173 Id. p. 4.
174 Id. p. 10.
175 Id. p. 9.

"no less favourable treatment standard"[176]. For example, in Article III of the GATT, the subject matter is the products of other Members, while in the GATS the subject matters can be both the services of other Members and the service suppliers of other Members[177]. Article XXVIII of the GATS has listed out the definition of the service suppliers, which includes natural persons of other Members, as well as local subsidiaries or branches of foreign-owned or controlled companies[178].

The national treatment standard in Article III of the GATT applies to internal taxes, laws and regulations including where they are collected or enforced at the point or time of importation[179]. The national treatment principle in the GATS, on the other hand, applies in respect of "all measures affecting the supply of services". Article I:3 makes it clear that such measures mean measures taken by central, regional or local governments and authorities, and non-governmental bodies in the exercise of powers delegated by such governments or authorities. Article XXVIII (c) defines "measures by Members affecting trade in services" to include measures in respect of: (i) the purchase, payment or use of a service; (ii) the access to and use of, in connection with the supply of one service, services which are required by those Members to be offered to the public generally; and (iii) the presence, including commercial presence, of persons of a Member for the supply of a service in the territory of another Member[180].

According to the WTO Secretariat, the interpretation of "no less favourable treatment standard" in Article III of the GATT requires equality of competitive opportunities between domestically produced and imported products. It prohibits measures that may adversely affect the conditions of competition facing imported products relative to domestically produced products on the internal market[181]. In the GATS, no less favourable treatment standards

176 Id. pp. 5–9.
177 Id. p. 5.
178 Id. p. 5.
179 Id. p. 6.
180 Id. p. 7.
181 Id. p. 7.

aims to ensure no less favourable conditions are built into the national treatment provision of the Agreement. As paragraph 3 of Article XVII states:

> Formally identical or formally different treatment shall be considered to be less favourable if it modifies the conditions of competition in favour of services or service suppliers of the Member compared to like service or service suppliers of any other Member.[182]

3.2.3 The Principle of Transparency

The principle of transparency requires the openness and impartiality of decision making in the design, introduction, administration and enforcement of new or amended regulations[183]. Such requirement is particularly important for the further liberalization of maritime transport services, especially in areas affecting access to port and coastal shipping. In most circumstances, these areas are heavily regulated by different levels of domestic laws and government policies, with various kinds of procedures, fees and formalities. Transparency in the domestic regulatory processes relating to maritime transport services is a key means of providing business with predicable conditions for access to and operation in foreign markets. It enables foreign business to obtain information on the conditions and constraints they will encounter in entering and operating in a market (such as port services and auxiliary services). It also enables them to acquire knowledge of the regulatory requirements and procedures that they need to comply with, as well as a more precise picture of the costs and returns on their presence or investment[184].

Moreover, transparency also helps to create additional incentives for governments to apply regulation in a non-discretionary

182 Id. p. 8.

183 OECD Working Party of the Trade Committee, "Strengthening Regulatory Transparency: Insights for the GATS from the Regulatory Reform Country Reviews", TD/TC/WP (99)43/FINAL, 11 April 2000, p. 4.

184 Id. p. 4

way, thus helping to reduce the incidence of arbitrary decisions at both regulatory policy-making level and regulatory implementation level[185].

The Rationale for Transparency

As regulatory measures affecting trade in services are inherently non-transparent, regulatory transparency is an important component to facilitate such trade. Transparency provides an essential tool to service providers in making clear on the discriminatory elements present in the measures affecting services trade and the regulatory requirements in place that govern the operation of all services providers in a given market. This includes making explicit the rationale behind regulatory decision-making, along with those procedures involved in administering, implementing and enforcing regulations[186].

In its paper "The Fundamental WTO Principles of National Treatment, Most-Favoured-Nation Treatment and Transparency", the WTO Secretariat has set out four ways in which transparency promotes the facilitation and liberalization of trade flows[187].

> (i) First, to promote a rules-based approach to trade policy and measures at the national level. A basic condition for the rule of law in this area is that of publication of all legal requirements and, wherever possible, their non-enforcement before persons subject to them have had a chance to become acquainted with them. The provisions concerning the impartial administration of such legal requirements and the scope for review by an independent body of decisions concerning their application also serve this function.
>
> (ii) Second, to provide information to economic actors so that they can take maximum advantage of the opportunities created by WTO rules and commitments, whether this concerns market access, protection of intellectual property or other relevant matters.

185 Id. p. 4.
186 Sherry Stephenson and Soonhwa Yi, "Transparency in Regulation of Services", paper prepared for the APEC Group on Services meeting held on 19–20 February 2002, p. 2.
187 WTO supra note 156, p. 15.

(iii) Third, to facilitate monitoring of compliance with obligations under the WTO and, through this means, the avoidance of disputes.
(iv) Fourth, to facilitate future trade negotiations with a view to further liberalization of international trade.

WTO Provisions to Ensure Transparency

Transparency provisions in the GATT include Article X and Article XXII. Article X of the GATT 1947 deals with "Publication and administration of trade regulations". It required that "laws, regulations, judicial decisions and administrative rulings of general application" affecting goods and products in various ways "shall be published promptly in such a manner to enable governments and traders to become acquainted with them". "Agreements affecting international trade policy ... shall also be published." Furthermore, the enforcement of more burdensome, restrictive rules, or prohibition, on imports and payments therefore shall not be made before any measure has been "officially published". Article XXII calls on each contracting party to "accord sympathetic consideration to, and shall afford adequate opportunity for consultation regarding, such representations ... with respect to any matter affecting the operation" of the GATT. If in this way "it has not been possible to find a satisfactory solution" then the contracting parties may consult with any party or group of parties[188].

Moreover, the GATT Annex 1A Agreements on TBT and SPS also require notifications to the WTO and other members[189]. In particular, the SPS Agreement requires members, upon request from other members, to provide through an official enquiry point, information about risk assessment procedures, factors taken into consideration therein and the determination of the appropriate level of sanitary or phytosanitary protection required. It is possible to view the risk assessment process as a specific form of regulatory impact analysis undertaken in the context of food safety regulation. In this sense, the SPS agreement is unique among the

188 OECD supra note 183, p. 6.
189 Id. p. 7.

WTO Agreements in requiring a risk assessment process before the implementation of new measures[190].

In the GATS, the concept of transparency is first reflected in its Preamble:

> Wishing to establish a multilateral framework of principles and rules for trade in services with a view to the expansion of such trade under conditions of transparency and progressive liberalization...

Article III of the GATS contains the general operational obligations regarding transparency of measures affecting the operation of the GATS. Its scope is broader than some other GATS obligations (e.g. market access and national treatment) in that all but one of its sub-paragraphs applies regardless of whether a Member has made specific commitments under the GATS. It is noteworthy that, apart from Article III:1, the focus of Article III is provision of information at the multilateral level. Hence its obligations in this regard relate to the provision of information from one Member to another on request and to the Council for Trade in Services. In particular, the requirement in Article III:4 to establish one or more enquiry points is aimed at facilitating responses to requests for information from other Members (i.e. central governments) and not more generally (e.g. from business and civil society)[191].

The other important provision on transparency is Article VI on domestic regulation, whose primary focus is the implementation and administration of domestic regulations affecting trade in services[192]. While the word "transparency" is not mentioned, several of the requirements of the Article in fact aim to create more transparent domestic regulatory decision-making, implementation, administration and enforcement. One noteworthy aspect of this Article is that the right of service suppliers to information on regulatory and administrative decisions, and to judicial and administrative review and appeals processes, is explicitly recognised (Article VI:2 and 3). Another is that Article VI contains no provi-

190 Id. p. 8.
191 Id. p. 9.
192 Id. p. 9.

sions on notifications to the WTO or on bilateral consultations with other WTO Members. The relevance of paragraph 4 of this article with maritime transport services will be discussed in the latter part of this section.

Some other GATS Articles provide for the exercise of transparency procedures between the WTO members such as notifications to the WTO and Member-to-Member consultations under the WTO auspice. However, these Articles contain no specific requirements on transparency in domestic regulatory decision-making and administration[193].

- Article VII (Recognition) addresses recognition of education and experience obtained in another country. It contains an obligation to inform the Council for Trade in Services of existing recognition measures, of the opening of negotiations on an agreement or arrangement on recognition and of the adoption or modification of any new recognition measure;
- Article VIII (Monopolies and Exclusive Service Suppliers) contains a provision whereby the Council for Trade in Services may, at the request of a Member, request another Member to supply specific information concerning a monopoly supplier of that Member, and a requirement to notify the Council of new monopoly rights regarding supply of a service covered by a Member's specific commitments;
- Article IX (Business Practices) obliges a Member to enter into bilateral consultations when another Member requests it to do so in order to eliminate "those practices that may restrain competition and restrict trade in services. The Member subject of such a request shall cooperate through the supply of publicly available non confidential information" and "provide other information subject to its domestic law and to the conclusion of a satisfactory agreement concerning the safeguarding of confidentiality";
- Article XIII (Government Procurement) and Article XV (Subsidies) at this time do not contain substantive disciplines. Based

193 Id. p. 10.

> on experience in GATT, procedures to promote transparency in trade-related decision-making could be an important element of efforts to create GATS disciplines in these areas.

The main transparency provisions of both GATT and GATS contain exceptions making it clear that Members are not required to disclose confidential information which would impede law enforcement or otherwise be contrary to the public interest, or which would prejudice legitimate commercial interests of particular enterprises, public or private[194]. Similar clauses can be found in many of the other WTO agreements that form part of Annex IA of the WTO Agreement.

Further Enhance Transparency Mechanism for Maritime Transport Services

The main type of transparency apparent in the GATS is the national schedules of specific commitments, which, some scholars argue, are non-transparent in nature[195]. The GATS provides the WTO members with great flexibility in the way and content in which they set out specific commitments. Analysis of these commitments indicates that most countries scheduled only a very limited part of their services sector. Furthermore, it is impossible to obtain information on any service sector that is not included in the national schedule. Additionally, the possibility of including the mention of "unbound" against conditions of either "market access" or "national treatment" with respect to any of the four modes of service supply or delivery means that even for included sectors, there is no obligatory transparency or disclosure of regulatory practices[196].

Furthermore, there is criticism that the schedules are not user-friendly and that it is both difficult and confusing to read and

194 WTO, supra note 156. GATT Article X:1, GATS Article III*bis*.

195 See for example, Sherry Stephenson, "Can Regional Liberalization of Services Go further than Multilateral Liberalization under the GATS?" paper prepared for the World Trade Review, Volume 1, Number 2, July 2002.

196 Id.

interpret them. The confusion is to some extent due to the complexity of disentangling trade protection, overly restrictive approaches to national regulation and the pursuit of legitimate public policy goals. It also can be traced to the interweaving of market access and national treatment measures in the commitments[197].

Some WTO member countries suggest that the most effective mechanism to ensure regulator transparency is through building up of an open, easily assessable and effective system which makes information on regulations affecting trade in services available to service providers[198]. It is also observed that the effective regulatory transparency mechanism should operate both as ex ante as well as ex post regulatory instruments: that is, regulatory transparency is a process by which market players can participate in the process of designing new regulations and regulations can be disclosed and clarified[199].

To be specific, when making regulations, two mechanisms, prior consultation and regulatory impact analysis, would contribute to minimizing the discretion of regulators and ensuring the benefits of regulations outweigh costs[200]. Regulations that are already implemented can be disseminated via publication, establishment of interactive enquiry points and the construction of central coding or registration system[201]. These mechanisms apply to maritime transport services.

More importantly, for maritime transport services, transparency helps to reveal covert discrimination in domestic regulation that arises from exemptions from competition laws, such as in liner shipping, as well as denial of access for foreign services suppliers to port access, port facilities and auxiliary services. The impact of GATS Articles VII, VIII and XI on restrictive business practices in

197 Feketekuty, G. "Improving the Architecture of the GATS", in Services Trade in Western Hemisphere: Liberalization, Integration and Reform, edited by S. Stephenson, Washington D.C.: Brookings Institution Press, 2001.

198 Stephenson and Yi, supra note 186.

199 Id.

200 Id.

201 Id.

liner shipping will be discussed in Part II of this work. Moreover, the regulations in GATS Article VI: 4[202] are closely relevant to maritime transport services and lists out three types of requirements aiming at enhancing transparency: firstly, qualification requirements and procedures; in maritime transport services, for public safety and security considerations, these requirements are often imposed on crew and officers under national registry systems. Secondly, technical standards[203]; besides requirements in shipbuilding and maintenance (usually also for public safety and security considerations), the IMO rules on maritime safety (such as SOLAS and MARPOL), as well as port state control as discussed in Chapter 2 of this work, are important international initiatives for technical standards. Thirdly, licensing requirements; in regard to harbour services, licensing requirements include general operating permits for the purpose of ensuring technical capability or financial soundness, and in some cases to implement quantitative restrictions[204].

202 GATS Article VI: 4: With a view to ensuring that measures relating to qualification requirements and procedures, technical standards and licensing requirements do not constitute unnecessary barriers to trade in services, the Council for Trade in Services shall, through appropriate bodies it may establish, develop any necessary disciplines. Such disciplines shall aim to ensure that such requirements are, *inter alia*:
(a) based on objective and transparent criteria, such as competence and the ability to supply the service;
(b) not more burdensome than necessary to ensure the quality of the service;
(c) in the case of licensing procedures, not in themselves a restriction on the supply of the service.

203 No definition of technical standards is made in the GATS, but work in accountancy suggests that services standards are being applied to both "production" and "process" methods, i. e. to the technical characteristics of the service (e. g. the format of financial reports) as well as to the way in which a service must be performed (e. g. the way in which an audit must be performed). See WTO, "International Regulatory Initiatives in Services, Background Note by the Secretariat", S/C/W/97, 1 March 1999, p. 13.

204 Id. p. 26.

3.2.4 *Multi-modal Transport and the GATS Negotiations*

The container revolution in shipping has greatly facilitated the integration of logistics operation and door to door services in international transport. As discussed in the previous sections of this Chapter, during the WTO negotiations on the three pillars of maritime transport services, some countries have proposed the inclusion of multimodal transport. However, although there were considerable discussions in this prospect, many substantive matters remained unsolved. As noted by the WTO Secretariat, the multimodal transport services reveal significant similarities with integrated express delivery services[205]. The integrated operations help to minimize the legal and physical fragmentation of the transport chain between the operators and the ensuing costs, coordination problems and inefficiencies.

Some WTO member countries proposed that under the GATS framework of negotiations on maritime transport services, in order to facilitate the inclusion of multi-modal transport, the multimodal component of maritime transport should be addressed by firmly linking these activities with the *"maritime leg"* of the movement of freight from origin to destination[206]. With this approach, the only multi-modal elements covered in the negotiations would be those activities in a transport chain that *include* a maritime leg. The transport activities where there was no maritime leg would be excluded from this scope, thus reducing concerns that by including multi-modal transport in the maritime services negotiations, this may have the effect of opening up the entire domestic transport system.

It was argued that this approach would provide an opportunity for negotiations to cover multi-modal activities where a sea leg was involved which could also include linkages between different modes of transport, such as terminal operations, for example, loading, unloading, storage and container stuffing[207].

205 WTO Secretariat, supra note 10, p. 26.
206 OECD information, supra note 7.
207 Id.

During the last round of negotiations, the issue of multi-modal was introduced and discussions were held on how this could be incorporated into an agreement on MTS. Australia produced a paper on *Scheduling Options for Multi-modal Transport*, which focused on how multi-modal should be treated if it were to included in discussions for an MTS agreement[208]. The paper provided a useful tool in determining how multi-modal may be treated in the coming round of negotiations. The options paper proposed three alternatives for treating multi-modal transport under the "three-pillar" model schedule[209]. One of the options for treating multi-modal would be as an additional commitment to the model schedule in the same way as access to and use of port services is treated, i.e., a "fourth pillar".

The other possible alternative was to expand the definition of maritime international freight transport as

> transportation of international freight by seagoing vessel from the port of loading in one country to the port of discharge in another country. This transportation may be combined with freight services from the point of loading in one country by a multi-modal transport operation to the point of delivery in another country under a multi-modal contract to provide a maritime transport service[210].

Still another option was to expand the definition of auxiliary services to include multi-modal which includes onward surface transport services directly supporting the movement of international cargoes by sea[211].

In the Doha Round of negotiations, a number of WTO Members emphasized the importance of multimodal transport and tabled proposals to that effect. In the light of recent trends in the field of trade and transport, many WTO Members have considered

208 Id.
209 "Negotiating Proposal for Maritime Transport Services", Communication from Australia. The paper is available at the website of Department of Foreign Affairs and Trade, Australia Government: http://www.dfat.gov.au revisited in May 2006.
210 OECD supra note 7.
211 Id.

commitments on multimodal transport services to be a necessity. Some of the proposals noted that when international transport services involve a sea leg, international services suppliers should be able to supply multimodal door-to-door transport services across the logistics chain. It is argued that consideration should be given to the possibility of allowing such activities without implying complete liberalization of road, rail and inland waterways[212].

This work argues that the integration of multi-modal transport into the WTO negotiations on transport would greatly facilitate the efficient and seamless movement of international trade. The WTO Members would benefit from addressing transport liberalization within a broader context, preferably in concert with trade facilitation negotiations. As its paper pointed out, the WTO may wish to consider exploring the linkages that prevail between these two areas of negotiations[213]. Developing countries would benefit particularly from building on the linkages between trade facilitation and trade liberalization. Moreover, technical assistance, capacity-building activities and special and differential measures that could be secured in the context of trade facilitation negotiations could contribute to achieving a more balanced and development-oriented set of commitments on transport and logistics services[214].

3.2.5 An Integrated Model Schedule

This work has identified some weaknesses in the all-in-one formula of the negotiation and the three-pillar approach, which have the potential to hinder the process of the negotiations.

212 WTO, "Council for Trade in Services – Special Session – Communication from the European Communities and their Member States – GATS 2000: Transport Services", S/CSS/W/41, 22 December 2000.

213 Id. p. 26.

214 Id. p. 26.

The weakness of the "all-in-one" formula delimitation

The issue of maritime transport services has been brought into the regime of WTO when the Uruguay Round negotiations resulted in the establishment of the GATS, by Article 10 (2), and Annex 1 B that set out the GATS principles of MFN, national treatment, transparency and voluntary commitment[215]. The Ministerial Decision at the end of the round provided for "negotiations to be entered into on a voluntary basis in the transport services sector within the framework of the GATS". The decision envisaged comprehensive negotiations to achieve commitments in the so-called three pillars: international shipping, auxiliary services and access to and use of port facilities[216]. The decision, however, does not provide any further interpretation of maritime transport services, or its so-called three pillars. As a matter of fact, the envisaged "comprehensive negotiations" is not only equivocal, but also fails to touch upon a number of fundamental services in maritime transport, such as marine insurance, subsidies and ship-building.

The weakness of the three-pillar classification approach

The previous negotiating round concentrated on three pillars comprising international shipping, auxiliary services and access to and use of port services. The discussion of multi-modal transport services formed an additional fourth pillar. This model failed to provide the means of reaching an agreement and therefore improvements to the model may need to be identified which would allow an agreement to be reached. The weaknesses of the three-pillar approach include:

Firstly, the over-wide scope of each pillar. Under the three-pillar approach, each pillar covers a number of maritime activities with highly diversified natures. For instance, the pillar of interna-

215 WTO, *The Result of the Uruguay Round of Multilateral Trade negotiations: the Legal Text*, WTO 1995, co-published with Cambridge University Press, pp. 325–364.

216 See Paragraph 1 of "Ministerial Decision on Negotiations on Maritime Transport Services".

tional maritime transport includes both bulk shipping and liner shipping. While bulk shipping has been a relatively liberal sector that does not need much work in the negotiation, liner shipping is complicated because of its privilege of antitrust immunity. Besides, it belongs to private restrictive practices that presently fall out of the scope of the GATS. Both in theory and in practice, it is not advisable to label them under the same sector.

The second weakness lies in the ambiguous delimitation between different pillars. This is especially the case in the distinction between maritime auxiliary services and port services. In making commitments, countries follow different classification schedules that add confusion and difficulties to the comparison of commitment coverage. For instance, the storage and warehousing services in port have been classified as maritime auxiliary services under draft schedule, while under GNS/W/120, they are put under the title of services auxiliary to all modes of transport.

Considering the extremely complex nature of maritime transport services, these problems have partially contributed to the impasse of the negotiations. In the Doha round, countries may engage themselves in clarifying these problems, including issues with negotiating modality and more standardized classification system.

Another approach of scheduling the models suggested by OECD Secretariat is worth noting[217]. It abandons the approach of pillars taken by the NGMTS, and replaces it by classifying maritime activities into three categories: access to port, access to cargo, and access to other maritime-related services. Each category is then divided into several smaller packages. The three categories cover the full range of activities of maritime transport services, including the landside transport with maritime leg.

Specifically, the classification may be arranged in the following pattern (the items listed out are not exhaustive)[218]:

217 OECD supra note 7.
218 Id.

1. Access to port
   - Navigation-related services
     i. Pilotage, shore-based navigational aid
     ii. Towing and tug assistance, anchorage, berthing, mooring, maintenance and repair
   - Cargo-related services
     i. Customs clearance, quarantine inspection, documentation processing
     ii. Cargo handling
     iii. Storage and warehousing
   - Agency services
   - Onward transport services
     i. Freight forwarding by road, rail or inland waterway
     ii. Inter-modal freight transfer
2. Access to cargo
   - Access to cargo in international shipping – liner shipping
   - Access to cargo in domestic shipping – cabotage
3. Access to other maritime-related services
   - Sales and marketing
   - Acquisition
   - Insurance
   - Subsidies
   - Ship-building
   - Other relevant services

This formulation has a number of merits[219]. By dividing each category into small packages, it avoids the potential problem that a single blockage with a certain activity would end up freezing the whole category. This problem could occur within the context of three pillars, where little flexibility exists and activities within one pillar have to be dealt with as a complete set. Moreover, it helps to avoid the confusion in labeling multi-modal transport into the original three pillars, which has been one of the major frustrations during the previous negotiations. The attempts in the past to either integrate it into the original three pillars, or to leave it out

219 Id.

as a separate fourth pillar, have added the complexity of the whole issue and blocked the negotiations to date. The above three-category formulation on the other hand, is able to deal with the entire process of maritime transport services as an integral and interrelated package.

Part Two

Analysis of Selected Issues

4 Access to Port

4.1 Access to Port in the Law of the Sea

4.1.1 Customary International Law

The right of access to port is one of the most difficult issues in the law of the sea, and there are no universally recognized rules on this matter. Although being a presumed and preferred right over decades, the right of access to port has not been formally established in customary international law. Its ambiguous status constitutes an un-harmonious link in the whole chain of freedom of the sea.

Except for certain law of the sea protocols such as those incorporated in the legislation of the flags for the avoidance of collision and pollution, ships on the high seas enjoy the freedom of navigation. In territorial and internal waters, however, shipping is subjected to the control of the coastal state in respect of the channels to be followed, compulsory pilotage, access to and conduct within port limits[220]. The issue of port access is usually related to the issue of internal waters, whose legal status is often assimilated to that of a state's territory[221]. Abundant literature in international

220 See for example, Mark J. Valencia, "Asia, the Law of the Sea and International Relations", *International Affairs (Royal Institute of International Affairs 1944)*, Vol. 73, No. 2, Asia and the Pacific (Apr., 1997), pp. 263–282.

221 Lowe, A.V., "The Right of Entry into Maritime Ports in International Law", San Diego Law Review, April 1977, Vol. 14, pp. 597–622; Baker, S., *First Steps in International Law*, Kegal Paul, Trench Trubner and Co, London, 1899, p. 61: "the maritime territory of each state extends to the ports, harbours, bays, mouths of rivers, and adjacent parts of the sea enclosed by headlands belonging to the same state". See also Oppenheim, L., *International Law (A Treatise)*, Vol. I, 8th edition, Lauterpacht, H., (eds), Longmans and Co, 1955, p. 460. Schwarzenberger, G. and Brown, E.D., *A Manual of*

law indicates consensus with the theory that ports constitute part of the territory of the country in which they are located[222]. In 1930, the Hague Conference for the Codification of International Law made one of the earliest attempts to define the delimitation of a port, where a text was produced on ports stating that in determining the breadth of the territorial sea, the outermost permanent harbour works in front of ports shall be regarded as forming part of the coast[223]. Later, the same terms were repeated in the 1958 Geneva Convention on the Territorial Sea and the Contiguous Zone[224]. The 1982 LOS Convention follows this formulation in Article 11[225], while adding that offshore installations and artificial islands shall not be considered as permanent harbour works[226].

International Law (6th edition), Professional Books Ltd, 1975, p. 100, that "the justification for the distinction between internal waters and the territorial sea lies in the limitation under customary international law of the coastal states' territorial jurisdiction in the territorial sea".

222 See for example: Whiteman, M.M., *Digest of International Law*, US Department of State Publication, vol. 4; Smith, H.A., *The Law and Custom of the Sea* (3rd edition), Stevens and Sons, London, 1959; Dunfee, G.E., "Territorial Status of Deepwater Ports", 15 San Diego Law Review 603 (1977–78), p. 613.

223 "Report of the Second Committee", Conference for the Codification of International Law, The Hague 1930, League of Nations Doc. C. 230 M 117–193. V., p. 12. It was also stated in the report that "the waters of the port as far as a line drawn between the outermost fixed works thus constitute the inland waters of the coastal state". See Whiteman M. M., *Digest of International Law*, US Department of State Publication, 1965, vol. 4.

224 The 1958 Geneva Convention on the Territorial Sea and the Contiguous Zone, 516 UNTS 205; 240 UKTS 94, Article 8 states that: "for the purpose of delimiting the territorial sea, the outermost permanent harbour works which form an integral part of the harbour system shall be regarded as forming part of the coast".

225 Article 11 on Ports: "For the purpose of delimiting the territorial sea, the outermost permanent harbour works which form an integral part of the harbour system are regarded as forming part of the coast. Offshore installations and artificial islands shall not be considered as permanent harbour works".

226 21 ILM 1982 1261; U.N. Doc A/CONF. 62/122 Also see O'Connell, D.P., *the International Law of the Sea,* Shearer, I.A., (ed.), Vol. I, Clarendon Press, London, 1983.

The uniqueness of ports lies in the fact that on one hand, they are part of national sovereignty and are under full jurisdiction of the port state; while on the other hand, ports represent a very special segment of territorial waters that are supposed to be open to international merchant ships in time of peace. There have been continuous controversies for many years seeking for the right balance of this subtle relationship.

4.1.1.1 General Principles on Port Entry

It is a well-established practice that the port state has the sovereign right of port nomination[227]. Moreover, port state's right[228] has also been established in state practices from early time, which are confirmed in many writings[229].

Ships seeking entry to foreign ports are subjected to the jurisdiction of the port state over its internal and territorial waters. Within the area of port authorities, ships are under special navigational regulations that they are required to observe. The existence of sovereignty over internal waters and the absence of any general right of innocent passage through them leads to the absence of right in customary international law in respect of foreign ships entering foreign ports. Except for ships in distress, there exists little support for this right. A famous case frequently cited for supporting the

227 Hakapää, K., *Marine Pollution in International Law (Material Obligations and Jurisdiction)*, Suomalainen Tiedeakatemia, Helsinki, 1981.

228 See for example A.V. Lowe, supra note 221, p. 602.

229 For state practices, see, for example., Newcastle v. Tinmouth, ch. VI, included in 1 Hargrave, *A Collection of Tracts Relative to the Law of England* (1787); Attorney General v. Bates (1610) 2 State Trials 371; the Bulgarian Decree of 10 Oct. 1951, U.N. Dec. ST/LEG/SER, B/6, at 84; the El Salvadoran Civil Code of 1860; the Guatemalan Act of 10 June 1934; the Roumanian Decree No. 39 of 28 Jan. 1956; the Yugoslavian Regulations of 2 Feb. 1949; the Chinese Law of 14 March 1957, cited in Tao Cheng, "Communist China and the Law of the Sea", 63 American Journal of International Law 47, 68 (1969); the Spanish Royal Decree of 20 June 1852; the Soviet Rules of Entry, 1926, quarterly rev. USSR Chamber comm., July 1932, at 75; the USSR Statute on the State Boundary, I New Directions in the Law of the Sea 29 (1973).

existence of the access right is the 1958 arbitration in "the Saudi Arabia v. Aramco" case, where the arbitrator asserted that "according to a great principle of public international law, the ports of every State must be open to foreign merchant vessels and can only be closed when the vital interests of the State so require"[230].

However, it is not clear whether the rule of international law to which the arbitrator of the above case referred is a rule that ports must be open to trade, or a rule that discrimination among foreign ships concerning the use of ports is unlawful. According to the definition of ports in the Geneva Convention on the International Regime of Maritime Ports, 1923[231], a maritime port is one frequented by sea-going vessels and used by foreign states. It could be concluded that the Geneva Convention aims at elimination of discrimination in respect of access to ports, rather than proclaiming a universal right of access. Although it is within a country's sovereignty to choose whether or not to open its ports, once it opens them, it is obliged to do this on a non-discriminatory basis.

The port authorities may withhold permission to access if a ship does not comply with the relevant regulations of the convention on safety at sea, which requires that ships carry valid safety certificates. Moreover, the port authorities may also deny access of foreign ships of some particular types, such as nuclear-powered ships, or ships equipped for electronic surveillance[232].

230 See for example, Stephen M. Schwebel, J. Gillis Wetter, "Arbitration and the Exhaustion of Local Remedies", *The American Journal of International Law*, Vol. 60, No. 3 (Jul., 1966), pp. 484–501.

231 The legal text of the Convention is available from Australian Treaty Series at: http://www.austlii.edu.au revisited in April 2006.

232 For example, the Australian Navigation Amendment Act, No. 60 of 1967 provides for special regulations to make sure that nuclear ships do not cause unreasonable radiations. Spain also has similar legislation which allows nuclear ships to enter their ports only under exceptional conditions, which covers the territorial sea as well. Source of information: Parliamentary Library, Parliament of Australia, at: http://www.aph.gov.au revisited in August 2006.

Port states enjoy a wide range of rights in regulating entry into their maritime ports, which could be deemed as a long established rule of customary international law. In the Nicaragua case, the International Court pointed out that internal waters are subject to the sovereignty of the State and it is "by virtue of its sovereignty that the coastal state may regulate access to its ports"[233]. The right of regulation, however, cannot be used in an unlimited way and may not be exercised to deny any right of entry that may exist to the ports of the State. The "Convention on Facilitation of International Maritime Traffic of 1965"[234] marks the first attempt of international regulation of this vital aspect of maritime activity.

Besides the relevant regulations in the 1982 LOS Convention which will be discussed in the following section of this Chapter, there are a number of other multilateral conventions that touch upon the issue of access to port, such as the 1965 Convention on Facilitation of International Maritime Traffic[235], the 1966 International Convention on Load Lines[236] and the 1952 International Convention for the Unification of Certain rules relating to the Arrest of Sea-going Ships[237].

4.1.1.2 Port Closure and Deny of Access

The right to close one's ports to foreign vessels is regarded as a natural extension to the principle of sovereignty. It is generally accepted that in order to protect its interests (such as national security considerations), a port state is entitled to close its maritime ports which are normally open to international traffic. As coastal states are entitled to suspend passage through their territorial seas when that passage was prejudicial to "peace, good order, or security"[238], states could also deny entry to its ports on basis

233 (1986) ICJ Rep. 14 at 111.

234 591 UNTS, 265.

235 55 UNTS. This Convention will be discussed further in this Chapter.

236 640 UNTS 133.

237 439 UNTS 193.

238 Art. 16 (1) of the Geneva Convention on the Territorial Sea and Contiguous Zone, 516 UNTS 205 (1958).

on similar considerations. The judgment of the International Court of Justice in 1986 in the *Nicaragua* case[239] confirms that

> The basic legal concept of state sovereignty in customary international law...extends to the territorial waters and territorial sea of every state...It is also by virtue of its sovereignty that the coastal state may regulate access to its ports.[240]

There also exists the issue of "foreign flag recognition", which means that the right of entry into port (if this right does exist) may be restricted to ships flying the flags of states which are recognized by the port state. This view was first put forward by Niboyet in his 1926 report to the International Law Association, which provided that "ships flying flags of a recognized State are granted access to ports"[241]. One example has been the position taken by the government of the People's Republic of China in 1950, which promulgated the Provisional Rules Governing the Entry of Merchant Vessels...of States Having No Diplomatic Relations with China[242]. The regulations required such merchant ships to obtain special permits from the government before entering its ports.

In most cases, the reason for a port state to execute its right on port closure and denial of access is potential or threatened marine pollution. In addition to the LOS Convention and the IMO regulations, there exist a number of multilateral treaties relevant to this subject. For example, the 1962 Convention on the Liability of Operators of Nuclear Ships regulates that nothing in that document shall affect any right that a party may have under international law to deny access to its waters and harbours to nuclear ships[243]. In the 1971 Amendments to the 1954 Convention for the Preven-

239 1986 International Court of Justice Report 14, p.111, Nicaragua v United States.

240 Id.

241 "Sont adm s dans les ports les navires battant pavillon d'un Etat reconnu", International Law Association, 34th Report 456 (Vienna, 1926).

242 UN Doc. ST/LEG/SER.B/6, at 112.

243 57 American Journal of International Law 268 (1963).

tion of Pollution of the Sea by Oil[244], Article VIbis (4) on tank arrangements and limitations of tank size affirms that

> if any Contracting Government has clear grounds for believing...that the tanker does not comply with Annex C, it may deny access to ports in its territorial waters or to offshore terminals under its control.

The 1973 International Convention for the Prevention of Pollution from Ships as amended in 1978 also provides certain safeguards in Article 5 (3): if a Party denies a foreign ship entry to the port or offshore terminals under its jurisdiction or takes any action against such a ship for the reason that the ship does not comply with the provisions of the present Convention...[245].

In addition, the judgment of vessels as substandard constitutes another important reason for foreign vessels to be excluded from port[246]. Canada and the US are among the first countries to establish such legislation with the purpose of preserving the Arctic regions[247].

244 "The 1954 International Convention for the Prevention of Pollution of the Sea by Oil", 327 UNTS 3; 1958 UKTS 56. For the 1971 Amendments see 11 ILM 1972 267; ND II p. 567; IMO Resolution A. 232 (7) and A. 246 (7).

245 17 ILM 1978 546 "The International Convention for the Safety of Life at Sea", 1980 UKTS 46, 14 ILM 1975 Chapter I of this Convention requires ships to carry safety certificates and states that "the port authorities may withhold permission to dock if a ship does not comply with the relevant provisions".

246 See for example, Articles 4 and 5 of the Finnish Act No. 300 of March 16, 1974.

247 Canadian Arctic Waters Pollution Prevention Act, Canada Gazette, Part II, Vol. 106, No. 15, SI/TR/72–76, ss. 11 and 12 For comments on the Act, see Beesley, J. A., "The Arctic Pollution Prevention Act: Canada's Perspective", 1 Syracuse Journal of International Law 226 (1973); Henkin, L., "Arctic Anti-pollution: Does Canada Make – or Break – International Law", 65 American Journal of International Law 131 (1971).
The pertinent US legislations include: United States Ports and Waterways Safety Act of 1972, as amended by Pub. L. 95–474 (1978); 1974 Deepwaters Ports Act, S. 19 (c).

4.1.1.3 Port Exit and Arrest of Ships in Port

The right of access does not automatically imply a right to exit from port. In fact, the right to leave ports could be subject to strict limitations. Port states may detain ships that are in unseaworthy condition. They may also require foreign ships to obtain clearing papers from the port authorities before being permitted to leave the port. Moreover, port states are entitled to arrest ships in port for customs offences, or as security in civil actions or actions "in rem". The arrest of ships in the case of maritime claims is regulated under the 1952 Brussels Convention on the Arrest of Sea-going Ships[248]. According to this Convention, "arrest" means the detention of a ship by judicial process to secure a maritime claim, but it does not include the seizure of a ship in the execution of a judgment[249].

17 kinds of maritime claims are listed out in this Convention where a ship could be arrested in the jurisdiction of any of the Contracting States[250]:

- Damage caused by any ship either in collision or otherwise;
- Loss of life or personal injury caused by any ship or occurring in connection with the operation of any ship;
- Salvage;
- Agreement relating to the use or hire of any ship whether by charterparty or otherwise;
- Agreement relating to the carriage of goods in any ship whether by charterparty or otherwise;
- Loss of or damage to goods including baggage carried in any ship;
- General average;
- Bottomry;
- Towage;
- Pilotage;

248 "International Convention Relating to the Arrest of Sea-Going Ships", Brussels, May 10, 1952 Full text available at: www.admiraltylawguide.com visited in December 2001 and revisited in August 2005.

249 Article 1 (2).

250 Article 1 (1).

- Goods or materials wherever supplied to a ship for her operation or maintenance;
- Construction, repair or equipment of any ship or dock charges and dues;
- Wages of Masters, officers, or crew; Master's disbursement, including disbursements made by shippers, charterers or agent on behalf of a ship or her owner;
- Disputes as to the title to or ownership of any ship;
- Disputes between co-owners of any ship as to the ownership, possession, employment, or earnings of that ship;
- The mortgage or hypothecation of any ship.

The Convention also makes it clear that a ship may only be arrested under the authority of a court or of the appropriate judicial authority of the contracting state in which the arrest is made[251].

4.1.1.4 Port Entry under Force Majeure

It is an established practice in the law of the sea that ships forced by unforeseen circumstances into the jurisdiction of other state are immune from its exercise[252]. The treaty practices have confirmed this practice, such as the 1795 US – Spain Treaty. The test of distress was laid down by Sir William Scott (Lord Stowell) in the Elenaor in 1809:

> It must be an urgent distress; it must be something of grave necessity; such as is spoken of in our books, where a ship is said to be driven in by stress of weather. It is not sufficient to say it was done to avoid a little bad weather, or in consequence of foul winds, the danger must be such as to cause apprehension in the mind of an honest and firm man... Then again, where the party justifies the act upon the plea of distress, it must not be a distress which he has created himself, by putting on board an insufficient quantity

251 Article 4.

252 For example, the 1818 Treaty of Commerce between Britain and US. There were also some exception cases, such as in Britain, an Order in Council of 1665 prescribed that enemy ships and goods entering port by stress of weather or other accident should belong to the Admiral and not the Crown. See Hay and Marriott's Admiralty Decisions (1801), p. 50, available at Bouvier's Dictionary of Law 1856, http://ecclesia.org revisited in July 2006.

> of water or of provisions for such a voyage, for there the distress is only part of the mechanism of the fraud, and cannot be set up in excuse for it; and in the next place the distress must be proved by the claimant in a clear and satisfactory manner[253].

The word "necessity" in the case of *force majeure* does not necessarily imply that a ship must be in a condition of total distress. In the case of The Rebecca[254], the US – Mexican Claims Commission held that a vessel that entered port under its own power was immune from local customs laws by virtue of prevailing weather conditions. This question arose in the Canadian Supreme Court in connection with the interpretation of the Treaty between Great Britain and the US of 1818, which authorized American fishermen to shelter and effect repairs on the coast of Canada[255].

Force majeure clauses are usually incorporated in shipping treaties and commercial contracts. The IMO conventions on shipping safety and marine environment protection typically contain such clauses. For example, Chapter V (Safety of navigation) of SOLAS 1974 includes the obligation for masters to proceed to the assistance of those in distress[256]. A ship claiming the benefit of *force majeure* usually lodges a statement of distress either with the consul of the flag state or with the port authority.

However, in recent years, arguments have intensified as to whether a port state is entitled to grant entry to a ship in distress out of political on environmental grounds. These arguments have challenged the traditional right of foreign ships' to access under *force majeure*[257].

253 Aldo E Chircop and Olof Linden, *Places of Refuge for Ships: Emerging Environmental Concerns of a Maritime Custom*, Martinus Nijhoff, 2006, pp. 186–187.

254 Kate A. Hoff (US) v. United Mexican States, UN Rep., Vol. IV, 444 (1929).

255 Supra note 253, Chircop and Linden, p. 189. The Treaty between Great Brain and the US is available at the website of Department of Foreign Affairs and International Trade, Canada, at: http://www.dfait-maeci.gc.ca revisited in March 2006.

256 SOLAS Convention will be discussed further in this Chapter.

257 See for example, Christophe F. Murray, "Any Port in a Storm? The Right of Entry for Reasons of Force Majeure or Distress in the Wake of the Erika and the Castor", Ohio State Law Journal, Vol. 63: 1465 (2002).

4.1.1.5 Controversial Interpretations over Port Entry Rights

It is universally accepted that a port state has full jurisdictional powers within its internal waters where its laws and regulations are fully enforceable[258]. However, while the right of a port state to exclude foreign vessels from most parts of its internal waters is not questioned[259], debate remains as to the right to deny access to its ports.

One of the earliest studies on this issue was made by Gentil and Grotius[260], where they expressed views on the existence of a general right of access to foreign ports. The Institute of International Law stated in 1928 that "as a general rule access to ports and roadsteads is open to foreign vessels"[261]. This view was supported by Colombos, who reiterated that

> prohibition of the use of ports to foreign nationals would imply a neglect of the duties for the promotion of international intercourse, navigation and trade which customary international law imposes upon it[262].

In his article "The Right of Entry into Maritime Ports in International Law"[263], Lowe classified several schools of arguments in favour of the existence of a right of entry. The first one is based on

258 Burke, K.M. and Deleo, D.A., "Innocent Passage in the United Nations Convention on the Law of the Sea", 9 Yale Journal of World Public Order 389 (1983); Smith, G.P., "The Politics of Lawmaking Problems in International Maritime Regulation –Innocent Passage vs. Free Transit", 37 University of Pittsburgh Law Review 487 (1976).

259 Degan, V.D, "Internal Waters", 17 Netherlands Yearbook of International Law, 3 (1986).

260 Grotius, H., *De Jure commentarius*, Vol. I: A translation of the original manuscript of 1604 by Gwladys L. Williams and Walter H. Zeydel, No 22 of the Classics of International Law, edited by James Brown Scott Publication of the Carnigic Endowment for International Peace (Washington) Oxford 1950.

261 Articles 2 and 3 The Institute restricted this view in 1957 when it declared that subject to the right of passage consecrated either by custom or convention, the coastal state may refuse foreign vessels access to interior waters.

262 Colombos, D.J., *The International Law of the Sea*, 6th edition, Longmans, London, 1967.

263 Lowe, A.V., supra note 221, p. 602.

the assumption that a right of entry flows from state practice; or, as Greenfield put it, "a discretion of a littoral state"[264]. Other writings[265] argued that the general commercial interests of a state, as well as requirements of competitiveness and communication, have led to the situation where the majority of maritime ports are open to international trade and traffic, as can be found in numerous bilateral treaties. This consequence reflects a common will between states, rather than a customary obligation[266].

The second school argues that a right of entry comes from the general right of navigation on the seas[267]. Scholars such as Lapradelle held the view that the juridical regime of all parts of the seas, including the territorial waters and ports, shall be assumed to form an integrated subject to the principle of freedom of navigation. Cundick pointed out that just like the high seas freedom of navigation is meaningless if states do not have access to the sea, it is also meaningless if vessels cannot cross the territorial sea of a state to enter the port of a third state which desires to trade with them[268].

264 Greenfield, L., *China and the Law of the Sea, Air and the Environment* Sijthoff and Noordhoff, the Netherlands, 1979.

265 Examples include: Valenzuela, M., "IMO: Public International Law and Regulation", in Johnson, D.M., and Letalic, N.G., "The Law of the Sea and Ocean Industry: New Opportunities and Restraints", 16th Annual Conference of the Law of the Sea Institute, University of Hawaii, 1983; Briggs, H.W., *The Law of Nations (Cases, Documents and Notes)*, Apleton Century Crofts, NY, 1952; Hyde, C.C., *International Law – Chiefly as Interpreted and Applied by the United States*, Little Brown and Company, Boston, 1922; Legatski, R.A., "Port State Jurisdiction over Vessel-Source Pollution", 2 Harvard Environmental Law Review 456 (1977); Akehurst, M., *A Modern Introduction to International Law*, George Allen and Unwin, London, 1982; Riphagen, W., "Some Reflections on Functional Sovereignty", 6 Netherlands Yearbook of International Law 121 (1975).

266 As Hakapää put it, "it might be desirable to keep the ports open anytime and anywhere, but from a legal point of view there is hardly any obligation to do so". Dubner also pointed out that state practices in recent centuries afford no indication that states may demand access to the ports of other states as a matter of right. Lowe, A.V., supra note 245, p. 610.

267 Lowe, A.V., supra note 221, p. 611.

268 Cundick, R.P., "International Straits: The Regime of Access", 5 Georgia Journal of International and Comparative Law 107 (1975).

However, with the acceptance by states of the principle of coastal sovereignty over coastal waters from the 1930s, it seems difficult to interpret the principle of freedom of the seas as including a right of entry into ports.

The third proposition regards a right of entry as based upon a right of free trade and commerce[269]. It argues that since the port entry right of foreign vessels is essential to the flow of international commerce, the self-interest of each state impels it to accord the privilege of entry to foreign merchant vessels. Foulke noted that

> the case where an independent state will prohibit the entry of merchant vessels to its ports except in time of war or under some particular temporary circumstances of quarantine etc., would be almost unthinkable[270].

However, the principle of free commerce has remained as a principle of foreign policy and has not been transformed into the rule of law. It was noted by Vattel that it is clear that each country is entitled to decide whether it conducts commerce and trade with other countries or not[271].

Arguments against the right of entry into port are often based on the theoretical justification in the protection of national sovereignty. Although the nature and the status of port entry issue remain the subject of debate, there seems to be consensus that the right of access could be reasonably restricted by the port state under certain circumstances. The idea of absolute right seems to be absent from most schools of thought.

269 The principle of free trade evolved as a precise theory from 19th century. One of the explicit argument on this principle and its relation with right of entry was made by J. N. Hyde in his *International Law* (1949): "as no State appears to be regarded as having the right to isolate itself wholly from the outside world, or to remain aloof from all commercial or economic intercourse with it, there would seem to be a corresponding obligation imposed upon maritime powers not to deprive foreign vessels of commerce of access to all its ports".

270 Foulke, R. R., *A Treatise on International Law*, Philadelphia: Winton, 1920. Lowe, A. V., supra note 221, p. 617.

271 Vattel E. de, *the Law of Nations or the Principles of Natural Law* (1758) (Classics of Int'l Law translation 1916).

Two cases supporting the right of port access can be found in the decisions of the Permanent Court of International Justice (PCIJ)[272]. The Oscar Chinn Case was a claim made by the Government of the UK in 1934 in respect of alleged loss and damages of Mr. Oscar Chinn, a British subject, on the Belgian government in connection with a company using the waterways of the Belgian Congo[273]. When considering the argument submitted by the UK concerning the inconsistency between the measures taken by the Belgian government and the freedom of navigation, the Court decided:

> According to the conception universally accepted, the freedom of navigation referred to by the Convention comprises freedom of movement for vessels, freedom to enter ports, and to make use of plants and docks, to load goods and transport goods and passengers[274].

The Convention referred to and the freedom of navigation elaborated upon in the above statement related to restricted navigation on international rivers regulated under international treaties. The freedom of navigation through international rivers is supported by alternative adjudication such as the Faber Case of 1903[275]. It is common for such treaties and agreements to hold the view that if

272 Also known as the World Court, PCIJ was established pursuant to Article 14 of the Covenant of the League of Nations. The protocol establishing it was adopted by the Assembly of the League in 1920 and ratified by the requisite number of states in 1921. By the time of its dissolution in 1945 when its functions were transferred to the newly created International Court of Justice, the Court had 59 member states. Established at The Hague, the Court was empowered to render judgments in disputes between states that were voluntarily submitted to it and to give advisory opinions in any matters referred to it by the Council or the Assembly of the League. For detailed description of PCIJ, see League of Nations Secretariat, *The Permanent Court of International Justice,* University of Michigan, 1930.

273 PCIJ (1934), "Oscar Chinn Judgement", Series A/B, No 63, p. 65.

274 Id., p. 83.

275 The case involves a Venezuela arbitration holding the view that a state can temporarily prohibit navigation on rivers flowing through its territory when necessary to peace, safety and convenience of her citizen. See Faber Case, Germany v. Venezuela, 10 Review of International Arbitral Awards 436, 463 (1903).

there is to be free navigation on international rivers, some degree of access to ports at the mouth of river shall exist[276].

The PCIJ Advisory Opinion upon the Danube Case[277] was directed to the competence and powers of the European Commission of the Danube, in regard not only to navigation, but also over the port of Braila. According to the Court, "the freedom of movement for vessels going to and from the sea also extends to ships coming into or leaving a port"[278]. The Court based its decision on the Treaty of Paris.

The right of entry into ports is reflected in many treaties or agreements. Most commonly, such rights are found in bilateral treaties or agreements as "Friendship, Commerce and Navigation". Contemporary examples include bilateral agreements giving rights of entry in connection with the voyages of the United States Nuclear Ship "Savannah" in 1964[279], the 1962 Treaty of Commerce, Establishment and Navigation between the United Kingdom and Japan[280], the provisions of the EEC Treaty on non-discrimination and free movement of goods. In these examples member states are given similar reciprocal right of access to each other's ports[281].

276 In the "Territorial Jurisdiction of the International Commission of the River Order", the PCIJ stated that: "this right, the essential features of which are the perfect equality of all riparian states in the use of the whole course of the river and the exclusion of any preferential privilege of any one riparian state in relation to the others..." PCIJ Series A, No. 23, 10 Sep. 1929.

277 "Jurisdiction of the European Commission of the Danube, Advisory Opinion", 1927 PCIJ Series B, No. 14.

278 Id., p. 65.

279 The Agreement of 19 June 1964 concerning the Use of the United Kingdom Ports and Territorial Waters by the Nuclear Ship Savannah, which provided that "entry of Savannah into any port in United Kingdom territory shall be subject to the prior approval of the Government of the United Kingdom".

280 This Treaty typically includes a provision on freedom of access to ports on basis of MFN or national treatment (Art. 20), and a provision on treatment of vessels entering internal waters in distress (Art. 21). For the Treaty see E.D. Brown, *The International Law of the Sea*, Dartmouth, 1994.

281 More discussion about EU regulations on free access to port between member countries is made in the latter section of this Chapter.

In most cases these agreements share the following characteristics[282]:

- Reciprocal recognition of the nationality of vessels, tonnage, certificates, other technical papers of the vessel;
- Granting of most-favoured-nation or national treatment as regards access to ports or use of the facilities of ports, dues and charges;
- Exclusion of cabotage, the performance of harbour services and national fisheries from the operation of the most-favoured-nation or national treatment;
- Treatment of crew;
- Treatment of vessels in distress and vessels wrecked or stranded off the port;
- Administrative, civil and criminal jurisdiction of the coastal state over the foreign merchant vessel;
- Jurisdiction and functions of consular officers in respect of fishing.

4.1.2 International Conventions and Treaties

4.1.2.1 Port Access Regulations in Ancient Treaties

Although not as universally accepted as the freedom of navigation, the right of foreign ships to enter into ports was also considered as an important principle from ancient times, as reflected in the forms of internal regulations within a country or in treaties or agreements between countries.

282 Information based on the 1975 UNCTAD report: "Economic Co-operation in Merchant Shipping – Treatment of Foreign Merchant Vessels in Ports", UNCTAD/TD/B/C. 4/136, 9 Sep. 1975.

Rome' Treaties of Commerce with Carthage & Persia, 508 B.C.–348 B.C.: right of entry into ports and certain internal waters

All of the three treaties between Rome and Carthage before the outbreak of the first Punic War (24 B.C.) all had provisions relating to navigation and commerce, in each of which, the Carthaginians insisted on prohibiting Roman vessels from entering the waters beyond the "Fair Promontory", which probably referred to Cape Fairna in the Bay of Tunis. The treaty of 348 B.C. mentioned a second geographical landmark of Mastia Tarseios, probably referring to a city replaced by Carthago Nova, today Cartagena in Spain. After Pyrrhus had failed in his last attempt to restore the fleet of Syracuse, the Carthaginian fleet dominated the entire western Mediterranean. As a result, the Carthaginians endeavoured to monopolize all maritime trade in this region against foreigners as well as against their own nationals. Consistent with this situation, the treaty of 348 B.C. allowed Roman vessels to enter Spanish, Sardinian and Libyan's ports[283], while by the treaty of 366 B.C., the Carthaginians closed all ports with the exception of port Carthage[284].

283 The provision reads: "There is to be friendship on the following conditions between the Romans and their allies and the Carthaginians, Tyrians, and the people of Utica and their respective allies. The Romans shall not maraud or trade or found a city on the farther side of Fair Promontory, Mastia, and Tarseum. No Roman shall trade or found a city in Sardinia and Libya nor remain in a Sardinian or Libyan post longer that is required for taking in provisions or repairing his ship. If he be driven there by stress of weather, he shall depart within five days. In the Carthaginian province of Sicily and at Carthage he may do and sell anything that is permitted to a citizen. A Carthaginian in Rome may do likewise". The treaty is available from: http://ancienthistory.about.com/ visited in January 2001 and revisited in July 2005.

284 The provision reads: "the Romans and their allies not to sail with long ships beyond the Fair Promontory unless forced by storm or by enemies: it is forbidden to anyone carried beyond it by force to buy or carry away anything beyond what is required for the repair of his ship or for sacrifice, and he must depart within five days. Men coming to trade may conclude no business except in the presence of a herald or town-clerk, and the price of

Treaty of Commerce between the Venetian Doge Morosini and the King of Tunis and Tripoli, 1251: Customs duties and taxes

Like her great rival Genoa, Venice tried to obtain security and freedom of trade by means of treaties and understandings with the Islamic rulers of the Mediterranean shores. Mario Morosini, elected Doge in 1240, managed to provide doges and admirals for the republic throughout the centuries. His contacting partner belonged to the Hafsides, a Berber family ruled over Tunisia and Tripolitania since 1100. In the opening paragraph of the treaty of Commerce of 1251, it was stipulated that "by obligation of this treaty all Venetians shall be safe and secure throughout the Kingdom" (of Tunis and Tripoli). The treaty elaborated the Venetians' rights in the following respects: duties and taxes on various kinds of goods by the Customs (Articles 5, 8, 9, 10, 13, 14, 24, 26), selling ships (Article 15), preparing ships for putting to sea (Article 16), claiming goods from ships that had suffered shipwreck in Barbary territory (Article 20), and the use of barges and lighters in a timely way (Article 25).

4.1.2.2 1923 Convention on the International Regime of Maritime Ports

One of the first international initiatives to deal with the issue of access to port was reflected in the "Convention on the International Regime of Maritime Ports of 1923 (the Geneva Statute 1923, hereinafter referred to as 'Statute' in this section)", which was signed in Geneva on December 9, 1923[285]. This Convention was

---

whatever is sold in the presence of such shall be secured to the vendor by the state, if the sale takes place in Libya or Sardinia. If any Roman came to the Carthaginian province in Sicily, he shall enjoy equal rights with others". The treaty is available from: http://ancienthistory.about.com/ visited in January 2001 and revisited in July 2005.

285 LNTS Vol. 58, pp. 285, *et seq*. See also Great Britain Treaty Series, No. 24 (1925).

held under the Communications and Transit Committee of the League of Nations[286].

The Statute aims to bring harmonization and co-operation to member countries concerning the access right of foreign merchant vessels into ports. It has not codified any pre-existing rules of customary law, nor has it passed into customary law itself. Instead, it remains a multilateral treaty with binding effects on its party members.

The core provision of the Statute on port access is Article 2 (1), which stipulates that subject to the principles of reciprocity, the contracting states to the Statute shall undertake to grant vessels of every other contracting States either national treatment or most favoured nation treatment, whichever is better. This covers the freedom of access to ports, the use of the port and the full enjoyment of the benefits as regards navigation and commercial operations that it affords to vessels, their cargo and passengers. This equality of treatment includes allocation of berths, loading and unloading facilities, dues and charges levied on account of the government, public authorities, or undertakings of any kind. A reservation is made respecting the liberty of the port provided that this conforms to the principles of equality of treatment.

Article 2 does not establish a right of entry to foreign ports. Instead it provides for equality of treatment of vessels in foreign ports on a most-favoured-nation or national treatment basis[287].

286 Before the establishment of the League of Nations Transit Organization, the work of preparing a draft regime of Maritime Ports was first undertaken by the Ports, Waterways, and Railways Commission of the Peace Conference and was subsequently continued by the Commission of Enquiry on Freedom of Communications and Transit. The Commission, after prolonged deliberation, came to the conclusion that a Convention was not necessary and thus it drafted a Resolution on Ports under an international regime. This Resolution was discussed by the Barcelona Conference of 1921 and it ultimately appeared in the form of a recommendation. It was therefore left to the Transit Committee of the League of Nations to draft a Convention on Maritime Ports, which was finally adopted by the 2nd General Conference on Communication and Transit held at Geneva in 1923. Source of information: the United Nations Office at Geneva, website: www.unog.ch revisited in August 2007.

287 Benjanmin Parameswaran, *The Liberalization of Maritime Transport Services: With Special Reference to the WTO/GATS*, Springer, 2004, pp. 130–131.

The Statute stipulates that all dues and charges levied for the use of maritime ports must be published before coming into force, and the same is true with the by-laws and regulations of the port[288]. Unless there are special reasons based on geographical, economical or technical conditions, customs duties at maritime ports may not exceed duties levied on other customs frontiers[289]. In addition, the provisions of the Statute only permit deviation from it for a limited period of time in the case of "grave incidents" which might influence the security or the vital interests of the port State[290]. These incidents may include industrial actions. Despite the rule of non-discrimination for ships in ports, that goal is not always achieved because shipping firms can be adversely affected by demurrage due to slow turn-round. Therefore, it would be desirable to have uniform rules simplifying the procedures and documentation pertinent to docking, discharge and loading.

A number of important provisions include: All maritime ports that are normally frequented by sea-going vessels and used for foreign trade shall be deemed maritime ports within the meaning of the present Convention (Art. 1). The nationals, property and flags of all contracting States shall have freedom of access to maritime ports situated under the sovereignty or authority of the contracting States. They shall be treated, in all respects, on the basis of absolute equality, particularly as regards to port facilities, and dues and charges. In particular, no distinction shall be made to the prejudice of the nationals, property or flag of any contracting State as between the said national, property or flag and those of the State under whose sovereignty or authority the port is situated, or of the State whose nationals, property or flag enjoy the most favourable treatment (Art. 2).

Moreover, in the absence of special circumstances justifying an exception on account of economic necessities, the customs duties levied in maritime ports situated under the sovereignty or authority of the contracting States must not be higher than those levied

288 Article 4.
289 Article 7.
290 Article 16.

on the other customs frontiers of the same State on goods of the same kind, source and destination. All facilities afforded by the contracting States to the import and export of goods by other routes shall be equally afforded to import and export through all maritime ports situated under their sovereignty or authority (Art. 6). The State under whose sovereignty or authority a port is situated may withdraw the benefits of the provisions of article 2 from any vessel if it is proved that the owner of the vessel discriminates systematically against the nationals of that State or against companies controlled by such nationals (Art. 7).

It was provided, however, that the Statute would not apply to the maritime coasting trade (Art. 8) or affect the right of a State to reserve to itself the exercise to towage in its ports or of pilotage (Art. 9)[291]. Should a State breach the Statute, other contracting parties may, after giving notice through diplomatic channels, withhold the benefit of equality of treatment from its vessels, their cargoes and passengers. In the event of action being taken under this article either State has the right to apply to the International Court.

One point should be noted is that the Statute was trying to secure equality of treatment for vessels in foreign ports, instead of attempting to establish any right of entry. This was demonstrated in the Preamble of the Convention

> in the fullest measure possible...freedom of communications...by guaranteeing in the maritime ports under the sovereignty or authority (of the Parties) and for the purposes of international trade equality of treatment between the ships of all the Contracting States, their cargoes and passengers.

The Statute was only ratified by a limited number of countries. Some traditional maritime countries such as Japan, US and Russia did not ratify it, which has obviously reduced the influence of the Statute. This may partially due to the fact that some countries

291 Other international regulations for the tonnage measurement have also been adopted at Geneva in 1939 by the "League of Nations Communications and Transit Organization", see supra footnote 51, "Research Guide to League of Nations Document and Publications", Northwestern University Library, US.

were not satisfied with the context of the Statute. On the one hand, more detailed and specified regulations are needed in the Statute, such as the procedures and timelines to prepare for the access, the relevant documentation and fees involved, the monitoring and surveillance of access and exit, and the circumstances under which access/exit can be postponed or denied. On the other hand, the ambiguous definitions of the types of ports[292] and vessels[293] concerned in the Statute may lead to open interpretation and add extra difficulties in coping with specific circumstances in practice.

4.1.2.3 1982 LOS Convention

4.1.2.3.1 Port State Jurisdiction

Through Article 94 (Duties of the flag States), the LOS Convention requires any state that allows the registration of vessels under its flag to effectively exercise its jurisdiction and control in administrative, technical and social matters over ships flying its flag. The flag state is to take such measures for ships flying its flag as are necessary to ensure safety at sea with regard to, *inter alia*, construction, maintenance and seaworthiness, manning, labour conditions and crew training, together with prevention of collisions. Specifically in relation to the monitoring of condition of vessels on the flag, such measures shall include those necessary to ensure that each ship is appropriately surveyed as to condition, equipment and manning. Article 94 (5) goes on to require that flag states take any steps that may be necessary to meet generally accepted international regulations, procedures and practices. The obligation is reiterated in relation to oil pollution in Article 211[294].

292 The definition of port is given in Article 1 as above mentioned.

293 Articles 9, 13 and 14 describe sea-going vessels as all vessels, whether publicly or privately owned or controlled, with the exception of warship, vessels performing police or administrative functions or exercising any kind of public authority; vessels temporarily used exclusively for military transport, fishing vessels, and coasting vessels.

294 Article 211: Pollution from vessels.

The LOS Convention requirement regarding flag state's duty in respect of its vessels' safety certificates and their compliance with international standards is further reiterated under the UN Convention on the Conditions for Registration of Ship[295], which emphasizes in its Article 5 that:

> A flag state should have a competent and adequate national maritime administration seeking to compel flag states to ensure that ships flying the flag of such state comply with its laws and regulations concerning registration of ships and with applicable international rules and standards concerning the safety of ships and persons on board and the prevention of pollution of the marine environment, and further that such ships are periodically surveyed by their authorized surveyors in order to ensure compliance with applicable international rules and standards.

However, in reality many flag states fail to fulfill their duties in regulating ships under their registration and the problems of substandard ships results. The concept of port state control has been introduced as a possible solution to the problem. Port state jurisdiction in the LOS Convention, which grants port states comprehensive jurisdiction to regulate issues of navigation, pilotage and pollution, is considered as an innovative expansion of jurisdiction in international law to provide a uniform mechanism of supervision and surveillance between countries. It contributes to the prevention and punishment of marine incidents which was previously left exclusively to the discretion of the flag state. Article 25 (Rights

295 The UN Convention on Conditions for Registration of Ships, signed in Geneva on 7 February 1986, was adopted mainly in order to stop the registration of ships in foreign States merely for financial purposes through flags of convenience, by strengthening the linkage requirement between the vessel and its flag state. It also aimed to ensure a better control of the flag state over the vessels that are registered under its jurisdiction. The Convention sets minimal norms, and states retain the power to adopt more exacting ones under domestic law. The Convention applies to any self-propelled vessel over 500 gross registered tons used in international seaborne trade for the transport of goods and/or passengers. The Convention is not yet in force (as of 31 December 2003). The legal text of the Convention is available at the website of Admiralty and Maritime Law Guide: http://www.admiraltylawguide.com visited in August 2007.

of protection of the coastal State) empowers states whose ports are used by vessels to take necessary steps to prevent any breach of the conditions to which such vessels may be subject[296].

The characteristics of port state enforcement under the LOS Convention include[297]:

- Port or offshore terminals. The exercise of port state enforcement power is limited to ports and offshore terminals. Internal waters are not included;
- Voluntary, investigative and adjudicative. Port state is not entitled to force a vessel on the high seas or in its own territorial waters or exclusive economic zones to proceed to its ports. In other words, the jurisdiction of port state is engaged solely by reason of a voluntary presence of vessel in its ports. The enforcement proceedings shall be primarily investigative and secondarily adjudicative;
- Discharge from ships. The enforcement powers are restricted to discharges from ships, which cover accidental and intentional discharges of oil, noxious and hazardous substances in bulk or packaged form; together with sewage and garbage such as reballasting, tank cleaning activities and leaking from engines;
- Applicable international standards and competent international organizations. The port state shall only enforce standards that are either part of customary international law or laid down in international maritime conventions. The generally accepted competent international organization is IMO;
- Role of the flag state. The flag state may request the investigation of discharge violations by its vessels on the high seas

296 For more elaboration on port state jurisdiction see Tatjana Keselj, "Port State Jurisdiction in Respect of Pollution from Ships: The 1982 United Nations Convention on the Law of the Sea and the Memoranda of Understanding", Ocean Development & International Law, Volume 30, Issue 2 June 1999 , pp. 127–160.

297 See for example, George C. Kasoulides, *Port State Control and Jurisdiction*, Kluwer Academic Publisher, 1993; Brian F. Fitzgerald, "Port State Jurisdiction and Marine Pollution under UNCLOS III", Journal of The Maritime Law Association of Australia and New Zealand, 1995 (11), pp. 29–35.

or foreign waters. Otherwise, it may pursue legal proceedings in its national courts. In case it decides to do so, the port state shall interrupt its own proceedings, subject to the safeguards of Article 228[298];

- Penalties. The Convention specifically refers to monetary penalties in Article 230, yet it further suggests by implication in paragraph 2 of Article 230[299] that imprisonment can be ordered as a sanction in the case of willful and serious pollution of the territorial sea.

The LOS Convention has not made substantial changes to the legislative powers of port states, except in Article 211 (3) which provides that states may set requirements as a condition for the entry of foreign vessels in their ports. It brought forward important changes concerning the enforcement jurisdiction of the port state, such as Article 218 (Enforcement by port States) which provides that:

1. When a vessel is voluntarily within a port or at an offshore terminal of a state, that state may undertake investigations and, where the evidence so warrants, institute proceedings in respect of any discharge from that vessel outside the internal waters, territorial sea or exclusive economic zone of that state in violation of applicable international law and standards established through the competent international organization or general diplomatic conference.
2. No proceedings pursuant to paragraph 1 shall be instituted in respect of a discharge violation in the internal waters, territorial sea or exclusive economic zone of another state unless requested by that state, the flag state or a state damaged or threatened by the discharge violation or unless the violation has caused or is likely to cause pollution in the internal waters, territorial sea or exclusive economic zone of the state instituting the proceedings.

298 Article 228: Suspension and restrictions on institution of proceedings.

299 Article 230: Monetary Penalties and the observance of recognized rights of the accused.

3. When a vessel is voluntarily within a port or at an offshore terminal of a state, that state shall, as far as practicable, comply with requests from any state for investigation of a discharge violation referred to in paragraph 1, believed to have occurred in, caused, or threatened damage to the internal waters, territorial sea or exclusive economic zone of the requesting state. It shall likewise, as far as practicable, comply with requests from the flag state for investigation of such a violation, irrespective of where the violation occurred.
4. The records of the investigation carried out by a port state pursuant to this article shall be transmitted upon request to the flag state or the coastal state. Any proceedings instituted by the port state on the basis of such an investigation may, subject to section 7, be suspended at the request of the coastal state when the violation has occurred within its internal waters, territorial sea or exclusive economic zone. The evidence and records of the case together with any bond or other financial security posted with the authorities of the port state, shall in that event by transmitted to the coastal state. Such transmittal shall preclude the continuation of proceedings in the port state.

Article 219 (Measures relating to seaworthiness of vessels to avoid pollution) further provides that:

> Subject to section 7[300], states which upon request or on their own initiative, have ascertained that a vessel within one of their ports or at one of their offshore terminals is in violation of applicable international rules and standards relating to seaworthiness of vessels and thereby threatens damage to the marine environment shall, as far as practicable, take administrative measures to prevent the vessel from sailing. Such states may permit the vessel to proceed only to the nearest appropriate repair yard and upon removal of the causes of the violation, shall permit the vessel to continue immediately.

300 Section 7 provides certain safeguards for the foreign vessel which include the facilitation of hearing of witness and the admission of evidence, the enforcement of any measures solely by officials or government vessels, as well as the obligation of the port state to exercise due care not to endanger the safety of navigation, create a hazard to the vessel, or bring it to an unsafe port or anchorage or expose the marine environment to an unreasonable risk.

Article 220 (Enforcement by coastal States) provides that the coastal state has the power to arrest and prosecute a vessel which violates its anti-pollution laws or applicable international rules, in its territorial sea or exclusive economic zone. This article further places an obligation on the coastal state to suspend any legal action taken against a foreign vessel, when appropriate procedures have been established through competent international organization or as otherwise agreed, to ensure that compliance with requirements for bonding or other appropriate financial security has been assured. The regulation under this article grants coastal states alternative methods of enforcement if the flag state fails to observe its international obligations concerning safety and pollution prevention for ships under its registration. This regulation has particular importance to ships with open registries or under flag of convenience[301].

Another important feature of the LOS Convention is that it provides detailed procedures for the investigation of foreign vessels. Article 226 (Investigation of foreign vessels) provides that:

1. (a) State shall not delay the foreign vessel longer than is essential for purposes of the investigation provided for in Articles 216, 218 and 220. Any physical inspection of a foreign vessel shall be limited to an examination of such certificates, records or other documents as the vessel is required to carry by generally accepted international rules and standards or of any similar documents which it is carrying; further physical inspection of the vessel may be undertaken only after such an examination, and only when:
   (i) There are clear grounds for believing that the conditions of the vessel or its equipment does not correspond substantially with the particulars of those document;
   (ii) The contents of such documents are not sufficient to confirm or verify a suspected violation;
   (iii) The vessel is not carrying valid certificates and records.

   (b) If the investigation indicates a violation of applicable laws and regulations or international rules and standards for the protection and preservation of the marine environment, release shall be made promptly subject to reasonable procedures such as bonding or other appropriate financial security.

301 Brian F. Fitzgerald, supra note 297.

(c) Without prejudice to applicable international rules and standards relating to the seaworthiness of vessels, the release of a vessel may, whenever it would present an unreasonable threat of damage to the marine environment, be refused or made condition upon proceeding to the nearest appropriate repair yard. Where release has been refused or made conditional the flag state of the vessel must be promptly notified, and may seek release of the vessel in accordance with Part XV.

2. States shall co-operate to develop procedures for the avoidance of unnecessary physical inspection of vessels at sea.

The LOS Convention reiterates the duty of the port state not to discriminate against foreign vessels in Article 227. Finally, the convention provides only for monetary penalties (Article 230), at the same time, it stipulates that port states are liable for damage or loss if their enforcement measures are unlawful or unreasonable (Article 231)[302].

The regulation relating to the legitimacy of port state control inspections in the LOS Convention is mainly focused on oil pollution preparedness and response. Although the Convention has given its highest priority to issues concerning marine pollution, there is no particular elaboration on a number of other pertinent issues, such as shipping safety, construction and equipment of vessels, crewing and working conditions on board vessels. Some scholars argued that the Convention seems to follow the traditional principle of non-intervention over issues of "internal economy" of the vessel[303] and leave the matters in the hands of the flag state[304].

302 Id.

303 Churchill R.R. and Lowe A.V., *the Law of the Sea*, 2nd ed., Manchester University Press, Manchester, UK, 1988, pp. 54–57; Brian F. Fitzgerald, supra note 297.

304 The LOS Convention stipulates duties of the flag state in several articles, such as Art. 94 entitled Duties of the Flag State. See also Art. 10 of the High Seas Convention which provides that every state shall take such measures for its vessels as are necessary to ensure safety at sea with regard to communications, the prevention of collisions, crew conditions and the construction, equipment and seaworthiness of ships, in conformity with generally accepted international standards.

However, the distinction between port state jurisdiction and flag state control of vessels is not clear-cut and further work of clarification is required.

4.1.2.3.2 Access Right of Landlocked State to Ports

Landlocked states refer to those without direct coastal access to the sea[305]. The precondition for considering the navigational rights of landlocked states and their rights of access to marine resources is whether or not they have the right of transit cross the territory of States lying between them and the sea. In customary international law, it is debatable whether such a general right of transit exists[306]. In addition, most treaties concerning this subject also seem to indicate the absence of such a rule[307].

The issue concerning the access of landlocked states was referred to in the 1958 Convention on the High Seas[308]. Article 3

305 UNECE 2003 "Trade Facilitation: The Challenges for Growth and Development". Geneva. United Nations Commission for Europe, p. 81.

306 Although opinion is divided, the majority of the scholars hold the view that under customary international law there is no right for vessels of one State – at least of a non-riparian State – to navigate a river passing through another State. See R.R. Baxter, *The Law of International Waterways*, Cambridge, Mass., Harvard University Press, 1964, p. 149–59. R. Jennings and A. Watts, *Oppenheim's International Law*, London, Longman, 9th ed., 1992, p. 582; see also the Faber case of 1903, where the German Commissioner of the Germany – Venezuela Mixed Claims Commission thought there was a general right of navigation on rivers (X RIAA 438, at 444–5), the Venezuelan Commissioner (pp. 448–9) and the Umpire (pp. 464–7) disagreed.

307 There are some scholars who consider that a right of transit does exist in customary law. See for example, J.E.S. Fawcett, *Trade and finance in international law*, 123 Recueil des Cours 215 (1968), at 266–7; E. Lauterpacht, "Freedom of transit in international law", 44 Transactions of Grotius Society 313–56 (1958–59).

308 The legal text of the High Seas Convention is available in the UN Treaty Series, vol. 450, p. 11. p. 82. For more discussion on the subject of landlocked states and their right of access to and from the sea, see Caflisch, L.C., "Landlocked States and their Access to and from the Sea", 49 British Yearbook of International Law 71 (1978).

of this Convention[309] reflects the rules contained in the 1923 Geneva Statute on this matter. Although access to port for other purposes is denied by the Convention, access for the landlocked countries is treated as a corollary to freedom of navigation on the high seas. Paragraph 2 referring to the use of maritime ports in general is subject to the conditions of reciprocity, while paragraph 4 of the Protocol of Signature specifies that the requirement of reciprocity is waived for contracting parties which have no reciprocal facilities to offer.

Since the adoption of the High Seas Convention in 1958, a number of bilateral treaties have been signed[310]. In addition, an important multilateral treaty was also signed – the Convention on Transit Trade of Landlocked Countries of 1965. Article 2 of the Convention grants the landlocked States the freedom of transit across a State lying between a landlocked State and the sea (the transit State) for goods traveling by road, rail or river between the landlocked State and the sea. No customs duties may be levied on goods in transit, and only dues to defray expenses and reasonable charges may be levied (Articles 3 and 4). Transit must not be hindered by administrative or customs practices (Article 5). Exceptions to all these provisions may be made on grounds of public health and security, or in case of emergency and war (Articles 11–13). By

309 Article 3 states that: 1. In order to enjoy the freedom of the seas on equal terms with coastal States, States having no seacoast should have free access to the sea. To this end States situated between the sea and a State having no sea-coast shall reach common agreement with the latter, and in conformity with existing international conventions, accord: (a) To the State having no sea-coast, on a basis of reciprocity, free transit through their territory; and (b) To ships flying the flag of that State treatment equal to that accorded to their own ships, or to the ships of any other States, as regards access to seaports and the use of such ports. 2. States situated between the sea and a State having no sea-coast shall settle, by mutual agreement with the latter, and taking into account the rights of the coastal State or State of transit and the special conditions of the State having no sea-coast, all matters relating to freedom of transit and equal treatment in ports, in case such States are not already parties to existing international conventions.

310 I. Delupis, "Landlocked States and the law of the sea", 19 Scandinavian Studies in Law 101–20 (1975).

September 1998, 36 countries had become parties to this Convention, of which 20 were landlocked. The low number of ratifications has reduced the impact of the Convention[311].

This right of access is further expanded in the LOS Convention[312], in which a guaranteed right of transit is provided for the landlocked States. Article 125[313] (1) provides that:

> Landlocked States shall have the right of access to and from the sea for the purpose of exercising the rights provided for in this Convention including those relating to the freedom of the high sea and the common heritage of mankind. To this end landlocked States shall enjoy freedom of transit through the territory of transit States by all means of transport.[314]

However, this right has been considerably limited in paragraphs 2 and 3 of Article 125, which provide:

> 2. The terms and modalities for exercising freedom of transit shall be agreed between the land-locked States and transit States concerned through bilateral, sub-regional or regional agreements.
> 3. Transit States, in the exercise of their full sovereignty over their territory, shall have the right to take all measures necessary to ensure that the rights and facilities provided for in this Part for land-locked States shall in no way infringe their legitimate interests.

In reality, whether or not the right of transit can be implemented depends largely on agreements between the transit states and the land-locked states, as well as the measures taken by transit states under Article 125 (3). In seeking to conclude a transit agreement, the transit state is expected to act in good faith, otherwise it is presumed to breach an international obligation and under such circumstances, the LOS Convention's provisions on settlement of

311 For more information on the Convention, see the website of International Maritime Law Institute under IMO, at: www.imli.org visited in June 2002 and revisited in August 2005.

312 See Part X of the Convention, Right of Access of Landlocked States to and from the Sea and Freedom of Transit.

313 Article 125: Right of access to and from the sea and freedom of transit.

314 "Means of transport" is defined in Article 124 as excluding pipelines and air transport, unless the States concerned agree to the contrary.

disputes could be provoked by the dissatisfied party[315]. Moreover, it is supposed that the terms and modalities of such agreements, together with any unilateral measures taken by a transit state cannot run contrary with the right of transit in principle. Furthermore, such terms, modalities and unilateral measures must comply with the regulations under Articles 127[316] and 130[317], which deal with customs duties and other charges and measures to avoid delays in a way similar to that of the 1965 Convention on Transit Trade of Landlocked Countries.

Apart from the LOS Convention, bilateral treaties are the most frequently applied mechanism to regulate transit rights in detail. Because most bilateral treaties are based on reciprocal conditions, a land-locked state is usually in a weak bargaining position when negotiating with a transit state because it has little to offer reciprocally. The lack of a general right of transit in customary international law or multilateral convention contributes significantly to this outcome[318]. Some issues remaining ambiguous in the LOS Convention needing further clarification, such as[319]:

315 According to Article 300 of the LOS Convention (Good faith and abuse of rights), where one party has not shown good faith, there is presumably breach of an international obligation In such case the Convention's provisions on settlement of disputes could be provoked by the dissatisfied party.

316 Article 127: Customs duties, taxes and other charges.

317 Article 130: Measures to avoid or eliminate delays or other difficulties of a technical nature in traffic in transit.

318 For more on this issue, especially on the efforts of balancing between multilateral treaties and bilateral treaties, see United Nations, "The Law of the Sea: Rights of Access of Land-locked States to and from the Sea, and Freedom of Transit – Legislative History of Part X, Articles 124–132, of the United Nations Convention on the Law of the Sea" (New York, United Nations), 1987; UN Secretariat, "The question of free access to the sea of land-locked countries", UNCLOS I, Official Records, Vol. I, pp. 306–35; UN Secretary General, "Study of the question of free access to the sea of landlocked countries and of the special problems of landlocked countries relating to the exploration and exploitation of the resources of the seabed, and the ocean floor beyond the limits of national jurisdiction", UN Doc. A/AC 138/37 (1971).

319 The ambiguous issues are discussed in many writings, see for example Churchill and Lowe, supra note 303.

Internal waters jurisdiction and right of access deny: Internal waters bear the same legal status of the territory of a state[320]. This represents the precondition by which port states can exercise full jurisdictional powers within their internal waters and full enforcement of their laws and regulations[321]. However, while the right of a port state to exclude vessels from other parts of its internal waters is not questioned, the right to deny access to its maritime ports used for maritime trade has been the subject of numerous debates[322]. The LOS Convention is also silent on this issue.

Right of innocent passage and right of access to port: Another issue that the LOS Convention does not clarify is the relationship between a foreign vessel's right of innocent passage in internal waters and its right of access to port. This work shares Jessup's viewpoint that the right of access to ports shall be treated as an independent right and be distinguished from the right of innocent passage through internal waters[323].

320 Baker, S., *First Steps in International Law,* Kegal Paul, Trench Trubner and Co, London, 1899, p. 61: "the maritime territory of each state extends to the ports, harbours, bays, mouths of rivers, and adjacent parts of the sea enclosed by headlands belonging to the same state"; Oppenheim, L., *International Law (A Treatise)*, Vol. 1, 8th edition, Lauterpacht, H., (ed.), Longmans and Co, 1955; Schwarzenberger, G. and Brown, E.D., *A Manual of International Law* (6th edition), Professional Books Ltd, 1975, p. 100, states that "the justification for the distinction between internal waters and the territorial sea lies in the limitation under customary international law of the coastal states' territorial jurisdiction in the territorial sea"; Jessup, P.C., *The Law of Territorial Waters and Maritime Jurisdiction*, E.A. Jennings Co, Inc., NY, 1927.

321 Smith, G.P., "The Politics of Lawmaking Problems in International Maritime Regulation – Innocent Passage vs. Free Transit", 37 University of Pittsburgh Law Review 487 (1976), pp. 515–518; Burke, K.M. and Deleo, D.A., "Innocent Passage in the United Nations Convention on the Law of the Sea", 9 Yale Journal of World Public Order 389 (1983), p. 390.

322 Degan, V.D., "Internal Waters", 17 Netherlands Yearbook of International Law, 3 (1986), pp. 10–13.

323 Jessup, P.C., "the United Nations Conference on the Law of the Sea", 55 Columbia Law Review 234 (1959).

4.1.3 International Organizations

4.1.3.1 IMO Regulations on Access to Port

It is an established legal practice in the law of the sea that a state has full jurisdiction over ships entering its waters and calling at its ports. Once a foreign ship enters a port, it is expected to fully comply with the laws and regulations of the port state and refrain from any activities that may be harmful to the port state.

However, from the 1970s, with the growth of flags of convenience, the incidence of sub-standard ships increased dramatically. In fields related to oil tankers in particular, with their potential threat to the environment, the international community started work to seek a coordinated international approach to solve the problem of sub-standard ships by means of new policy and regulatory mechanism.

The concept of port state jurisdiction and control was first introduced at an international level through the 1973 IMO Conference on Marine Pollution[324]. Since then the formulation of the port state authority of a coastal state has been included in a number of maritime conventions, such as the Load Line Convention 1966[325], the MARPOL 73/78[326], the SOLAS[327], the 1976 ILO Convention No. 147[328], the 1978 STCW Convention[329], the 1969 Convention on Civil Liability[330], and the 1986 United Nations Convention on Conditions for Registration of Ships[331].

324 Writings on IMO efforts to cope with marine pollution, see for example: Brian F. Fitzgerald, supra footnote 297; Douglas Cormack, *Response to Marine Oil Pollution: Review and Assessment,* Springer, 1999; Kasoulides, G. C., "The Port State Enforcement Regime Through International Organizations", Proceedings of the 23rd Annual Conference of the Law of the Sea Institute, 12–15 June 1989, The Law of the Sea Institute, University of Hawaii, Honolulu, 1990.
325 Art. 21.
326 Art. 5 (2).
327 Regulation 19 of Chapter I Regulation II of Chapter VIII.
328 Art. 4.
329 Art. X (1).
330 Art. VII (11).
331 Art. 6 (4).

In addition to the promotion of international conventions, the IMO has passed its own assembly resolutions that bind the member states of the IMO. These resolutions have coupled with international conventions to impose obligations on port states and implement the supervision and monitoring envisaged by the resolutions.

The IMO discipline on port state control was further strengthened by the introduction of the SOLAS requirements for ISM certification. Coupled with a Safety Management System, this certification came into effect on July 1st 1998 and imposes upon ship-owners definitive standards of operation and management that becomes the benchmarks against which port state control inspectors may assess compliance.

Although the IMO is the most influential international organization for the drafting, implementation and supervision of maritime safety standards, including those for port state control, several other international organizations have also played active roles in applying pressure upon maritime states to apply relevant safety conventions and regimes. These include International Labour Organization (ILO), International Chamber of Shipping (ICS) and International Shipping Federation (ISF). The 1948 SOLAS convention was actually the first time a permanent international authority enacted international conventions to regulate shipping. During the 1950s, the IMO played a leading role in the preparation of the LOS Convention[332], and it has since sponsored the various subsequent SOLAS conventions establishing and improving load lines, navigation, watch-keeping, building and registration requirements of all ships.

4.1.3.1.1 SOLAS 1974 and MARPOL 73/78

The SOLAS Convention (International Convention for the Safety of Life at Sea) is universally regarded as one of the most influential international treaties concerning the safety of merchant ships. In

332 John Hare, "Port State Control: Strong Medicine to Cure a Sick Industry", available at: http://www.uctshiplaw.com visited in December 2001 and revisited in August 2005.

addition to what it is SOLAS Convention 1974 and its amendments that are in force today[333], there were several previous versions between 1914 and 1960, with the 1960 Convention seen as a major step towards reinforcing the regulations on shipping safety against the background of technological progress from the 1960s (such as containerization).

The SOLAS Convention is aimed at specifying minimum standards for the construction, equipment and operation of ships which are compatible with their safety standards. The Convention requires the flag states to ensure compliance of their ships with these standards which need to be proven by certain certificates. The Convention also sets up the procedure of port state control, which allows port state to inspect foreign ships if there are clear grounds to believe that the ship (and its equipment) does not substantially comply with the requirements and standards of the Convention[334].

The MARPOL Convention (International Convention for the Prevention of Pollution from Ships) is one of the most important international marine environmental conventions under the IMO. It is aimed at minimizing pollution of the seas, including dumping, oil and exhaust pollution, which includes both accidental pollution and the pollution from routine operations. The original 1973 version of the MARPOL Convention (signed on 17 February 1973)

333 SOLAS 1974 includes Articles setting out general obligations and amendment procedure which are following by annex divided into 12 chapters. The 12 chapters of SOLAS Convention are: chapter I – General Provisions; chapter II-1 – Construction – Sub-vision and stability, machinery and electrical installations; chapter II-2 – Fire protection, fire detection and fire extinction; chapter III – Life-saving appliances and arrangements; chapter IV – radio-communications; chapter V – Safety of Navigation; chapter VI – Carriage of Cargoes; chapter VII – Carriage of Dangerous Goods; chapter VIII – Nuclear ships; chapter IX – Management for the safe operation of ships; chapter X – Safety measures for high-speed craft; chapter XI-1 – Special measures to enhance maritime safety; chapter XI-2 – Special measures to enhance maritime security; chapter XII – Additional safety measures for bulk carriers.

334 IMO, International Convention for the Safety of Life at Sea (SOLAS), 1974. The legal text of the convention is available at IMO website www.imo.org revisited in August 2007.

did not come into force. The current Convention is the combination of the 1973 Convention and its 1978 Protocol, which entered into force on 2 October 1983[335].

The Convention currently includes six technical Annexes[336]. States Parties must accept Annexes I and II, but the other Annexes are voluntary. The six annexes are: Annex I – Regulation for the Prevention of Pollution by Oil; Annex II – Regulation for the Control of Pollution by Noxious Liquid Substances in Bulk; Annex III – Prevention of Pollution by Harmful Substances Carried by Sea in Packaged Form; Annex IV – Prevention of Pollution by Sewage from Ships: Annex V – Prevention of Pollution by Garbage from Ships; and Annex VI – Prevention of Air Pollution from Ships.

4.1.3.1.2 1965 Convention on Facilitation of International Maritime Traffic

The objective of the IMO Convention on Facilitation of International Maritime Traffic of 1965 is to prevent unnecessary delays in maritime traffic, to aid cooperation between Governments and to secure the highest practicable degree of uniformity in formalities and other procedures[337].

Under this Convention, Contracting Parties undertake to adopt all appropriate measures to facilitate and expedite international

335 As at 31 December 2005, 136 countries were parties to the MARPOL Convention, representing 98% of the world's shipping tonnage.

336 IMO, International Convention for the Prevention of Pollution from Ships, 1973, as modified by the Protocol of 1978 relating thereto (MARPOL 73/78). The legal text of the convention is available at IMO website www.imo.org revisited in August 2007.

337 IMO Secretariat, Convention on Facilitation of International Maritime Traffic, 1965, available at IMO website www.imo.org revisited in July 2006. This Convention is an important addition to the achievements of the Inter-Governmental Maritime Consultative Organization at whose invitation a conference was held in London in March 1965 to draw up a convention to facilitate international maritime traffic. The Convention was signed in London on April 9, 1965, marking the first attempt in the field of international regulation of this vital aspect of maritime activity. The Convention came into force on March 5, 1967.

maritime traffic and to prevent unnecessary delays to ships and to persons and property on board[338]. They are also expected to co-operate in the formulation and application of measures for the facilitation of the arrival, stay and departures of ships. Such measures are to be not less favourable than measures applied in respect of other means of international transport. The measures in question cover formalities, documentary requirements and procedures in all matters in which uniformity will facilitate and improve international maritime traffic and keep to a minimum the formalities required. The co-operation is to be effected through the IMO and the contracting parties remain free to apply temporary measures considered necessary to preserve order and security and for quarantine purposes. The provisions of the Convention do not apply to warships or pleasure yachts[339].

The Convention draws a distinction between Standards, which are the uniform application of measures, and Recommended Practices, which are desirable measures[340]. Annexed to the Convention are lists of measures distinguished as either Standard or Recommended. In the Standard measures, it is provided that public authorities shall not require the retention, on arrival or departure of ships, of any documents other that General Declaration, Cargo Declaration, Ship's Stores Declaration, Crew's Effects Declaration, Crew List, Passenger List, UPU document for mail, and Maritime Declaration of Health. The General Declaration, signed by master or agent, shall be the basic document on arrival and departure and it shall be the same form on arrival and departure[341].

It is recommended in the Convention that the General Declaration contain no more information than that listed in the schedule, including name and description of ship, nationality of registration, tonnage, master's name, name and address of agent, description of cargo, number of crew and passengers, brief particular of voyage, date and time of arrival and date of departure, together

338 Id. Article I.
339 Id. Article II.
340 Id. Article VI.
341 Id. Annex Section 2 A.

with port and dock location.[342] Similarly, the Cargo Declaration shall be the basic document and contains only the listed basic document including name and nationality of ship, name of master, port arrived from, port where report is made, marks and numbers, number and kind of packages, quantity and description of goods, bill of lading number for cargo to be discharged, ports of discharge of remaining cargo and original ports of shipment of goods shipped on through bills of lading. There are similar recommended practices in respect of the other six documents listed above, as well as standard requirements respecting the number of copies of each document to be completed[343].

With respect to the arrival and departure of persons, it is a standard requirement that a valid passport shall be the basic document for passengers. A Recommended Embarkation/Disembarkation Card should require only the additional information listed. Similarly, an International Certificate of Vaccination in the forms provided for in the International Sanitary Regulations of the World Health Organization shall be Standard and it is recommended that medical examination on board be limited to persons arriving from an area infected with one of the quarantinable diseases within the incubation period of the disease concerned. As to customs inspection, it is Recommended Practice that only sampling or selective inspection be carried out and that written declarations in respect of accompanied baggage be dispensed with as far as possible[344].

The measures to facilitate clearance of cargo, passengers, crew and baggage are all Recommended Practice to achieve satisfactory port traffic flow for rapid clearance. Public authorities should require ship-owners to ensure that ship's personnel take all necessary measures to help expedite arrival procedures for passengers and crew. The only Standard requirements are that public authorities shall, without unreasonable delay, accept passengers and crew for examination as to their admission into the State and shall not impose any penalty upon ship-owners in the event that any con-

342 Id. Annex Section 2 B.
343 Id. Annex Section 2 B.
344 Id. Annex Section 2 C & D.

trol document in possession of a passenger is found to be inadequate, or if for any reason the passenger is found to be inadmissible to the State[345].

Amendments to the Convention were adopted in 1971 concerning cruises and cruise passengers, passengers in transit and ships in scientific services, shore leave for crew members, graphical symbols and signs. Moreover, general amendments were adopted in 1973, and were elaborated in 1977, when a few more recommendations were incorporated, such as a standard simple declaration for re-export of containers and pallets; acceptance of documents produced by automatic data techniques; arrival of ships with sick persons; use of standard signs and symbols; exemption of transit passengers on board from routine control; permission of shore leave for crew without visa; and facilitation of arrival and departure of vessels engaged in natural disaster relief work[346].

4.1.3.1.3 Regional Co-operation under the Guidance of IMO

As discussed in the above sections, the international conventions under IMO have greatly facilitated the harmonization of international regulations on maritime safety and marine environmental protection. They have also provided strong support and guidance for port states to exercise port state control. However, there was the possibility that port state control as empowered by the IMO conventions could create frictions and conflicts between countries. This made it necessary to seek for co-ordinations to achieve the feasible enforcement of this new system. At the same time, because of the diversified regulatory and management systems of ports around the world, it could be difficult to implement a unified system of application for port state control on global scale[347].

Against this background, an alternative was for countries to undertake regional cooperation in the application of port state control. Regional initiatives were established in which states work

345 Id. Annex Section 2 E.

346 IMO, supra note 337.

347 K.C. Chung and T. Tsutsumi, "Port State Control", Transportation, Water and Urban Development Department, World Bank, May 1994.

together in their port state control activities in form of memoranda of understandings (MOUs). These regional co-operations have been effective in implementing port state control[348]. A number of typical advantages of these regional co-operations have been noted. Firstly, they provide certainty of the applicable instruments for ship-owners under different legal systems. Secondly, they help to balance the different levels of port state control regime within a certain area. Thirdly, they enable neighbouring countries in a region to exercise a more effective control of vessels visiting the region. Information gathered during inspection carried out by one country can be shared with others and to avoid unnecessary duplication of work as well as unnecessary inconvenience for the vessels being inspected.

The 1982 Paris MOU[349] is the most prominent regional initiative for establishing a comprehensive system of regional co-operation for the exercise of port state control. Member states have agreed that the purpose of the Paris MOU "was intended to enforce and reinforce IMO agreed standards and not to develop new standards"[350]. The setting up of the Paris MOU demonstrates the wish of the participating countries to co-ordinate their efforts for the enforcement of international standards within their ports. The approach is mainly conducted through the adoption of uniform procedures for carrying out inspections, exchanging the gathered information and implementing of the new regime in general. The executive body of the Paris MOU is the Port State Control Committee[351] and the administration is undertaken by the Netherlands[352].

348 For elaboration on the advantages of regional cooperation on port state control, see for example: R. Shiferli, "Regional Concepts of Port State Control: A Regional Effort with Global Effects", Ocean Yearbook, Vol. 11, 1994, p. 202; Heike Hoppe, "Port State Control – an Update on IMO's Work (2000)", available at IMO website: http://www.imo.org/Circulars revisited in July 2006.

349 The text and introduction of Paris MOU is available from its website at: http://www.parismou.org revisited in March 2006. According to the 2007 Annual Report of Paris MOU, it had 27 members by 2007.

350 IMO, C. 50/II, 25 Feb. 1983, para. 13.

351 Sections 6.1 and 6.4 of the MOU. Apart from the 14 participating authorities, a representative of the EC also participates in the Committee.

352 Id, Section 6.4.

The Paris MOU focuses on the need to increase maritime safety, the protection of the marine environment and the importance of improving living and working conditions on board the ship. The key to the MOU is a requirement that each contracting state will ensure through an effective system of port state control that foreign merchant ships calling in its ports comply with the international instruments listed in the MOU. The Paris MOU requires that each contracting authority, within three years to inspect an annual total of 25% of foreign merchant ships calling at its ports, and each authority shall consult, co-operate and exchange information with other authorities. Moreover, authorities shall seek to avoid inspecting ships that have been inspected by any of the other authorities within the previous six months unless they have clear grounds for inspection[353].

The Paris MOU requires that port state control would be conducted without discrimination as to flag. It also requires that each state ensure that no more favourable treatment is given to ships flying the flag of a state not party to the memorandum. It sets out detailed guidelines as to inspection procedures and detention, the prime purpose of which is to ensure rectification of defects in vessels. In Section 3, it provides that:

> In the case of deficiencies which are clearly hazardous to safety, health or the environment, the Authority will, ..., ensure that the hazard is removed before the ship is allowed to proceed to sea. For this purpose appropriate action will be taken, which may include detention or a formal prohibition of a ship to continue an operation due to established deficiencies, which, individually or together, would render the continued operation hazardous[354].

The Paris MOU provides that there must be "no more favourable treatment" of ships registered in a state that is not a party to the applicable instruments in section 2.4. This section has the potential of leading to an attempt by participating authorities to enforce the provisions of relevant instruments even in cases where the conventions themselves do not specifically provide for such a

353 Id, section 3.
354 Id. section 3, 3.10.1.

possibility. This has led the Secretariat to declare that this section applies only in cases where the relevant convention contains a no more favourable treatment clause[355]. In practice, if a ship is inspected and found not to be in compliance with any of the relevant instruments, the master will be given notice to carry out the necessary repairs and rectifications before leaving the port.

No exercise of such control may "unduly detain or delay a ship"[356]. Section 5 extends the authority of the port state to apply "not to the condition of the ship, but to its activities". It provides that the participating authorities must do their best to gather evidence of suspected violations to the requirements of Rule 10 of MARPOL 73/78 when the request is made by another participating authority. Even though this is pursuant to the provisions of the LOS Convention, it restricts the role of the port state by allowing it merely to offer its assistance in the process of collecting evidence. The port state is not in a position to take any measures of enforcement against a vessel. The collected evidence may result in action being brought against the vessel only in the flag state or in the state requesting the inspection, provided that the vessel calls in one of the ports of that state in the future.

One of the most effective provisions of the Paris MOU is the obligation imposed upon each authority to publish quarterly information about detentions under PSC procedures. This information is required not only to nominate the name of the ship concerned, but also to name her owner and operator, her flag state and her classification society. The declaration also needs to state reasons for the detention[357].

The Paris MOU is based on the spirit of the main IMO Conventions. Annex 1 provides for the inspection procedures to be followed by the participating authorities and makes extensive references to a number of IMO resolutions[358]. However, it adopted

355 See an information booklet published by the Paris MOU Secretariat: "Memorandum of Understanding on Port State Control", 1986, p. 7.

356 Supra note 349, section 3.11.

357 Supra note 349, section 3.17–18.

358 Supra note 349, 1.1 of annex 1.

more general provisions than those adopted by the proposed Directive by avoiding the provision of an exhaustive list of clear grounds. Section 3.2.1 provides that the authorities will regard as clear grounds, *inter alia*, the following:

- A report of notification by another authority;
- A report or complaint by the master, a crew member, or a person or organization with a legitimate interest in the safe operation of the ship, shipboard living and working conditions or the prevention of pollution, unless the authority concerned deems the report or complaint to be manifestly unfounded;
- Other indications of serious deficiencies, having regard in particular to annex 1.

However, the authorities are expected to include control on compliance with on-board operational requirements in their control procedures[359]. Clear grounds for the control of operational requirements are comprehensively listed[360]. The IMO recognizes that it is not necessarily the deliberate intent of flag states to allow substandard ships to operate under their flags. Some flag states, particularly developing countries with new registers, suffer from a lack of adequate resources for monitoring the fleet. The IMO thus provides assistance in training government officials in improving their maritime inspectorates and plays a leading role in maritime education[361].

359 Supra note 349, section 3.1.

360 Supra note 349, sec. 3.2.2.

361 The IMO's role in relation to port state control is summarized by its Director, Mr. William O'Neil in his speech on World Maritime Day in 1996: "shipping is an international industry which is proud of its tradition of freedom of the seas, but that does not mean that ships can sail wherever they like regardless of their condition. The maritime world has the right to expect that ships of all nations meet the levels of safety and environmental protection that have been internationally agreed upon. It is up to the shipowners to make sure that their ships are safe, properly manned and do not pollute the seas and it is the duty of governments to make sure that ships which fly their flag comply with the standards laid down in the IMO treaties which they have ratified. If they fail to do so, then the IMO – which has the stewardship of these standards – has not only the right but the obliga-

The Paris MOU has undergone progressive improvements since its introduction[362]. Since 1993, it has given further incentives to flag states to carry out their obligations in respect of the implementation of international standards. These efforts have exercised a direct pressure on the flag state. They also indirectly promoted a more effective implementation since the targeting of a specific flag could result in a decrease in the tonnage of that flag and shipowners, whose vessels are in general complying with international standards, would not allow their ships to be subject to more inspections simply because they fly the flag of certain states[363].

The Paris MOU has proven to be a pioneer for a port state control regional co-operation scheme that seeks to enforce existing international standards, such as those set by the relevant international organizations, in particular IMO and ILO.

4.1.3.1.4 1976 Legal Committee Report on Port Entry Right

The IMO's work on the issue of port access conducted through its Legal Committee was initiated by a proposal from the USSR in 1974, in which it was suggested that some sort of international convention concerning the regime of vessels in foreign ports should be adopted[364]. This subject was discussed in 1975 at the

---

tion to take further action", available at: http://www.imo.org revisited in July 2006.

362 For Paris MOU efforts to improve itself over years, see for example: Paris MOU report for 2002: the 20th anniversary report of the Paris Memorandum has been published and details two major inspection campaigns that identified room for improvement in issuing STCW certificates and implementation of the ISM Code, available at: www.allbusiness.com revisited in April 2006.

363 FAO Corporate Document Repository: "Element of a possible MOU", http://www.fao.org revisited in July 2006.

364 "Proposal on an International Convention on the Regime of Vessels in Foreign Ports" Note by the Government of the Union of Soviet Socialist Republics (IMO Doc C/XXXIII/14/1) The text is reproduced in "Consideration of Recommendations to the Council on Possible Work on a Convention on the Regime of Vessels in Foreign Ports", LEG XXVI/2, Annex, 24 Dec. 1974.

26th session of the Legal Committee, where it was suggested that it would be useful to have governments' views on the issue raised in the proposal and the draft convention[365]. Later, at its 31st session in 1976 the Legal Committee reconsidered the issue and the replies from governments on the proposal, as well as the draft convention and the related work undertaken by some other organizations[366].

The summarized replies from governments reflected the fact that countries held highly divergent views on the Geneva Statute 1923. Some countries like Denmark, Finland and Norway explicitly expressed their support for adopting such a convention, while others such as Argentina suggested their support only on condition of certain reservations. Countries including China and Madagascar, however, disagreed with the adoption of any such convention. Still other countries such as France believed that it was premature to discuss this issue at this moment[367].

Given these circumstances, the Legal Committee decided to put the issue aside until the majority of countries considered it appropriate to develop it at an international level[368]. At the same time, the Committee felt that it was premature to pick up this issue when the LOS Convention was still in preparation and did not have chance of undertaking any work on this issue. Although no substantive progress was made, the IMO Assembly approved at its 13th regular session to integrate the subject for consideration in the long-term work plan of IMO[369].

It is interesting to note that in making comments on the draft convention proposed by the USSR, despite many objections on the

365 The recommendations of the Legal Committee were endorsed by the IMO Council at its 44th session held in June 1975, as well as by the IMO Assembly at its 9th regular session in Nov. 1975.

366 IMO Doc., LEG XXXI/3.

367 "Report of the Legal Committee on the work of its thirty-first session", Doc. LEG XXXI/7, paragraph 16; LEG XXXI/3, Annex I: Comments by Governments: General Comments.

368 IMO Doc., LEG XXXI/7.

369 Resolution IMO A. 554 (13); the statement was reiterated in Resolution A. 591 (14), 20 Nov. 1985.

articles of the convention[370], no country raised objection to Article 3 – "Admittance to Ports", which stipulated that "coastal State shall have the exclusive right to declare the ports under its sovereignty or jurisdiction open to the entry of foreign vessels and to regulate such entry"[371]. This consensus implied an absence of support for foreign vessels' absolute port access right in customary law.

4.1.3.2 UNCTAD Works on Port Access Issues

For decades, shipping issues have been an area of focus for the UNCTAD, in particular from the perspective of safeguarding the interests of developing countries. Founded in 1964, the Trade and Development Board of the UNCTAD gave special consideration to the appropriate institutional means for dealing with problems of shipping[372]. In April 1965, the Board passed its resolution of establishing the Committee of Shipping. A wide variety of issues have been discussed under the Committee, ranging from freight rates, discriminatory practices, improvement of port facilities, expansion of merchant marines of developing countries, to the complicated legal issues of revising the present international conventions of merchant shipping[373].

Among the achievements of the Shipping Committee, there are two conventions that deserve particular attention, namely, the Convention on a Code of Conduct for Liner Conferences (the Liner Code Convention) 1974[374] and the United Nations Convention on International Multi-modal Transport of Goods (the Multi-modal

370 IMO Doc., LEG XXXI/3, annex I, Part B, Comments on specific issues and provisions.

371 IMO, Draft USSR Convention, Art. 3.

372 UNCTAD, basic documents, http://www.unctad.org revisited in July 2006.

373 See "Proceedings of the United Nations Conference on Trade and Development", Vol. 1, Final Act and Report, p. 54.

374 The legal text of the Convention is available at the website of Admiralty and Maritime Law Guide: http://www.admiraltylawguide.com revisited in December 2005.

Transport Convention) 1980[375]. The Liner Code Convention was aimed to set up the orderly development of liner trades and its provisions dealing with cargo sharing, shippers' interests, freight rate changes, consultations and procedures for conciliation. The Multi-modal Transport Convention aimed at the development of international multi-modal transport to facilitate international trade. It established liabilities for multi-modal transport operators and consignors, laying down procedures for claims, juridical proceedings and arbitration in respect of international multi-modal transport.

An annual publication of the UNCTAD, Review of Maritime Transport, has the purpose of identifying the main developments in world maritime transport and providing relevant statistical data[376]. It focuses on developments of maritime activities in developing countries as compared with other groups of countries. In addition, it also highlights the correlation and coordination between development of global trade and maritime transport activities in general.

From the middle 1970s, the UNCTAD studied the treatment of foreign merchant vessels in ports as well as the status of the Geneva Statute 1923. This work was reflected in the 1975 report (the Report) on the evaluation of the relevant jurisprudence and the legal status of foreign merchant vessel's entry into maritime port in international law. It concluded that the status of this issue remained under debate and insufficient evidence existed for it to be recognized as a custom in international law[377]. The Report stated that "the very existence of the Convention and bilateral treaty clauses on the subject shows that countries still deem it necessary to stipulate in a treaty that they grant access to their ports". This argument is not valid if it can be proved that the convention is a

375 DOC. TD/MT/CONF/16. The legal text of the Convention is available at UNCTAD website.

376 The annual review on maritime transport is available from the Digital Library of UNCTAD at its website: www.unctad.org revisited in May 2006.

377 "Economic Co-operation in Merchant Shipping – Treatment of Foreign Merchant Vessels in Ports", UNCTAD/TD/B/C.4/136, 9 Sep. 1975 (UNCTAD 136).

codification of an existing custom or that it consequently passed into customary international law[378].

The Report pointed out that a relatively small number of countries had ratified or acceded to the 1923 Ports Convention, but that certain important maritime countries and many developing countries had not done so. Some of the respondents to the UNCTAD questionnaire stated that they had not given any considerations to the question of accession, but the principles of the 1923 Ports Convention were generally adhered to in the treatment of foreign merchant vessels in their ports[379].

The Report concluded that the 1923 Geneva Statute did not state explicitly that all merchant vessels have a right to come to a port with lawful purpose, regardless of their nationality or ownership and prior/subsequent ports of call. Therefore, the Report suggested that the Committee on Shipping consider whether problems with the 1923 Convention justified a new multilateral convention on the port issue. It further suggested that a certain number of important subjects be elaborated upon under some new multilateral convention, if it proved to be premature to undertake a comprehensive convention for the time being[380]. The important subjects concerned may include the treatment of officers and crews, together with vessels in distress. The Report was discussed by the Committee on Shipping at its 7th session[381] and it was decided that the question of treatment of foreign merchant vessels in ports should be kept under consideration. However, no decision was reached as to whether there was a need to revise the 1923 Ports Convention. At its 8th session, the subject was again considered and decision was taken to defer consideration of the matter and wait the relevant developments of other international organizations.

In view of new developments which had emerged from the establishment of arrangements on treatment of merchant vessels in ports

378 Id. UNCTAD Report 136, para. 70.
379 Id. para. 65.
380 Id. para. 117.
381 TD/B591 – TD/B/C.4/147, paras 70–87.

at the regional level, the Committee on Shipping decided to reconsider this issue at its 10th session in 1983. The session came to the conclusion that different standards at regional level concerning the treatment of foreign ships in ports may act as barriers to the smooth flow of international trade. Therefore, it was recommended that the establishment of relevant arrangements should receive the attention of the Committee on Shipping. Subsequently, the Committee adopted Resolution 49 (X), requesting the UNCTAD Secretariat to submit a report on the above-mentioned issue. The report was later presented at the 11th session[382].

4.1.4 Regional Arrangements under the European Union

Four important EU Regulations, Nos 4055/86[383], 4056/86[384], 4057/86[385] and 4058/86[386], set out to apply the principles of freedom to provide services, competition, and free access to the market in maritime transport. Another Regulation, No 3577/92, deals specifically with freedom to provide services in sea transport within Member States (maritime cabotage)[387].

382 International Maritime Legislation: "Treatment of Merchant Vessels in Ports at the Regional Level", TC/B/C.4/275, 1 Oct. 1984.

383 Council Regulation (EEC) No 4055/86 of 22 December 1986 applying the principle of freedom to provide services to maritime transport between Member States and between Member States and third countries (Official Journal L 378 of 31.12.1986).

384 Council Regulation (EEC) No 4056/86 of 22 December 1986 laying down detailed rules for the application of Articles 85 and 86 of the Treaty [*now Articles 81 and 82*] to maritime transport (Official Journal L 378 of 31.12. 1986).

385 Council Regulation (EEC) No 4057/86 of 22 December 1986 on unfair pricing practices in maritime transport (Official Journal L 378 of 31.12.1986).

386 Council Regulation (EEC) No 4058/86 of 22 December 1986 concerning coordinated action to safeguard free access to cargoes in ocean trades (Official Journal L 378 of 31.12.1986).

387 Council Regulation (EEC) No 3577/92 of 7 December 1992 applying the principle of freedom to provide services to maritime transport within Member States (maritime cabotage) *Official Journal L 364, 12/12/1992.*

In December 1997, the EC issued the "Green Paper on Sea-ports and Maritime Infrastructure"[388], the aim of which was to remove restrictions that hampered access to current or future service providers, to ensure a more systematic application of Treaty rules and to improve the quality of service to port users and to help reduce costs[389]. The basic approach of the paper was reflected in a Proposal for Directive on market access to port services that aimed to liberalize these services (hereinafter referred to as the Proposal)[390]. Some of the key points of the Proposal are:

- Member states must designate "competent authorities" to implement the Directive. The competent authority would be responsible for deciding whether or not the number of service providers should be restricted, considering applications for authorizations and deciding the outcome of a competitive tendering process[391];
- Member states would have an obligation to ensure that providers of port services and self-handlers have access to the port facilities that they need for their activities. Member states may require providers of port services and self-handlers to obtain prior authorization. Eligibility criteria can be best summarized as aiming to ensure fitness for purpose. The authorization may also impose public service requirements relating to issues such as safety and quality[392];

388 COM (1997) 678 (final) 10 December 1997. The paper is available at the EU website: http://europa.eu.int revisited in June 2005.

389 Communication from the Commission to the European Parliament and the Council "Reinforcing Quality Service in Sea Ports, a Key for European Transport, Proposal for a Directive of the European Parliament and of the Council on Market Access to Port Services". COM (2001) 35 (final), 13 February 2001.

390 Commission of the European Communities, "Proposal for a Directive of the European Parliament and of the Council on market access to port services", COM (2004) 654 final, Brussels, 13.10.2004.

391 Id. Article 7.

392 Id.

- The competent authority may decide to limit the number of service providers in any port should there be good reason in terms of constraints on space, capacity and/or maritime safety. In such cases there must be a minimum of two providers for each category of cargo handling unless there are exceptional circumstances relating to traffic volume or type[393];
- The competent authority must run an open and accountable tendering process to select such restricted service providers. This must be publicized in the Official Journal. All concessions would be subject to a maximum period of 25 years or less, depending on the type of investment involved. As long as opportunities are advertised the Commission sees no problem if the offer to tender for provisions of specific port services is not taken up[394];
- Where the number of port service providers is to be limited and a system of competitive tendering introduced, transitional rules would apply to protect the interests of existing providers who have made significant investment in moveable and immovable assets[395];
- There is no bar to port authorities being designated as the competent authority and/or for acting as a service provider. However, if the competent authority wishes to limit the number of service providers and the port authority wishes to tender to provide the services, the port authority cannot be the competent authority deciding the outcome of the competition[396].

The Proposal attempts to prohibit limitations on the number of port service providers, except for grounds such as safety. Authorization procedures should be fair, transparent and non-discriminatory. The harbour authorities should not participate in the selection process if they provide themselves commercial services and their commercial accounts should be separated from regulatory activi-

393 Id.
394 Id. Article 8.
395 Id. Article 9.
396 Id.

ties. Self-handling of ship-owners would be permitted. Port service providers would be allowed to use personnel of their choice, subject to relevant national legislation. However, public service obligations related to safety, regularity, continuity, quality and prices could be imposed on them.

It can be seen from the above regulations that instead of dealing with the issue of port access, the purpose of these internal arrangements is mainly concentrated on regulating the conditions for market access to port services.

4.1.5 Summary

Under most circumstances, countries have reciprocal interests in the use of each other's ports, and port states are expected to grant foreign merchant vessels access to their maritime ports under normal situations. In most cases, foreign merchant vessels receive the right of access to maritime ports and due consideration is given to circumstances under which access is either denied or controlled. In addition, access is ordinarily granted to any foreign vessel that comes to a maritime port with a lawful purpose, for example, to land and discharge cargo, to embark and disembark passengers, to obtain bunkers, supplies and repairs. As was discussed earlier in this Chapter, Report 136 of the UNCTAD urged that such access should be granted regardless of the nationality and ownership of the foreign merchant vessel and regardless of its prior or subsequent ports of call[397].

The authority of the port state is limited by the reasonable expectation that excessive measures by a port state would result in retaliatory measures by other states[398]. At the same time, there is

397 Supra note 377, UNCTAD Report 136, para 5, UNCTAD/TD/B/C.4/136, 9 Sep. 1975.

398 See for example Burke, W.T., Legatiski, R. and Wodhead, W.W., "National and International Law Enforcement in the Ocean", Washington Sea Grant Publication, International Marine Studies, University Press, Washington, Seattle/London, 1977.

little debate as to the sovereign right of a state to declare which of its ports are, or will in the future, be open for access to foreign merchant vessels[399]. A port state is actually capable of granting access to its maritime ports on the condition that its merchant vessels receive reciprocal treatment and subject to the provision that access may be denied when the peace, good order or security of the coastal state is endangered. This would include merchant vessels sailing under the flag of a country with which that country is at war. There are also occasions when denial of access is necessitated for reasons of health precautions prevailing at the port[400]. Moreover, a number of sanitary conventions have incorporated agreements not to exclude vessels from ports solely because of disease or sickness on board the vessel[401].

4.2 Access to Port in the WTO

Because of the crucial roles of maritime transport services to international trade, countries' right to port and port services is a fundamental subject in the WTO regulatory framework for trade in services. In his book "Access to Maritime Ports"[402], Gero Brugman asks the question: do commercial interests break the barriers? Indeed, in an era of globalization, countries are constantly confronted with the challenge of balancing between their commercial inter-

399 Id. Access may be forbidden to maritime ports or sections thereof, which are exclusively used by war vessels, for the handling of strategic cargoes, by cabotage vessels and national fishing vessels, etc.

400 See for example, "International Health Regulations including the International Sanitary Regulations", Geneva 1951, as amended by the World Health Assemblies 1955, 1956 and 1961, in Singh, N. (ed.), *International Conventions on Merchant Shipping*, 1973, British Shipping Laws, Vol. 8, Stevens, London.

401 See for example, Hydeman, L.M. and Berman, W.H., *International Control of Nuclear Maritime Activities*, Ann Arbor, Michigan, 1960, p. 140.

402 Brugman G. *Access to Maritime Ports*, Angus & Robertson, Australia, 2003.

ests and the sovereignty right over port access. As discussed earlier in this work, maritime transport services under the GATS have been grouped into the so-called three pillars, with the latter two pillars closely relevant to the issue of access to port. Auxiliary services cover cargo handling, storage and warehousing, stevedoring, freight forwarding, customs clearance services, container-station and depot services. The GATS negotiations also deal with foreign operators' rights to establish their own facilities and supply these services. Access to port and use of port facilities include services such as pilotage, towing and tug assistance, provisioning, garbage collection, port captain's services and anchorage. The GATS negotiations focus on the rights of foreign ships to gain access to these services without discrimination.

Discriminatory limitations on the access to, and use of port facilities may take several forms. Port state may discriminate in favour of domestic flag shipping either by giving domestic ship-owners preferential berthing rights or by charging lower prices to domestic ship-owners. The range of such limitation includes various port charges such as berthing charges, cargo handling charges, demurrage and pilotage, as well as bunker charges or taxes on bunkers[403]. Some port states may also discriminate against foreign ship-owners by granting domestic owners priority in leasing port facilities or by forbidding foreign ship-owners to invest in the landside facilities. Besides discriminating against ships of another state, different charges may also be levied in favour of a certain group of states[404]. Some of the concessions, exemptions and permissions in bilateral agreements may also lead to differential treatment of trading partners.

It is possible that vessels from certain states are denied access to port because the port state takes retaliation measures for other

403 OECD, Maritime Transport Statistics 1998.

404 For example, in the response to the 1994 Negotiating Group for Maritime Transport Services, the US states that: "the US maintains a differential vessel tonnage tax collected on entry to US ports and based on gross registered tonnage. Vessels entering US ports from North or parts of South America, irrespective of the vessels' country of ownership or registry, are assessed at lower duty than vessels entering US ports from other foreign ports".

actions by the flag state that are perceived to impede the operation of free trade of the port state in the flag state. Most states require navigation in the port zones and certain other maritime zones to be restricted where there is no reciprocity between countries[405].

Apart from discriminatory limitations, access to and use of port facilities may also be granted on a non-discriminatory basis with burdensome conditions. Some of the typical conditions may include[406]:

- Restrictions on the number of ports that may be accessed. As mentioned earlier in this Chapter, port state has the right to decide and nominate which of their ports are opened to international trade, usually out of considerations of national security or avoidance of excessive dependence on foreign feeder services;
- Requirement to use port services. In most instances, foreign vessels visiting a port are required to use certain port services, such as towage services[407];
- Imposition of unjustified charges. Although they vary in forms (some charges are directly related to the use of port facilities or services, while some others are not directly related to port services such as tonnage tax of goods), unjustified charges imposed on foreign vessels in port may act as impediment to trade and be regarded as an exploitation of monopoly power.

The following sections of this Chapter will discuss GATT/GATS principles and provisions which have close relevance to the right of access to port and the use of port facilities. Some of them may constitute non-tariff barriers to international trade on the grounds

405 Warren, T and Findlay, C "How Significant are the Barriers? Measuring Impediments to Trade in Services" paper presented at the "Services 2000: New Directions in Services Trade Liberalization" Conference at the University Club in Washington DC, 1–2 June 1999.

406 See for example, Warren and Findlay, id.

407 Information source of this passage: "Assorted Response to Transparency Exercise Questionnaire, question 10 on access to and use of ports, related port services and onward transport services". The Questionnaire is available at the website of Institute of Transportation of Taiwan: http://www.ito.gov.tw revisited in September 2005.

of sovereignty right and/or the considerations of environment, safety, sanitary and technical standards.

4.2.1 *The WTO Regulations Relevant to Access to Port and Port Services*

There are a considerable number of WTO regulations that are relevant to a country's handling of imports, which have substantial influences to other countries' access to port and use of port facilities. The impact of some clauses such as GATT Articles V, VIII, XI, XIII, XX & XXI, will be discussed in this section. In addition, other measures that directly affect imports include: measures on registration and documentation requirements such as Agreement on Preshipment Inspection; agreements on non-tariff barriers such as on customs valuation and rules of origin; agreements on standards and safety such as SPS and TBT Agreements; import prohibition, restrictions and licensing; contingency measures such as anti-dumping, countervailing measures, safeguards and agreement on government procurement.

The specific impact and implications of these rules on international trade varies from country to country. In addition to the principles and provisions discussed below, the agreements on TBT and SPS are frequently resorted to as disguised obstacles to the free flow of international trade, including access to port. This is partially due to their wide coverage on a country's legitimate policy objectives, such as national security, prevention of deceptive practices, health, safety and environment.

The latest WTO Panel Report on *Colombia – Indicative Prices and Restrictions on Ports of Entry*[408], has elaborated the relevance of the Customs Valuation Agreement in determining the ports of entry measures in certain Member countries' customs regulations, including the application of indicative prices in customs procedures and port entry restrictions.

408 WT/DS366/R, 27 April 2009.

4.2.1.1 GATT Article V

4.2.1.1.1 Freedom of Transit

Although a general right of transit does not exist under customary international law, such a right has been granted in a number of treaties. One early example was the Convention and Statute on Freedom of Transit of 1921, which obligated the parties to facilitate free transit of goods and persons across their territory by rail or waterway for international transit, without distinction as to nationality[409]. Only dues to defray expenses and reasonable tariffs may be charged[410].

The more specific of these obligations were subsequently taken up in the Havana Charter[411] and later were embodied in paragraphs 1 to 4 of Article V of the GATT 1947. The relationship between these two treaties is of particular relevance, as the GATT 1947[412] was originally only meant to apply under the Havana Charter's entry into force. In the case of Article V, the original 1947 version was never altered, whereas the corresponding articles of

409 See Barcelona Convention, Articles 1–3 particularly, which were subsequently taken up and largely addressed, in the Havana Charter, whose Articles 1 to 4 essentially embodies the same precepts as originally laid out in the Barcelona Convention. For Barcelona Convention itself, see UN. Doc. E/PC/T/C.II/54/Rev. 1.

410 The Convention is made up of 9 articles, and the Statute is made up of 15 articles. The goal of the Convention and Statute, as declared in its Preface, is to secure and maintain freedom of communications and of transit, and to develop cooperation between States without prejudice to their rights of sovereignty or authority over routes available for transit. The Convention and Statute are general in scope and do not mention specifically landlocked states or access to the sea. Till the end of September 1998, there were 48 contracting parties to it, of which 12 were landlocked. Full text of the Convention and Statute is available at: www.jurisint.org visited in January 2001 and revisited in August 2005.

411 The Havana-Charter for an International Trade Organization; it was designed to set up a forerunner of the WTO but failed to come into force. Its Article 33 was very similar to that of GATT Article V. See "the GATT years: from Havana to Marrakesh", http://www.wto.org revisited in March 2006.

412 Article XXIX of the GATT 1947: "Part II of this Agreement shall be suspended on the day that the Havana Charter enters into being".

the Havana Charter underwent several modifications, which were not brought into the GATT when Members negotiated the 1948 protocols that amended some of the provisions in order to achieve conformity with the Havana Charter.

There exist some differences between the Havana Charter and the GATT on this provision[413]. For example, instead of including the interpretative note as contained in the GATT, the Havana Charter comprises three different interpretative notes to its Article 33[414]. In addition, unlike the Havana Charter, the GATT does not have provision to recommend that the organization

> ... undertake studies, make recommendations and promote international agreement relating to the simplification of customs regulations concerning traffic in transit, the equitable use of facilities required for such transit and other measures designed to promote the objectives of this Article. Members shall cooperate with each other directly and through the Organization to this end[415].

This provision was added to the Havana Charter at the Havana Conference in the view of the significance of this matter to many countries, particularly those countries that have no access to the sea[416].

The objective of GATT Article V is to allow the freedom of transit through the territory of each member for transport movements to or from the territory of other members. The Article fo-

413 Nora Neufeld, "Article V of the GATT 1994 – Scope and Application". This paper is available at the website of UNCTAD: http://www.unctad.org revisited in August 2007.

414 Id. p. 2. The notes were annexed to the Havana Charter.

415 Id. p. 3. Article 33 (6) of the Havana Charter. It consequently also lacks the interpretative notes related to this Article, which held that, if, as a result of negotiations in accordance with paragraph 6, a Member grants to a country which has no direct access to the sea more ample facilities than those already provided for in other paragraphs to Article 33, such special facilities may be limited to the land-locked country concerned unless the Organization finds, on the complaint of any other Member, that the withholding of the special facilities from the complaining Member contravenes the most-favoured-nation provisions of this Charter.

416 Id. p. 3.

cuses on the freedom of transit dealing with goods, vessels and other means of transport in transit across the territory of a contracting party. It regulates the conditions a Member may impose on goods transported through its territory by another party to a foreign destination. The two obligations under this Article are, firstly, not to hinder traffic in transit by imposing unnecessary delays or restrictions or by imposing unreasonable charges, and secondly, to accord MFN treatment to transit goods of all members[417].

The definition and scope of "traffic in transit" are given in paragraph 2 of the Article, which states that goods (including baggage) together with vessels and other means of transport, shall be deemed to be in transit across the territory of a contracting party when the passage across such territory, (with or without transshipment, warehousing, breaking bulk, or change in the mode of transport), is only a portion of a complete journey beginning and terminating beyond the frontier of the contracting party across whose territory the traffic passes. The Article goes on to say that there shall be freedom of transit through the territory of each contracting party, via the routes most convenient for international transit, for traffic in transit to or from the territory of other contracting parties.

The specific requirements on freedom of transit are listed out in paragraph 2, which requests each member to allow for free transition through its territory for traffic in transit to or from the territory of another member. Such transit shall be granted via the routes most convenient for international transit. According to Neufeld, this condition constitutes a serious restriction, as it means that the duty to grant free transit does not extend to all routes[418]. Furthermore, parties are required not to make distinctions based on differences in the flag of vessels, the place of origin or departure, entry, the point of exit or destination together with circumstances relating to the ownership of goods, of vessels or of other means of transport[419].

417 Id. p. 3.
418 Id. p. 4.
419 Id. p. 4.

Paragraphs 3 and 4 set up a number of rights and obligations for the port state on customs issues, which grants the contracting party to require traffic in transit be entered at the proper custom house, without any unnecessary delays or restrictions except in cases of failure to comply with applicable customs laws and regulations. Furthermore, such transit shall be exempt from customs duties and from all transit duties or other charge imposed in respect of transit, except charges for transportation or those commensurate with administrative expense entailed by transit or with the cost of services rendered. The Article also rules that all relevant charges and regulations imposed on traffic in transit as mentioned above shall be reasonable as to the conditions of traffic[420].

Paragraph 5 of the Article requests that countries granting most-favoured-nation treatment of traffic in transit to other contracting countries, with respect to all charges, regulations and formalities in connection with transit. Paragraph 6 requires each party to treat products, which have been in transit through the territory of another member, no less favourably than products transported from their place of origin to their destination without going through the territory of such other member. An exception is made for certain direct consignment requirements existing at the time of this Agreement, where that they are a condition for goods to be eligible for preferential duty rates or relate to a party's prescribed method of valuation for duty purposes. The inclusion of this provision is considered necessary as several countries have required the direct shipment to their territory from the country of origin as a condition of eligibility for certain preferences[421]. Paragraph 7 exempts the operation of aircraft in transit from the application of this Article. Finally, there is an interpretative note in Annex I stating that with respect to transportation charges, the MFN principle refers to like products being transported on the same route under like conditions.

420 Id. p. 5.
421 Id. p. 6.

In addition to the basic obligations of non-discrimination, Article V contains a number of important elements aimed at ensuring the smooth flow of trade across borders for the purpose of transit. For example, it provides a very broad definition of "Traffic in transit", by making it encompassing not only the goods transported, but also the vessels or other means of transport. It imposes a general obligation on WTO members to facilitate transit instead of simply permitting transit, by obliging members to provide freedom of transit through their territories via the routes most convenient for international transit for traffic in transit to or from the territory of other contracting parties. In addition, Article V emphasizes the principle of non-discrimination in the transit context and specifies the obligation of parties to ensure that transit is not subject to unnecessary delays or restrictions and charges shall be commensurate to services rendered.

While the basic obligations in this Article are aimed at ensuring optimal conditions for transit, there are still indications that in reality the freedom of transit is not sufficient. A number of obstacles do exist in relation to transit[422], such as:

- non-standardized documentation requirements, excessive documentation and physical checks on transiting goods, vehicles and vessels;
- non-application of international, regional or bilateral instruments for transit such as the TIR system[423];

422 WTO Trade Facilitation Symposium, 9–10 March 1998. Report by the WTO Secretariat G/C/W/115 and the International Forum on Trade Facilitation: 29–30 May 2002. More information is available at: www.unece.org visited in June 2002 and revisited in August 2006.

423 The TIR system has been devised to facilitate to the maximum extent the international movement of goods under Customs seals. The system provides transit countries with the required guarantees to cover the Customs duties and taxes at risk. A balance is struck between the responsibilities of the Customs authorities and those of the international trading community. The system offers various benefits to the different stakeholders involved in the international movement of transit goods. For more information on the system, see website of International Road Transport Union, under its website: www.iru.org visited in October 2001 and revisited in August 2006.

- onerous customs requirements for transiting cargoes than for final destination imports;
- unjustifiable restrictions on transiting vessels, vehicles or their drivers, and
- unwarranted restrictions on the entry of non-national transport operators; unjustifiable restrictions on the nature of goods that are allowed to transit.

For years countries have proposed means of simplifying, limiting and standardizing customs procedures and documentation requirements, as well as clarifying fees and charges for customs services[424]. The proposals of the EC to WTO Secretariat cast some lights on the simplification and clarification of this Article for the facilitation of international trade[425]. The impact of this Article on access to port will be discussed in the following section of this Chapter.

4.2.1.1.2 Right of Access to Port

Article V is particularly significant in respect of landlocked states which are geographically disadvantaged. Their right to port access under the law of the sea is discussed earlier in this Chapter. Although the 1982 LOS Convention provides the right of access to and from the sea and the freedom of transit for landlocked states, it also provides the sovereign state with the right to take necessary measures to ensure that the transit right given to landlocked countries does not infringe their legitimate expectations. Thus, there need to be an appropriate balance between the right to transit and sovereignty of states to ensure that this right will not be abused under the pretext of legitimate expectations. It is not sufficient for landlocked countries to depend on the goodwill

424 A detailed analysis of these proposals for trade facilitation is made by Zanamwe, G. in his paper: "Trade Facilitation and the WTO: a critical analysis of the proposals on trade facilitation and their implications for African countries", tralac Working Paper, No. 5/2005, September 2005, available at: www.tralac.org visited in February 2006.

425 WTO, "Negotiating Group on Trade Facilitation – Communications from the European Communities – Freedom of Transit", TN/TF/W/35, 29 April 2005.

of their neighbours to access world markets. Improving Article V may be one way of achieving this objective.

The EU-Chilean Swordfish Case, which will be discussed later in this work as illustrative of dispute settlement between international institutions, shows the interaction of trade agreements and port access. Although this case highlights the problem of forum shopping and the relationship between the WTO law and other branches of international law, due to the fact that it was settled through bilateral negotiations outside both the WTO panel and the ITLOS, it has not helped to clarify the issue. Another aspect of this case is whether or not GATT Article V implies a right to port. Based on the following reasons, this work argues that Article V does not imply such a right.

Firstly, as the International Court of Justice noted in the Nicaragua case, it is "by virtue of its sovereignty that the coastal State may regulate access to its ports"[426]. The issue of port access, as discussed previously in this Chapter, has never attained the status of customary international law, nor has it been qualified as a general principle of law. Therefore the main applicable law regarding port access is domestic law rather than international law or international agreements. Even if the Swordfish case was referred to the WTO panels, the disciplines of GATT Article V have not changed the nature of this issue.

Secondly, until now GATT Article V has not been applied to issues regarding fisheries and port access, which, according to Marcos Orellana, are matters respectively "ruled by the customary law of the sea and bilateral treaties of 'Friendship, Commerce and Navigation'"[427]. Besides domestic law, fisheries are regulated by a series of conventions and agreements on different levels within the realm of the law of the sea. The relationship between these conventions/agreements and the WTO is beyond the scope of this work.

426 Military and Paramilitary Activities (Nicaragua v. US), 1986, ICJ 14 at 111.
427 Marcos Orellana, "The Swordfish in Peril: the EU Challenges Chilean Port Access Restrictions at the WTO", BRIDGES, August 2000, available at www.ictsd.org revisited in August 2006.

Thirdly, judging from the current WTO negotiations on maritime transport services, it is not clear as to what extent WTO members agree to open their ports under GATT Article V. However it is clear that during the WTO negotiations on maritime transport services, based on the specific commitments of member countries on access to port and auxiliary services, most countries hold cautious attitudes on making commitments in this area. As discussed in Part I of this work, access to port and use of port services (as one of the three pillars of maritime transport services) are listed merely as "additional commitments" in the negotiation schedules. This gives countries sufficient flexibility not to make any commitments on port services.

Fourthly, on the issue of the freedom of transit, the effectiveness of Article V is reduced in a number of ways. For example, if a party to the GATT wishes to exercise its right of freedom of transit, its nationals or their goods must not only pass through the territory of a party to the GATT, but both the State of origin and the State of destination must also be parties to the GATT. This has obviously limited the applicable scope of this article. In addition, as stated in paragraph 1, the provision is focused transportation (traffic in transit), rather than on the right of port entry. Access to port may merely constitute a possible segment of the activities during the process of the transit, such as when transshipment or warehousing, are bound to be necessary. Furthermore, even when port entry is made necessary for the journey, this provision limits its scope of application to the purpose of "transit" only. The numerous situations in international trade when the port state is also the destination state of the same journey are excluded from the scope of this provision. Therefore this work argues that although GATT Article V contributes to facilitate the freedom of transit in international trade, it does not bring substantive change to the right of port, which is still under the realm of domestic regulations.

4.2.1.2 GATT Article VIII

Although its purpose is to facilitate trade, Article VIII of the GATT also has important implications for the facilitation of access to port and port services. Its regulations in respect of fees and formalities connected with importation and exportation are broad in scope, extending to "fees, charges, formalities and requirements imposed by governments in relation to importation and exportation". The disciplines on Article VIII apply to all fees and charges imposed on imports or exports but do not cover import and export duties and internal taxes within the scope of Article III of the GATT. Examples of these fees and charges, formalities and requirements are set out in paragraph 4 of this Article[428].

Countries such as New Zealand, Norway and Switzerland, as well as regional arrangements such as the EC[429], have in recent years put forward proposals to clarify and improve Article VIII to make it more operational. These proposals focus on the following aspects[430]:

Firstly, the diversity of the fees and charges shall be reduced. Article VIII merely recognizes the need to reduce the number and diversity of fees and charges but does not actually oblige Members to do so. The EC and Australia (TN/TF/W/23), the US (TN/TF/W/14), Japan and Mongolia (TN/TF/W/17), Chinese Taipei (TN/TF/W/25) and Hong Kong China (TN/TF/W/31) proposed that there should be parameters or disciplines on fees and charges[431].

428 Such as consular transactions, consular invoices and certificates, quantitative restrictions, licensing, exchange control, statistical services, documents, documentation and certification, analysis and inspection and quarantine, sanitation and fumigation.

429 WTO, Negotiating Group on Trade Facilitation, "Clarifications and Improvements in the GATT Article VIII, Proposals on Simplification, Reduction and Standardization of Trade Documents", Communication from New Zealand, Norway and Switzerland, TN/TF/W/36, 29 April 2005.

430 Supra note 425.

431 The EC and Australia (TN/TF/W/23) proposed that (a) the service provided must be related to the product in question; (b) the fees or charges levied must refer to the approximate cost of the service rendered; (c) the fees or charges in question may not be calculated on an ad valorem basis; (d) the

They suggested these fees and charges should be reviewed, consolidated, justified, notified and published[432]. Furthermore, the EC and Australia (TN/TF/W/23) proposed the establishment of a list of permissible fees and charges, and time intervals between their publication and entry into force, and also the discontinuation of the levying of "consular fees" or "consular invoices". A recent OECD study[433] indicated that most customs fees and charges on imports were excessive and unjustified because they were applied on an *ad valorem* basis and were not limited to the underlying costs of the services rendered.

Secondly, the incidence and complexity of import and export formalities needs to be simplified. The EC (TN/TF/W/46), Japan and Mongolia (TN/TF/W/17), Korea (TN/TF/W/18), Canada (TN/TF/W/20) and Hong Kong China (TN/TF/W/31) proposed that in order to reduce the incidence and complexity of import and export formalities, Members should be encouraged to use international standards to the extent possible[434], accept copies in

---

administrative or operational costs not associated with the treatment of imports or exports respectively may not be imposed on such imports or exports; (e) there should be non-discrimination in the design and application of fees and charges. They also proposed that these general disciplines apply not only to customs authorities but also to other agencies involved in the imposition of import and export charges.

432 Chinese Taipei (TN/TF/W/25) proposed that periodic review should be done at least once every three years. It also proposed a scientific method for calculating fees and charges and wants the costs of services rendered to be broken down into direct and indirect costs using the Generally Accepted Accounting Principles.

433 OECD Trade Policy Working Paper No. 22, "The Role of Automation in Trade Facilitation", TD/TC/WP (2003) 12/FINAL, 17 October 2005.

434 Korea proposed that Members must use the UN Layout Key for Trade Documents to align documents and the WCO Customs Data Model to harmonize and standardize the format of documents and accept commercially available information. New Zealand (TN/TF/W/24) proposed that all Members must use the WCO Convention on the Harmonized Commodity Description and Coding System (HS Convention) for classifying goods to ensure that tariff classification decisions are not used as disguised protection of domestic industries. It suggested that where it was not possible to determine accurately the classification of a product using the HS system, an objective test must be developed.

certain cases, accept commercially available information and establish a single one-time presentation of data to one agency. They also emphasized that there should be coordination of physical inspections between relevant authorities to the extent possible and integrated border controls through single, shared physical infrastructure in which the neighbouring countries' customs services operate side by side. The EC (TN/TF/W/46) called for the application of the non-discrimination principle in the design and application of import and export procedures and formalities, in respect of licensing of customs brokers and an obligation to phase out the mandatory use of customs brokers[435]. Japan and Mongolia (TN/TF/W/17) proposed the use of least trade restrictive import and export documentation requirements and a periodic review of these documents based on comments from the private sector. In addition, they suggested that the documentary examination and physical inspection must be conducted without delay and documents must not be rejected because of minor breaches.

Thirdly, fast clearance procedures should be adopted. The EC (TN/TF/W/46)[436], Japan and Mongolia (TN/TF/W/17), Korea (TN/TF/W/18), Canada (TN/TF/W/20), the US (TN/TF/W/15), and Chinese Taipei[437] called for the simplification of import and export procedures by adopting fast clearance procedures involving automation, risk assessment, authorized traders' facilities and the use of pre-arrival and post-audit clearance systems. Australia and Canada (TN/TF/W/19) made suggestions on the separation

435 The EC also supported the periodic review of procedures or formalities, the use of international standards and instruments, the use of a least trade restrictive test, the principle of a single, one-time presentation to one agency, normally the customs, of all documentation and data requirements for export or import, the use of risk analysis methods and the elimination of Pre-Shipment Inspection Arrangements. Source of information: WTO document TN/TF/W/46.

436 The EC recommended progressive implementation of simplified and standardized import and export procedures, based on international standards and instruments, including the WCO Kyoto Convention and all Members to introduce simplified customs release and clearance procedures.

437 Chinese Taipei also called for speedy clearance for express consignments using the WCO Customs Guidelines for Express Consignments.

of the process of fulfillment of customs obligations including payment of duties from the actual release of goods[438], which could be done by the use of collateral or monetary securities like bonds or other financial guarantees. The US proposed that Members should provide specific expedited procedures for express shipments[439]. It argued that the lack of reference in Article VIII regarding how express shipments should be treated reflected a major difference between the trading world of 1947 and 2005. Chinese Taipei (TN/TF/W/44) and Turkey (TN/TF/W/45) also submitted detailed proposals on how to expedite procedures for express shipments.

4.2.1.3 Exceptions Clauses

Both the GATT and the GATS contain articles on general exceptions and security exceptions which may have implication for maritime transport services, in particular with port access and cabotage. The relevance of Articles XX and XXI of the GATT, as well as GATS Article XIV, will be discussed in this section. The other clause, Article XIVbis of the GATS on security exception, will be analyzed in the next Chapter.

Article XX of GATT contains general exceptions that apply to all provisions, including maritime transport services. The most relevant regulations in this article are paragraphs (b) and (g). Especially on the issues of access to port and maritime cabotage restriction, these paragraphs are frequently used as hindrance against free trade[440].

438 Security can be given where delays are encountered in completion of final clearance procedures because the trader will be waiting for a decision on the correct tariff classification or where goods are imported to fulfil a specific purpose and subsequently duty paid or exported after use (as in cases where there is authorization to import goods for "inward processing" without payment of duties and taxes, provided that the finished goods are subsequently exported).

439 It suggested that there should be *de minimis* procedures for low value shipments, an absence of weight or value restrictions on what is considered "express", and the submission of import data in advance for goods to be released rapidly. Source of information: WTO document TN/TF/W/15.

440 Examples include the EU-Chilean Swordfish Case which will be studied in Part III of this work.

The purpose of Article XX is to establish a balance of rights and duties, which was interpreted by the Appellate Body in the *US – Shrimp* case[441]:

> A balance must be struck between the *right* of a Member to invoke an exception under Article XX and the *duty* of that same Member to respect the treaty rights of the other Members. The task of interpreting and applying the chapeau is, hence, essentially the delicate one of locating and marking out a line of equilibrium between the right of a Member to invoke an exception under Article XX and the rights of the other Members under varying substantive provisions (e.g., Article XI) of the GATT 1994, so that neither of the competing rights will cancel out the other and thereby distort and nullify or impair the balance of rights and obligations constructed by the Members themselves in that Agreement. The location of the line of equilibrium, as expressed in the chapeau, is not fixed and unchanging; the line moves as the kind and the shape of the measures at stake vary and as the facts making up specific cases differ.[442]

Paragraph (b): necessary to protect human, animal or plant life or health

The Panel on *US – Gasoline*, presented the following three-tier test in respect of Article XX (b)[443]:

> As the party invoking an exception the United States bore the burden of proof in demonstrating that the inconsistent measures came within its scope. The Panel observed that the United States therefore had to establish the following elements:
> (1) that the *policy* in respect of the measures for which the provision was invoked fell within the range of policies designed to protect human, animal or plant life or health;
> (2) that the inconsistent measures for which the exception was being invoked were *necessary* to fulfil the policy objective; and
> (3) that the measures were applied in conformity with the requirements of the *introductory clause* of Article XX.
> In order to justify the application of Article XX (b), all the above elements had to be satisfied.[444]

441 WTO, Interpretation and Application of the GATT provision, at: http://www.wto.org revisited in August 2007, p. 516.
442 Id. p. 516.
443 Id. p. 540.
444 Id. p. 540.

In addition, in *US – Gasoline*, the Panel addressed the question of which specific aspect of a measure under scrutiny should be justified as "necessary" within the meaning of paragraph (b) of Article XX. The Panel held that

> it was not the necessity of the policy goal that was to be examined, but whether or not it was necessary that imported gasoline be effectively prevented from benefiting from as favourable sales conditions as were afforded by an individual baseline tied to the producer of a product.

The Appellate Body did not address the Panel's findings on paragraph (b). However, in addressing the Panel's findings on paragraph (g), more specifically the Panel's statements concerning the terms "relating to" and "primarily aimed at", the Appellate Body was critical that "the Panel (had) asked itself whether the 'less favourable treatment' of imported gasoline was 'primarily aimed at' the conservation of natural resources, rather than whether the 'measure', were 'primarily aimed at' conservation of clean air." The Appellate Body found that "the Panel ... was in error in referring to its legal conclusion on Article III: 4 instead of the measure in issue."[445]

Paragraph (g): relating to the conservation of exhaustible natural resources if such measures are made effective in conjunction with restrictions on domestic production or consumption

In *US – Shrimp*, the Appellate Body reviewed the Panel's finding concerning a US measure which banned imports of shrimps and shrimp products harvested by vessels of foreign countries, where such exporting country had not been certified by US authorities as using methods that would not lead to the incidental killing of sea turtles above certain levels. The Panel had found that the US could not justify its measure under Article XX (g). The Appellate Body made the following comment:

> We do not pass upon the question of whether there is an implied jurisdictional limitation in Article XX (g), and if so, the nature or extent of that

445 Id. p. 542.

> limitation. We note only that in the specific circumstances of the case before us, there is a sufficient nexus between the migratory and endangered marine populations involved and the United States for purposes of Article XX (g).[446]

To summarize, by allowing governments to act on trade in order to protect human, animal or plant life or health, provided the measure is not used to discriminate or introduce disguised protectionism, Article XX of the GATT may be used by port countries to hinder the port access right of other countries.

Similarly, Article XIV of the GATS on General Exceptions endorses member countries to adopt or enforce any measures that are necessary to protect human, animal or plant life or health (paragraph (b).

As for GATT Article XXI, paragraph (c) allows any party to take action that violates the agreement if it is "...in pursuance of its obligation under the United Nation Charter for the maintenance of international peace and security." It seems that this provision suggests security concerns may in some cases be permitted to override other sections of the GATT disciplines. Therefore, if a port state sets up a security regime targeting certain vessels and cargo seeking access to its ports, and if such regime finds its foundation in international agreements for maritime safety and marine environment (such as MARPOL or SOLAS under IMO[447]), it may be regarded as a security exception under Article XXI instead of constituting a violation of the GATT[448].

446 Id. p. 555.

447 These Conventions are analyzed in 4.1.3.1 "IMO Regulations on access to port" of this Chapter.

448 Claude Pohlit, "New Developments in Maritime Security and Their Impact on International Shipping", available at: http://lawspace.law.uct.ac.za revisited in August 2007.

5 Access to Cargo in Coastal Shipping – Cabotage

5.1 General Background

The original meaning of the term "cabotage" was the navigation and trade along the same stretch of coast belonging to the same State. Now this term comprises sea trade between any two ports of the same country, regardless of whether or not on the same or different coasts[449]. For decades, most countries with a coastal shipping trade reserved those trades for the national fleet under a cabotage regime. It is only in recent years that the combination of an increasing liberalization of international trade in services and the loss of competitiveness of the fleets of developed countries has seen such reservation policies being challenged.

Cabotage policy can be implemented through any measures which have the effect of excluding foreign shipping or crews from engaging in a country's coastal trades[450]. From a historical perspective, cabotage was related to the cargo sharing under the so-called "mercantilist model" which dated back as early as the 17th century (British "Navigation Acts", the French régime of the Colbert ordinances and of the *"exclusif colonial"*)[451]. Under such regimes, the external trade of a country had to be transported by ships flagged in the country manned with nationals and where colonial traffic was reserved to the flag of the country. The UK abolished this model in 1847, but traces of it remain in the legislation of

449 F.L. Oppenheim, *International Law* 493 Vol. I, Eighth edition, Lauterpacht, H., (eds), Longmans and Co, 1955.

450 UNESCAP, publication on national shipping fleets and access to shipping market: http://www.unescap.org revisited in June 2006.

451 WTO Secretariat background note, supra note 8, p. 3.

many other countries. However, during the 1960's and 1970's, the "mercantilist model" largely disappeared as a result of decolonization, of the "deflagging" of bulk fleets effectively severing the link between flag and ownership and of the development of "third traffics" meaning trade between two countries carried in ships belonging to neither[452].

The English "Navigation Acts" were a series of laws which, beginning in 1651, restricted foreign shipping[453]. The 1651 Act banned foreign ships from transporting goods from outside Europe to England, and banned ships from third countries from transporting goods from a country in Europe to England. In France, the trade called cabotage applies to ships sailing in the territorial seas between ports of the same state. Originally, it was confined to voyages on the same sea coast, but subsequently France distinguished between this "petit cabotage" and voyages between ports on two different seas, or "grand cabotage"[454]. France has also restricted the trade between French ports and Algeria to French ships, but not under the term of cabotage. Likewise, Portugal reserves the trade between Portugal and the adjacent islands and Portuguese West Africa to its national ships, but the trade between Portugal and other Portuguese possessions is open to foreign ships.

In most cases, ships engaged in cabotage trades are required to meet the following conditions: manned by the country's own citizens; wholly or majority owned by domestic nationals; vessels built at domestic shipyards and registered under the country's national flag. Consequently, in return for meeting such requirements, owners operating ships on cabotage routes do not have to compete with foreign flag ships. Besides, some countries also provide fleet subsidies or other financial benefits to such ship-owners[455].

452 Id. p. 3.

453 Carl Stephenson and Frederick George Marcham (eds.), *Sources of English Constitutional History*, Harper & Row Publishers, New York, USA, 1937, p. 538.

454 Information source: Maritime History Archive, Memorial University of Newfoundland at: http://www.mun.ca/mha/ revisited in August 2006.

455 Supra note 7, OECD paper, pp. 39–40.

Many countries apply restrictive regulations that discriminate against foreign shipping in cabotage trades. National laws relating to migration, employment, customs and taxation can also impact on the ability of, or attractiveness for, foreign ships or crews operating national coasts. National migration and employment laws often contain clauses restricting the occupations that foreign workers can engage in or the period of time they are allowed to engage in such work, or specify the wage rates that are payable. Customs laws may regard a foreign ship operating on the coast as an import and liable for duty. Taxation laws may require the payment of commercial taxation on income or wages derived on the national coast or bring the ship within the liability of local indirect taxes such as fuel excise. Any of these areas of law either individually or in combination can act as an impediment to foreign shipping engaging in coastal trades.

Governments typically apply cabotage policies on the basis of national security or economic considerations[456]. More significantly, it is argued that cabotage is essential to preserve the domestic transport capability, to maintain essential maritime skills that may be required in time of conflict, to create employment in the shipping and ship-building industries and to strengthen balance of payments by preventing an outflow of foreign exchange in the form of profits earned by foreign ship-owners providing domestic shipping services.

However, cabotage may have negative impacts on the technical efficiency of shipping services and lead to lower standards of services[457]. If domestic shipping trades are opened, larger and more efficient ships operating on international routes may include coastal trading as a leg of their overseas voyages, and replace small, inefficient ships engaged in coastal shipping. Cabotage also may lead to monopoly by domestic ship-owners, who may face less competi-

456 Id. p. 40. Besides, the Maritime Cabotage Task Force of the US is one of the strongest proponents for reserving the cabotage protection. Its website: http://www.mctf.com (revisited in July 2006) contains many writings defending the cabotage system.

457 For analysis on the positive and negative impacts of cabotage, see for example supra note 21, Hoekman B., Carlos A. and Primo B.

tion than if the market was open to international competition. This could lead to the establishment of cartels and decline of services levels to customers.

Cabotage still remains as issue for debate, whose values and negative effects remain under discussion, but do need to be seen in the context of broader policy objectives of the country in question.

5.2 Cabotage under Multilateral and Domestic Regulatory Frameworks

5.2.1 Cabotage under Multilateral Institutions

5.2.1.1 The OECD

In its paper "Regulatory Issues in International Maritime Transport"[458], the OECD Secretariat described cabotage as

> widely practiced, both by OECD and non-OECD members, and is generally considered, but never demonstrated, to be crucial to ensure the maintenance of domestic transport capability, as well as acting as an inhibitor to foreign influence in domestic transport services.

Liberalization of cabotage trades in OECD member countries has not progressed to the same extent as liberalization in international maritime trade. Cabotage regulations are still maintained in many countries such as the US, Japan, Korea, Turkey, Canada and Australia[459].

It has been argued that any concessions by major maritime markets such as the EU, Japan and the US would contribute to improved efficiency in fields like lower transportation costs for bulk commodities and environmental benefits arising from the trans-

458 OECD, supra note 7.
459 Id. p. 65.

fer of some traffic from land transport[460]. The main obstacle to such reforms comes from the pressure to retain cabotage policies as a means of preserving related employment and maritime skills necessary in cases of external emergencies[461]. It is recommended by the OECD that in view of the benefits that have resulted from domestic liberalization in other economic sectors, it may be valuable to examine cargo reservation and/or cabotage provisions and to see whether there is the political will to roll-back existing barriers. If an immediate total roll-back meets significant political obstacles, some time frame for such roll-back could be examined. Under such circumstances all privileges derived from such arrangements and enjoyed by one member country should be extended to all other member countries in order to ensure free and non-discriminatory treatment of all OECD countries[462].

The OECD has progressively adopted important maritime agreements, such as the Common Shipping Principles, which provide guidelines for the regulation of maritime transport services, including cabotage. These agreements will be further discussed in the following Chapter 6.

5.2.1.2 The WTO

Some fundamental WTO principles such as general exceptions and security exceptions have implications for cabotage. Their actual and potential impacts on this area of maritime transport services will be examined in Section 5.3 of this Chapter.

In addition, the existence of grandfather clauses constitutes a striking feature of the GATT in respect of cabotage[463]. The GATT

460 Id. p. 65.
461 Id. p. 65.
462 Id. pp. 65–66.
463 Grandfather clause refers to GATT provision that allows the original contracting parties to exempt from general GATT obligations mandatory domestic legislation which is inconsistent with GATT provisions, but which existed before the GATT was signed. Newer members may also "grandfather" domestic legislation if that is agreed to in negotiating the terms of accession. This definition is from "Glossary of Trade & Shipping Terms" at: http://www.tradeport.org visited in July 2006.

1994 includes a permanent grandfather clause for the US build requirement of the Jones Act and other cabotage laws. Article 3 of GATT 1994 stipulates that[464]:

3. (a) The provisions of Part II of GATT 1994 shall not apply to measures taken by a Member under specific mandatory legislation, enacted by that Member before it became a contracting party to GATT 1947, that prohibits the use, sale or lease of foreign-built or foreign-reconstructed vessels in commercial applications between points in national waters or the waters of an exclusive economic zone. This exemption applies to: (*a*) the continuation or prompt renewal of a non-conforming provision of such legislation; and (*b*) the amendment to a non-conforming provision of such legislation to the extent that the amendment does not decrease the conformity of the provision with Part II of GATT 1947. This exemption is limited to measures taken under legislation described above that is notified and specified prior to the date of entry into force of the WTO Agreement. If such legislation is subsequently modified to decrease its conformity with Part II of GATT 1994, it will no longer qualify for coverage under this paragraph.
(b) The Ministerial Conference shall review this exemption not later than five years after the date of entry into force of the WTO Agreement and thereafter every two years for as long as the exemption is in force for the purpose of examining whether the conditions which created the need for the exemption still prevail.
(c) A Member whose measures are covered by this exemption shall annually submit a detailed statistical notification consisting of a five-year moving average of actual and expected deliveries of relevant vessels as well as additional information on the use, sale, lease or repair of relevant vessels covered by this exemption.
(d) A Member that considers that this exemption operates in such a manner as to justify a reciprocal and proportionate limitation on the use, sale, lease or repair of vessels constructed in the territory of the Member invoking the exemption shall be free to introduce such a limitation subject to prior notification to the Ministerial Conference.
(e) This exemption is without prejudice to solutions concerning specific aspects of the legislation covered by this exemption negotiated in sectoral agreements or in other forums.

During the first review, Panama, Japan, and the EU questioned whether the exemption should continue to exist. The WTO report

464 The legal text of General Agreement on Tariff and Trade 1994 is available at WTO website: www.wto.org revisited in August 2007.

issued after the review in 2000 stated that the maritime transport sector "continues to rank among the most protected sectors of the US economy" and cited the cabotage laws that reserve domestic routes to US operators, US maintenance of cargo preference requirements and the provision of "a fixed payment to US flag vessel operators" through the Maritime Security Program[465]. Countries that have urged the WTO to put maritime services on the table include Japan, Korea, Norway, Hong Kong, the EC, Singapore, Chile, Australia and Columbia[466]. However, there has been no substantive liberalization in the US cabotage restriction.

5.2.2 Cabotage under Select Domestic Legislations and Policies

5.2.2.1 New Zealand

The change of cabotage legislations and policies of New Zealand is among the most comprehensive in the world, which serves as a good example of cabotage deregulation.

Until 1995, the carriage of coastal cargoes in New Zealand was restricted to vessels under the New Zealand register. The Maritime Transport Act 1994[467] which came into effect in 1995 re-

465 Magee Kathleen, "US Cabotage Laws: Protective or Damaging?" Monterey Institute of International Studies, April 2002, available at: http://www.commercialdiplomacy.org revisited in July 2006 p. 35.

466 Id. p. 35.

467 Maritime Transport Act 1994, No. 104, has been taken up with the purposes of: continues the Maritime Safety Authority of New Zealand; enables the implementation of New Zealand's obligations under international maritime agreements; ensures that participants in the maritime transport system are responsible for their actions; consolidates and amends maritime transport law; amends the law relating to the health and safety of seafarers; protects the marine environment; continues, or enables, the implementation of obligations on New Zealand under various international convention relating to pollution of the marine environment. The Maritime Transport Act 1994 was later amended by: the Maritime Transport Amendment Act 1996, No. 79; the Maritime Transport Amendment Act 1998, No. 53; the Maritime Transport Amendment Act 1998 (No. 2), No. 116; the Maritime Trans-

laxed this restriction. The driving force that led the New Zealand Government to support the introduction of the policy was the promise of "an increase in choice and competition, and the potential to lower domestic transport costs"[468]. This was in keeping with the general direction of economic reform in New Zealand over the 1980s and 1990s, which included the introduction of a wide range of deregulatory measures in many previously protected industries.

The original intention of the government was the total removal of all restrictions on coastal cargo operations by foreign operators[469]. Clause 240 of the Transport Law Reform Bill of 1993 read:

> Coastal shipping – (1) Cargo loaded, or passengers embarking, at any port in New Zealand intended to be finally unloaded or to finally disembark at any port in New Zealand may be carried by any ship where all appropriate maritime documents are held in respect of the ship and any maritime products and seafarers on board the ship.

However, there was strong opposition to the policy from a number of quarters. Those opposed to the policy argued that the costs of liberalizing cabotage would be high, impacting on employment opportunities, equity in employment conditions, GDP, balance of payments, regional development, service levels, the environment, primary industry and national defence.

Opponents also argued that the different tax environment faced by foreign and domestic ship-owners gave an unfair competitive

---

port Amendment Act 1999, No. 68; and, the Maritime Transport Amendment Act 2000, No. 71. For more information on this Act and other relevant Acts, see the website of Maritime Safety Authority of New Zealand, at its website: www.msa.govt.nz visited in April 2002 and revisited in August 2005. The legal text of the Maritime Transport Act is available from: http://www.legislation.govt.nz revisited in April 2006. It is also available at the website of Ministry of Transport of New Zealand: http://www.transport.govt.nz revisited in April 2006.

468 Kirsten Knudsen, "Zero Taxation of World Shipping Industry", Maritime Policy and Management, 1997, Vol. 4, No. 1.

469 R.Y. Cavana, "Policy issues relating to coastal and international shipping in New Zealand", GSBGM Working Paper Series 2/95, Victoria University of Wellington.

advantage to foreign vessels. Foreign crew would have higher wages due to the fact that they did not pay income tax, were not subject to New Zealand labour laws and in most cases, received subsidies and/or fiscal incentives from their own governments. New Zealand vessels were subject to much less attractive conditions and it was feared the policy would considerably weaken the shipping industry in New Zealand.

The legislation was later amended to allow only foreign vessels that transit the New Zealand coast in the course of their international trading to carry coastal domestic cargoes. Specifically, Section 198 of the Maritime Transport Act provides that[470]:

> No ship shall carry coastal cargo unless the ship is:
> - A New Zealand ship; or
> - A foreign ship that:
>   (i) Has disembarked at a port in New Zealand passengers who embarked at a foreign port or unloaded at a port in New Zealand goods loaded at a foreign port, and has not visited a foreign port since that disembarkation or unloading; or
>   (ii) Will, before departing from a port in New Zealand for a foreign port, disembark such passengers or unload such goods; or, a foreign ship that has embarked at a port in New Zealand passengers who are to be disembarked at a foreign port or loaded at a port in New Zealand goods that are to be unloaded at a foreign port, and has not visited a foreign port since that embarkation or loading; or
>   (iii) Will, before departing from a port in New Zealand for a foreign port, embark such passengers or load such goods.

Even without the provision of the Maritime Transport Act, it would not be possible for a foreign-crewed vessel to operate continuously on the New Zealand coast. Immigration provisions which apply to all industries limit the time that a foreign-crewed vessel can spend continuously on the New Zealand coast to a maximum of 28 days[471].

470 Supra note 467.

471 According to the agreement between Australia and New Zealand, this restriction would not apply to Australian crew, as Australian citizens have the right to work in New Zealand for unlimited periods.

The impact of liberalization of the coastal shipping regime in New Zealand has been felt most in the container shipping sector, and particularly in the carriage of domestic containers between the North and South Islands[472]. The 2003 WTO Trade Policy Review on New Zealand gave a detailed description on the impact of cabotage liberalization and identified a number of foreign carriers that began carrying domestic containers[473].

Freight rates for coastal containers were reported to have dropped fairly quickly in the period immediately following the liberalization, but to have stabilized to some extent since that time. Southbound freight rates were reported to have fallen from around NZ $1200–$1500 per TEU prior to liberalization to around NZ $950–$1000 per TEU. Similar changes appeared to have occurred in northbound freight rates for dry box cargoes, but reductions for refrigerated box cargoes did not appear to have been as large[474].

Although there is little official data on the share of the domestic market that has been secured by international carriers, an informal estimate by the Ministry in 1998 put the likely share at around 10 percent of the inter-island trade. Sources interviewed during the case study program typically put the international carriers share at around 3 percent to 5 percent of total domestic maritime container movements. Consequently it appeared that the domestic carriers have in general been able to retain the vast majority of the market, but in order to do so they have had to substantially lower freight rates[475].

472 New Zealand, Ministry of Transport, "Brief to the Minister of Transport 2006", paper available at the website of the Ministry of Transport: http://www.mot.govt.nz revisited in August 2007.

473 WTO, Trade Policy Review – New Zealand – Report by the Secretariat, WT/TPR/S/115, 14 April 2003, p. 106.

474 Supra footnote 472, New Zealand 2006 Transport Brief. See also WTO, Trade Policy Review – New Zealand – Report by the Government, WT/TPR/G/2115, 14 April 2003, p. 5.

475 The information and updated figures are available from the website of Ministry of Transport, New Zealand at: http://www.transport.govt.nz revisited in July 2006.

One of the fears held by opponents was that the deregulation would lead to a dramatic reduction in the number of dedicated coastal operators[476]. However, the Trade Policy Review conducted by the government of New Zealand showed that this was not the case[477]. The number of commercial vessels permanently deployed on coastal routes in New Zealand remained largely unchanged in the six years since the Maritime Transport Act came into force. The only sector in which there was a decline in the number of vessels deployed was the liquid bulk sector. Given the restrictions that were placed on the carriage of coastal cargoes by international operators, and the general view that the impact of competition from foreign vessels principally felt in the container sector, it appeared unlikely that this decline could be attributed to competition from foreign operators.

In New Zealand, following liberalization, some foreign shipping lines took the opportunity to provide domestic services to local procedures. Liberalization led to a fall in coastal freight rates of approximately 20–25 percent between 1994 and 2000[478]; an intensification in competition for domestic cargoes between coastal shipping, rail and road; a significant increase in the frequency of services between the major ports of the South and North Islands of New Zealand; an increase in the number of vessels operated by New Zealand's only coastal shipping line, and a modest increase in hubbing at Auckland, to the benefit of shipping lines moving maritime containers to and from out-ports[479].

The deregulation of coastal shipping, introduced by the Maritime Transport Act 1994, and the removal of cabotage policies, appears to have provided the New Zealand economy with signi-

476 Supra note 474. The Maritime Union of New Zealand argued that Section 198 of Maritime Transport Act on cabotage liberalization should be repealed. For its opinion see http://www.munz.org.nz/cabotage.html revisited in July 2006.

477 Supra note 472, p. 6.

478 Supra note 473.

479 Supra note 472, New Zealand 2006 Transport Brief.

ficant benefits[480]. Cabotage reform in New Zealand has resulted in reduced domestic transport costs. Competition in shipping, rail and road for the domestic carriage of goods has provided lower prices and a range of new shipping options to cargo owners. Furthermore, it has also improved the quality of service offered by dedicated operators[481]. Without liberalization and the entry of foreign vessels into domestic trade, the economic impetus to provide quality service at a reasonable cost may not have presented itself[482].

5.2.2.2 The European Union

Regulation 4055/86

As part of the process of completing the European internal market, the freedom to provide services to maritime transport was ratified in 1986. As was briefly described earlier in this work, four relevant Regulations, Nos 4055/86, 4056/86, 4057/86 and 4058/86, were set out to apply the principles of freedom to provide services, competition, and free access to the market in sea transport among member states. Regulation 4055/86[483] gives Member State nationals (and non-Community shipping companies using ships registered in a Member State and controlled by Member State nationals) the right to carry passengers or goods by sea between any port of a Member State and any port or off-shore installation of another Member State or of a non-Community country. Any current national restrictions which reserve the carriage of goods to vessels flying the national flag are to be phased out. Some of the major disciplines of Regulation 4055/86 are stipulated by Articles 2, 3 and 4:

480 Id.

481 Id.

482 Supra note 472, New Zealand 2006 Transport Brief.

483 Council Regulation (EEC) No 4055/86 of 22 December 1986 applying the principle of freedom to provide services to maritime transport between Member States and between Member States and third countries, O J L 378, 31/12/1986 P. 0001–0003, Brussels, 24 November 1992. The text is also available at "Summary of Legislation" under: http://europa.eu.int revisited in June 2006.

Article 2 of the Regulation stipulated that all relevant national restrictions on the carriage of goods must be phased out in accordance with a certain timetable[484]. Articles 3 and 4 obliged Member States to either phase out or adjust cargo-sharing arrangements in bilateral agreements between Member States and third countries[485]. Where these arrangements were not phased out, compliance, adjustment or modification was distinguished by whether or not the trade concerned was governed by the UN Code of Conduct for Liner Conferences. Where trades governed by the Code were concerned, the Regulation stated that cargo-sharing arrangements shall comply with the Code and with the obligations of Member States under Regulation (EEC) No. 954/79. Action by a Member State in Pursuance of the above must be notified immediately to all Member States and to the Commission. The Commission provided the Member States with draft texts for an exchange of letters which could satisfy the requirements of the Regulation Article 4 (1) (a)[486]. For non-Codist trade, adjustment or modification was expected to be completed by 1 January 1993, so as to provide free, fair and non-discriminatory access by all Community nationals to the cargo-shares due to the Member States concerned[487].

The Commission concluded that the implementation of this Regulation by Member States was slow, uneven and incomplete[488]. It had encountered considerable difficulties in obtaining information which, under the Regulation, it should receive automatically. The Commission believed the biggest success of the Regulation was the fact that Member States had concluded no new agree-

484 Id. p. 1. Article 2. The timetable provides that: carriage between Member States by vessels flying the flag of a Member State: 31 December 1989; carriage between Member States and third countries by vessels flying the flag of a Member State: 31 December 1991; carriage between Member States and between Member States and third countries in other vessels: 1 January 1993.

485 Id., Articles 3 and 4, pp. 5–6.

486 Id. p. 5.

487 Id. p. 5.

488 Id. p. 16.

ments since the previous report containing cargo-sharing clauses forbidden under Article 5. In addition, most of the unilateral restrictions on the carriage of goods had been phased out[489].

Regulation 3577/92

In order to eliminate restrictions on the freedom to provide maritime transport services within the EU Member States, the Community took the decision on December 7 1992 to apply "Council Regulation No 3577/92 applying the principle of freedom to provide services to maritime transport within Member States"[490]. This Regulation grants freedom to provide maritime transport services within a Member State (maritime cabotage) for Community shipowners operating ships registered in a Member State and flying the flag of that Member State, subject to these ships complying with all the cabotage conditions within that Member State[491].

The Regulation defined "maritime transport services within a Member State (maritime cabotage)", "Community shipowners", "public service contract", "public service obligations", and "serious disturbance of the internal transport market"[492]. Depending on the kind of transport service, matters relating to manning were the responsibility either of the Member State of registration or of the Member State in which the cabotage service was performed. Member States may make the right to provide transport services subject to public service obligations in the interests of maintaining adequate cabotage services between the mainland and its islands and between the islands themselves. Safeguard measures may be taken by the Commission where the internal market was seriously disrupted by the liberalization of cabotage. Such measures may include the temporary exclusion of the area concerned from the scope of the Regulation. Persons providing maritime transport

489 Id. p. 16.

490 The full text of the Regulation is available at: http://eur-lex.europa.eu revisited in July 2006.

491 Article 1.

492 Article 2.

services may do so temporarily in the Member State in which the transport services operated on the same terms as those applied by the Member State in question to its own nationals[493].

Maritime cabotage was liberalized in the EU on 1 January 1993. In the case of France, Italy, Greece, Portugal and Spain mainland cabotage would be gradually liberalized according to a specific timetable for each type of transport service. Mainland-island and inter-island cabotage was not liberalized until 1999 for these countries. This exemption continued to apply until 2004 for scheduled passenger and lighter services and services involving vessels of less than 650 gross tonnages in the case of Greece[494]. In the years after the Regulation was made, the Commission conducted a number of examinations to ensure that the Regulation was duly implemented.

The Commission Report on the implementation of Regulation (EEC) 3577/92 applying the principle of freedom to provide services to maritime transport within Member States – 1993–1994, which was the first report on implementation of the Regulation 3577/92. It consisted of three parts: a description of implementation of the Regulation by Member States, an analysis of the effects of admission to the market of ships that did not meet the conditions for admittance to cabotage in the flag State and an overview of the cabotage fleets of the EFTA countries considering crew costs and participation in EU coastal traffic during the period 1993–94 when Sweden and Finland were still members of EFTA[495].

The Commission Report for 1995–96 on the implementation of Regulation 3577/92 applying the principle of freedom to provide services to maritime transport within Member States (maritime cabotage), and on the economic and social impact of the liberalization of island cabotage, was published as the second report on implementation of the Regulation. It consisted of four parts:

493 Articles 3–8.
494 EU, "Freedom to provide services within the Member States (ocean trade)", Summaries of Legislations, available at: http://europa.eu revisited in July 2006.
495 Id.

an analysis of the economic development of the cabotage industry compared with the period 1993–94, a study on the involvement of certain ships in cabotage trades within the European Union and the question of extending Regulation 3577/92 to EEA countries, a comparison of crew costs and an analysis of the economic impact of liberalizing of island cabotage[496].

The Commission report of February 2000 on the implementation of Regulation 3577/92 applying the principle of freedom to provide services to maritime cabotage, which covered the period 1997 to 1998, dealt with legal and market developments in the EU Member States and EFTA States, the extension of the Regulation to the EEA and the comparative manning costs for cargo vessels[497]. In respect of the legal developments in the Member States under this Regulation, all the Member States' first registers had access to EU cabotage. The northern Member States had already fully liberalized their cabotage when the Regulation came into force. The southern Member States reserved domestic cabotage to the national flag. Therefore the Regulation provided for a gradual opening of the Southern Member States' cabotage markets. During the period 1997–1998, two cabotage segments were liberalized in the southern Member States, services involving the transport of strategic goods (oil, oil products and drinking water) and services by ships smaller than 650 gross tons[498].

In 1993, the Regulation was partially extended by Commission Decision 93/396/EEC[499], which prolonged the exemption accorded to mainland Spain from the implementation of Regulation (EEC) No 3577/92 for a period of six months as from 17 August 1993 in

496 Id.

497 Id.

498 Id.

499 93/396/EEC: "Commission Decision of 13 July 1993 on Spain's request for adoption by the Commission of a prolongation of safeguard measures pursuant to Article 5 of Regulation (EEC) No 3577/92 applying the principle of freedom to provide services to maritime transport within Member States (maritime cabotage)", Official Journal L 173, 16/07/1993 P. 0033–0035, full text of the Decision is available at: http://eur-lex.europa.eu revisited in July 2006.

respect of the following cabotage services for break-bulk general cargo, dry bulk cargo (except for the transport of cement or clinker in specialized cement carriers) and chemical products in specialized tankers. The remaining mainland cabotage trades, with the exception of those referred to in Article 6 (1) of Regulation (EEC) No 3577/92 which was subject to special derogations, were liberalized as from 17 August 1993. The exclusion did not apply to feeder services. In the event that no Spanish vessel could meet a specific demand for cabotage services, other Member States' vessels may offer such services.

On 3 June 1998, the Commission put forward a Proposal for a Council Regulation (EEC) amending Council Regulation (EEC) No 3577/92 applying the principle of freedom to provide services to maritime transport within Member States (maritime cabotage)[500]. The Proposal altered the allocation of responsibilities between the flag State and the host State for matters relating to the crew[501]. Article 1 of the Proposal read:

> Article 3 of Regulation (EEC) No 3577/92 is hereby replaced by the following:
> Article 3
> (1) For vessels carrying out cabotage services other than those referred to in paragraph 2, all matters relating to manning shall be the responsibility of the State in which the vessel is registered (flag State), except for ships smaller than 650 gt, where the conditions in force in the State in which the vessel is performing its services (host State) may be applied.
> (2) For vessels carrying out regular passenger and ferry services, including mixed passenger/cargo services and scheduled cruise services, the rules concerning the required proportion of Community nationals in the crew (namely all staff employed on board) as in force in the host State shall apply. All other matters relating to manning shall be the responsibility of the flag State.
> (3) Where host States allow non-member-country nationals to be employed on board ships carrying out cabotage services as referred to in paragraph 2, they shall require that those crew members shall be treated in the terms and conditions of their employment as residents of the Mem-

500 *Official Journal C 213, 09/07/1998 p.0016. The full text of the Proposal is also available at:* http://eur-lex.europa.eu revisited in August 2006.

501 Article 1.

ber State being the flag State. The host State shall apply its own terms and conditions of employment to non-member-country seafarers on board its national vessels carrying out such services.

(4) Member States' measures implementing the provisions of this Article shall be notified to the Commission in accordance with Article 9.

In addition, the Proposal also distinguished between ships providing regular passenger transport and ferry services, for which the rules of the host State (i.e. the country in which the ship provides its services) applied in respect of the proportion of Community nationals in the crew; and the rules of the flag State applied to any other matters relating to the crew and other ships engaged in cabotage (except ships of less than 650 gross ton), for which the rules of the flag State applied in all matters relating to the crew.

5.2.2.3 The United States

The cabotage protection under the US legislative system is among the most frequently cited. The Jones Act and associated legislation require that ships used to carry cargoes and passengers between ports in the US must be owned by US citizens, built in US shipyards and manned by US crews. The US domestic water-borne trade comprises freight movement on the Great Lakes, inland waterways, and the domestic ocean trades[502].

The most important legislation impacting domestic waterborne trade in the US is the Jones Act, which applies to Section 27 of "the Merchant Marine Act 1920"[503], It stipulates that foreign-built (or rebuilt) vessels are prohibited from engaging in coastwise trade either directly between two points of the US or via a foreign

502 US Department of Transport, "Domestic Shipping: Vital to the Nation's Economy, Security and Transportation", paper available at the website of the Department: http://www.marad.dot.gov revisited in August 2007.

503 This particular piece of legislation is briefly discussed in Chapter 2 of this work as example of restrictive practices in trade in services. For a detailed study of Jones Act, see Jesse S. Reeves, "The Jones Act and the Denunciation of Treaties", *American Journal of International Law*, Vol. 15, No. 1 (Jan., 1921), pp. 33–38.

port. Trade with US island territories and possessions are included in the definition of coastwise trade. Moreover, the definition of vessels has been interpreted by the US Administration to cover hovercraft and inflatable rafts. Limitations on rebuilding act as another discrimination against foreign materials: the rebuilding of a vessel of over 500 gross tones must be carried out within the US if it is to engage in coastwise trade. A smaller vessel may lose its existing coastwise rights if the rebuilding abroad or in the US with foreign materials is extensive[504].

The authorities responsible for the interpretation and enforcement of US cabotage laws are the US Customs Service and the US Coast Guard. The Maritime Administration (MARAD) is responsible for the effects of the cabotage laws on the US domestic fleet. MARAD has argued that the cabotage laws, together with the Maritime Security Program and the National Ship-building Initiative have promoted the US merchant marine so that critical national security requirements are met[505].

The US coastal trades remain protected from competition by foreign flag carriers, and there have been no significant or substantive changes in its cabotage regime over the past several decades. The Act of December 27, 1950 provided for an administrative waiver whenever such waiver could be in the best interest of national defense[506]. In enacting the Coast Guard Authorization Act of 1998, the 105th Congress further established an administrative process for Jones Act waivers. The Secretary of Transportation, under certain conditions, is authorized to issue certificates of documentation with an endorsement for employment in the coastwise trade to certain small passenger vessels and un-inspected passenger vessels carrying no more than 12 passengers for hire.

504 Jones Act, Section 27, Merchant Marine Act, 1920 § 861, Maritime Cabotage Task Force, available at: http://www.mctf.com revisited in July 2006.

505 Maritime Administration, Department of Transportation, "A Report to Congress on US Maritime Policy" Washington: Maritime Administration, May 1998, p. 44.

506 Explanation of the waiver can be found in the website of American Maritime Officer at: http://www.amo-union.org revisited in August 2007.

The waiver, which is subject to notice and public comment, may not be granted if it would adversely affect US ship-builders or the coastwise trade business or any person who employs US-built vessels. This administrative process is not applicable to larger passenger vessels and to cargo vessels. Any other waivers of the Act must be obtained legislatively[507].

The Jones Act and related US coastwise trade laws have been amended several times to provide exceptions from their basic requirements[508]. In September 1998, the Senate of Commerce, Science and Transportation Committee held a full Committee Hearing on S. 2390, the Freedom to Transport Act of 1998 (the Hearing)[509].

The Hearing[510] received evidence suggesting that despite Jones Act protection and subsidies, the record of the US ship-building industry remained poor. Not only had the Jones Act failed to protect the American merchant fleet, it also failed to preserve jobs. Competition, on the other hand, would benefit the domestic shipping industry, by forcing inefficient and high cost producers to streamline and cut costs wherever possible, from both domestic and foreign sources. The Hearing was advised the negative effects of Jones Act in undermining the competitiveness of the US steel industry, through prohibiting the steel industry from using the full range of transportation options available to the foreign competitors, leading to artificially high rates to ship steel and raw materials by water, constricting transportation options for steel companies and thereby straining the demand for truck and rail services[511].

The Hearing was further advised that section 2390 was able to provide a substantial revival of port jobs, lower consumer costs and a more favourable trade balance between the US ports including the Great Lakes. Taxpayer subsidies to American ships should

507 Id.
508 Magee Kathleen, supra note 465.
509 Full text of the Hearing can be found at the US Senate website: http://commerce.senate.gov revisited in July 2006.
510 Id.
511 Id.

be abolished and water transportation should be freed to compete with railroads and trucks[512].

Soon after the Hearing, it was announced that a bill would be introduced to allow foreign-built US-flag cruise ships into the US domestic trades. Unfortunately, the bill failed to generate support and did not progress beyond the stage. However, pressure has been increasing for US domestic reform. The 1999 OECD report noted a strong lobby has emerged in the US seeking reform of the Jones Act[513]. Besides, ship-owners were reported to oppose the Jones Act because ships built in the US shipyards were three to four times more expensive than those built in competitive foreign shipyards, which led to the result that they could not afford the price and many ships trading on the US coast were more than 25 years old[514]. Other major business groups favouring the reform of the Jones Act include the National Industrial Transportation League and the Jones Act Reform Coalition.

In the 1980s, during US-Canada negotiations on a free trade agreement, Canada tried to limit the US cabotage law which was rejected by the US[515]. Later, in the NAFTA negotiations, Canada proposed a "North American Jones Act" under which the vessels of each nation could compete for domestic cargoes within the three countries. Mexico also agreed to relax its own cabotage restrictions on a reciprocal basis. Unfortunately once again the proposals failed to make a breakthrough due to US's resistance[516].

OECD has also tried to curb the Jones Act in the field of shipbuilding subsidy by subjecting new Jones Act projects to OECD

512 Id.

513 Maritime Transport Committee, OECD, "Discussion Document on Regulatory Reform in International Maritime Transport, Paris: OECD", 1999, p. 44. See also "Containerization International", November 1995, p. 101.

514 Cargo Systems, "the Future of the Container Shipping Industry", London: Cargo Systems, 1999, p. 29.

515 Mary R. Brooks, "The Jones Act under NAFTA and its Effects on the Canadian Shipbuilding Industry", research paper for the Atlantic Institute for Market Studies (AIMS), September 2006. The paper is available at: http://www.aims.ca revisited in August 2007, pp. 12–13.

516 Id. p. 13.

approvals[517]. Moreover, it proposed in 1994 to set up regional maritime services agreements with the purpose of limiting or eliminating cabotage requirements[518].

The most important initiatives to address US cabotage policies, however, have been undertaken in the multilateral trade negotiations within the GATT/WTO[519]. From early 1990s, the EU and Japan started to negotiate possible ways to liberalize and gain access to Jones Act markets. They wished to win some concessions on US cargo preference laws that set aside certain amounts of US government-financed imports and exports for US-flag vessels. However, the US government refused these proposals by arguing that US shipping markets were already liberalized enough, and that the shipping services agenda shall be limited to the authority of the Federal Maritime Commission who was entitled to respond unilaterally when foreign policies discriminated against US-flag vessels in port access, auxiliary services and high-sea trade[520]. But at the same time, the US agreed to a maritime policy stand-still, which prohibited parties from adopting any measure affecting trade in maritime transport services, except in response to measures applied by other countries, and with a view to maintaining or improving the freedom of provision of maritime transport services, nor in such a manner as would improve their negotiating position and leverage[521]. In a later negotiation, Japan won a WTO pledge to review the Jones Act and rule on its legitimacy within five years. A favourable Jones Act determination would then let the law stand and pending WTO review every two years[522].

In May 1999, the Consultative Shipping Group representing cargo ship-owners in 13 European countries and Japan sent a dele-

517 OECD Ship-building Agreement, available at OECD website: http://www.oecd.org/document revisited in June 2005.

518 Source of information: OECD website at: http://www.oecd.org revisited in May 2005.

519 McKay M.R., "Jones Act is always at Risk in Trade Pact Negotiations", American Maritime Officer, http://www.amo-union.org revisited in July 2006.

520 Supra note 515.

521 Id.

522 McKay M.R., supra note 519.

gation to Washington and held talks with the Maritime Administration of the Department of Transportation, trying to persuade the US to repeal the Jones Act in the interest of free trade. In July 1999, a report by the WTO Secretariat charged that the US restricts competition in maritime transportation where domestic services are limited to US carriers[523].

The above examples demonstrate the determination of the American industry and other countries to address the US cabotage policy and the difficulty in finding resolution on this issue. The WTO negotiations on maritime transport services are particularly difficult given the reluctance of the US representatives to make the issue negotiated at a multilateral level.

523 Id.

6 Access to Cargo in International Shipping – Liner Shipping

6.1 General Background

6.1.1 Liner Conference and Its Evolution

Liner shipping refers to shipping services that are provided on a regular schedule basis to pre-determined ports[524]. It is distinct from bulk shipping services which carry non-containerized raw materials such as crude and refined oil, grain, coal, cement or liquefied gas provided only on demand made by individual shippers on non-scheduled routes. While bulk shipping is generally believed to be a fairly competitive market, liner shipping services were traditionally involved in a cartel-like price fixing and capacity allocating arrangements.

As noted in Chapter 2 of this work, in contrast to bulk shipping, liner shipping companies offer scheduled services predominantly moving containers, and providing transport services to third party logistics service suppliers or cargo owners whose markets are increasingly global in scope. Moreover, liner shipping is also capital-intensive, with fixed costs often exceeding 80% of the total costs[525]. The adjustment of supply to demand can be difficult because the market demands regular, fixed-day sailing schedules. Load factors are quite variable, with directional imbalances and cyclical and seasonal variations. Supply must be maintained to

524 For interpretations of liner shipping, see for example, "International Organizations and the Law of the Sea: Documentary Yearbook", p. 548, edited by Netherlands Institute for the Law of the Sea; "Antitrust Aspects of the Ocean Shipping Reform Act of 1998", p. 64, United States, Congress House Committee on the Judiciary, 2000.

525 Supra note 8, WTO Secretariat background note, p. 14.

service peak demand. The resultant excess capacity can tempt firms to engage in discount pricing when demand is not at the peak, but lower rates do not result in significantly more demand. Finally, as the same with other service industries, the value of unsold capacity is lost when not used. It was generally accepted that the conference system lended some measure of stability to the industry, a measure that shippers sought in order to engage in long-term transport supply relationships[526].

By contrast to other transport sectors, liner shipping has for a long period of time enjoyed the privilege of self-regulation, where national carriers and liner conferences have a major influence on issues such as whether competition in the market shall be allowed or not. This means that the economic control of maritime markets has been left in the hands of private companies, while in other sectors like air and rail transport, it is usually the government who has control over the market[527]. There is much debate on whether such self-regulation in liner shipping has been successful and more beneficial to consumers than the normal governmental regulation in other areas.

There has been a long tradition of maritime carriers entering into various types of agreements, which could help them enjoy benefits that arise from cooperation on technical or commercial matters. Conferences, the oldest form of ship-owner cooperation, first appeared in the 1870s[528]. Conferences exist where two or more vessel-operating carriers providing international liner services for the carriage of cargo on particular routes, reach agreement to apply uniform or common freight rates and any others conditions for these routes (e.g. coordination of sailing dates and dates of call,

526 World Shipping Council, "International Liner Shipping Regulation: Its Rationale and Its Benefits", March 2001, p. 7. The paper is available at the website of World Shipping Council: http://worldshipping.org revisited in August 2006.

527 Id. p. 17.

528 For more on the history of liner conference, see: Douglas K. Fleming, "Selected Pages from the History of US Cargo Liner Service", available at the website of University of Washington at: http://www.sma.washington.edu revisited in June 2006.

determination of frequencies, regulation of capacity and allocation of cargo and revenues)[529]. By joining carrier agreements[530], shipping companies retain their juridical independence, while consenting to common practices with the other members regarding pricing, traffic distribution and/or vessel capacity utilization[531].

Conference agreements are made between two or more ocean common carriers and provide for the fixing of and adherence to uniform tariff rates and conditions of service[532]. Conferences are the most widespread type of rate-binding agreements which can be roughly divided into two groups. In the US, conferences are required by law not to restrict the entry and exit of any shipping company and are called "open" conferences. By contrasting conferences covering other routes are mostly "closed" to outside carriers[533].

Prior to containerization, the majority of shippers supported the argument that conferences contributed to the efficiency of trade. This support was based on the understanding that without some degree of cooperation, liners would find it difficult to maintain efficient and sustainable services.

529 See Articles 1.3 (b) and 3 of Council Regulation (EEC) 4056/86 of 22 December 1986 "Laying Down the Detailed Rules for the Application of Articles 85 and 86 of the Treaty to Maritime Transport", Official Journal L378 of 31 December 1986. Definitions in other jurisdictions are similar. However, US legislation increasingly denies conferences price fixing authority.

530 Some examples of carrier agreements that were recognized in US regulation by the end of 1998 include: conference agreements, cooperative working agreements, joint services agreements, pooling agreements, space charter agreements, and transhipment agreements.

531 Felix Dinger, "What Shall We do with the Drunken Sailor? EC Competition Law and Maritime Transport", European Institute of University of Basel. Paper available at: http://www.europa.unibas.ch revisited in August 2007, p. 6.

532 Fink, Mattoo and Neagu, supra note 150, pp. 8–9.

533 In November 2002, the EC claimed that the steps taken by the Trans-Atlantic Conference Agreement (TACA) to comply with the open conference obligations of US law had constituted an abuse of their dominant position. It was alleged TACA offered inducements to certain shipping lines to enter the transatlantic trade as parties to the conference, rather than as independents. For more information see the Press Release of TACA at: http://www.tacaconf.com/ revisited in August 2006.

The introduction of containerization and the development of independent liner service operators have to some extent reduced the influence of conferences in international shipping[534]. Shipping lines merged their conference rights into consortia and subsequently formed global alliances. Apart from the harmonization of schedules and ports of call, liner operators share transport capacity in consortia, while in alliances, price setting is being increasingly favoured because regulators do not disapprove of the practice[535].

At the same time, the perception of shippers also took a dramatic shift. More rational, market-oriented philosophies in the shipping industry gradually replaced the historical support for the conference system[536]. In addition to the arrival of containerization, this erosion in the power of conferences was caused by[537]:

- The trend of deregulation in other modes of transport such as railways has given shippers an opportunity to witness the benefits of improved efficiency brought by the independent actions of carriers and shippers;
- The entrance into the market of strong and efficient independent shipping companies, has made it possible for outsiders to supply the same services as the conferences at lower costs to consumers;

534 See for example, European Shippers' Council: "Containerization International Conference: Deregulation Takes Hold – What are the Implications?", March 2000, available at: http://www.europeanshippers.com/docs revisited in August 2006.

535 Felix Dinger, supra note 531, p. 6.

536 For instance in Canada, prior to the passage of the revised Shipping Conferences Exemption Act in 1979, most shippers considered it naïve for the Department of Consumer and Corporate Affairs to oppose conferences. While by late 1980s, a majority of shippers were opposed to conferences themselves. See Trevor Heaver, "The Shipping Conferences Exemption Act: Review and Suggestions of Positions Appropriate for the Panel". April 2001, Research conducted for the Canada Transportation Act Review, available at: http://www.reviewcta-examenltc.gc.ca revisited in August 2006. For similar change of views from shippers of US and of UK, see US Federal Maritime Commission: "Section 18 Report on the Shipping Act of 1984", September 1989.

537 Id. Trevor Heaver, pp. 13–15. See also Fink, Mattoo and Neagu, supra note 150, pp. 9–10.

- The erosion of the power of conferences through legislative changes has increased the efficiency and quality of services without diminishing the profitability of lines. A notable example is the US Ocean Shipping Reform Act (OSRA) of 1998 that amended the Shipping Act on 1984. While preserving the antitrust immunity of the rate-setting conference system, OSRA allows for the confidentiality of key contractual features (including price) between shippers and carriers, creating a higher level of competition in all respects;
- Shippers engaged in international trade are more sophisticated in dealing with risks than before. Besides, they have realized that being able to enter into contracts with individual carriers provides flexibilities absent from collective arrangements;
- The globalization of competition gives the shippers greater opportunity to observe the liberalization of the shipping industry in other countries. Globalization also makes shippers more inter-dependent among countries and their dependence on railways and trucking firms, on manufacturers and retailers is also much strengthened;
- Some radical changes occurred in the shipping industry itself also speed up the process of erosion[538].

Moreover, the changes in shipping patterns and the powerful new entrants have also contributed to the erosion of traditional conferences. For instance, the expansion of feeder and relay alternatives to traditional direct shipping operations has strongly undermined the ability of conferences to control capacity and rates in trade lanes. Several new powerful shipping lines have been growing out-

538 The changing characteristics of liner shipping are manifested by: the cost structure of lines with the development of containerization; the decline of the number of lines on routes under the pressures of globalization and the increased competition that follows; the increased quality of non-conference services which has decreased the percentage of traffic carried by conference lines; the emergence of alliances and other forms of operating agreements, which have contributed to the reduction in the number of vessels required and narrowed the cost differences among lines; and, the changing business strategy of liner shipping.

side the conference system, including China Shipping Group and Mediterranean Shipping Company. Some other non-conference operators such as COSCO and Evergreen also managed to increase their market presence[539].

Another force for change stems from the rapid growth of East Asian economies from the 1970s[540]. Developing countries in Asia doubled their share of world ship registration from 7.8 percent in 1980 to 16.8 percent in 1997, while the figure for industrial countries dropped from more than 50 percent to 27.4 percent in the same period. In the case of open-registry countries, the UNCTAD found that developing countries' share has also increased since 1980 when such open-registered tonnage was negligible, reaching one-quarter in 1997[541]. On the other hand, industrial economies' overall share has fallen, representing two-thirds of the total tonnage registered in 1997. In the 1990s, competitive pressure from new developing countries and the growing demand for global logistics brought about the disintegration of the consortia and the advent of huge global alliances that united the Asia-Europe transpacific and transatlantic trades[542].

6.1.2 *Consortia and Alliances*

Consortia are agreements between liner shipping companies aimed primarily at operating joint services by means of technical, operational or commercial coordination, such as joint use of ships, port installations and marketing organizations[543]. They emerged in response to the increased capital requirements of ship-owners seeking to obtain larger and more efficient vessels necessitated by

539 Information source: Containerization International, 2000, at http://www.worldcargonews.com revisited in August 2006.

540 UNESCAP, "Changes in International Container Shipping and Port Environment". Paper available at: http://www.unescap.org revisited in August 2006.

541 Id. See also supra note 10, WTO Secretariat background note, p. 5.

542 Id.

543 WTO, supra note 8, p. 18.

the trend of containerization in international maritime transport[544].

The regulation of consortia varies in different jurisdictions. For example, in countries like the US, Japan, Australia, Canada and New Zealand, consortia are granted immunity from anti-trust law by legislations[545]. Under EU regulations, consortia are not granted price fixing authority, except if they obtain an individual exemption under Regulation 4056/86 to that effect. Regulation 870/95 allows group exemptions for consortia whose market share does not exceed 35 per cent if members are not part of a conference (30 per cent if members are part of a conference)[546]. For market shares between 30–35 per cent and 50 per cent, a simplified opposition procedure applies. Consortia benefit from group exemption unless the Commission objects within six months of notification. In the event of higher market shares, the consortium may apply for individual exemption[547].

There has been longstanding debate over the nature of liner consortia and what kind of regulation should be utilized. Questions such as the commonality and difference between liner consortia and liner conference, the relationship between liner consor-

544 According to the Economic and Social Committee on the proposal for a Council regulation on the application of Article 85 (3) of the treaty to certain categories of agreements, decisions and concerted practices between shipping companies (OJ 1991 C 69/16), consortia are fairly recent phenomena born out of the container revolution in the 1960s/70s which called for the building of much larger ships to effect economies of scale and increase ship productivity. The degree of investment needed to re-equip to meet such technology innovation was beyond the capability of most single ship-owners. It became clear then that the vast majority of existing liner companies were no longer the optium commercial unit for raising the huge capital sums involved. Many of the shipping lines which once provided conventional liner-cargo services grouped together to form consortia, first at national level and then also internationally.

545 WTO, supra note 8, p. 18. See also OECD DSTI/DOT/MTC (99) 8, "Discussion Document on Regulatory Reform in International Maritime Transport".

546 WTO, supra note 8, p. 18.

547 Id. p. 18.

tia and merger or whether consortia should be defined as operational agreement or technical agreement have all been attracting increasing interest and research under different jurisdictions.

Alliances, or sometimes referred to as global strategic alliances, are usually categorized as operational agreements[548] in which two or more carriers operate on a continuing basis in several major trade lanes. Alliances allow the participating lines to integrate their ocean, shore-side and inland operations (under some jurisdictions) in a way that lets them offer their customers access to a large transportation network, while keeping costs relatively low for participating lines, reducing risk, and freeing capital for other uses[549].

Typically, the parties involved in an alliance agree on conditions such as joint vessel route assignments, itineraries, sailing schedules, additions and withdrawal of capacity, ports and port utilities. The alliance usually covers charters, space charters, use of joint terminals and containers, pooling of containers, establishment of container stations, vessel feeder routes, co-ordination of inland services where permitted, information exchanges and relevant procedures[550]. On the other hand, items usually not covered included: joint sales, marketing or joint maritime or multi-modal pricing, joint ownership of vessels or maintenance or insurance, joint or common bills of lading, common tariffs, joint management and executive functions, revenue pools or cargo pools and sharing of profits and losses.

Alliances have not yet been challenged by national competition authorities for they are not very much different from consortia if considered from a legal point of view. Many governments regard alliances as an alternative way to avoid mergers that may lead to

548 Operational agreements include mostly vessel-sharing arrangements, in which carriers are permitted not only to share vessels, but also to integrate their operations so as to reduce the cost of terminal and shore-side service, equipment use and information and electronic data management. Such agreements offer an opportunity for greater efficiencies in the marketplace and improve rational use of carriers' assets. See infra footnote 659, FMC interim report, p. 29.

549 WTO, supra note 8, p. 18.

550 Id. p. 18.

concentration and oligopoly[551]. For example, the relevant US authorities tend to develop a positive view of the effects of alliances concerning rationalization and customer benefits[552].

6.1.3 New Developments

Mergers and acquisitions emerged in the liner industry in mid 1990s with a process of transnational consolidation, a trend clearly visible in statistics on the degree of concentration in the liner shipping industry[553]. In the US, most of the major international liner shipping companies have passed into foreign control, involving Singaporean, Danish, German and Anglo-Dutch companies[554]. The FMC has repeatedly stated in this context that it would not change its policy with regard to the use of section 19 of the 1920 Shipping Act and its related instruments[555], the mission of the FMC was not limited to pursuing US beneficial interests in shipping, but more widely to defend US flags and maritime trade objectives.

551 See "Liner Shipping: Market Developments and Government Action – the EU Competition Policy Perspective", delivered by Jean Francois Pons, Deputy Director-General of the Competition Directorate of the EC at the 1st Lloyd List International Shipping Convention, 18–22 October 2000.

552 For more information see the website of US Federal Maritime Commission at its website: www.fmc.gov visited in June 2002 and revisited in April 2006.

553 WTO, supra note 8, p. 20. In 1988, the top 20 container lines controlled around 35 per cent of the total global TEU capacity. In 1996 the figure has crept up to around 50 per cent of total global shipping capacity. Later, from 1996 to 1998, the share of the top 20 lines leapt to approximately 70 per cent. Ever since 1998, there has been a further increase in this trend and nearly 80 per cent of the total global capacity is now under the control of the top 20 lines. For more information see Containerization International, November issues of every year, available on its website: http://www.ci-online.co.uk/ revisited in July 2006.

554 WTO Trade Policy Review, Report for the United States from the Secretariat (WT/TPR/S/88), para. 41.

555 See, for example, remarks of the Chairman of the FMC before the 88th Annual Convention of the American Association of Port Authorities, on 28 September 1999 www.fmc.gov revisited in March 2005.

Compared with other industry fields, mergers and acquisitions in the liner shipping industry have not been particularly concentrated, which explains the fact that they yet to be objected to by national competition authorities, although they are submitted to such authorities for authorization and subject to certain thresholds[556].

Discussion agreements came into being and became prevalent from late 1980s as a forum within which conference lines managed to participate with non-conference rivals to discuss and act together with respect to rates, capacity as well as various charges and fees[557]. Such new agreements were put into effective operation on both trans-Atlantic and trans-Pacific lines[558]. Discussion agreements have also been established in the US/South American and US/Caribbean trading lines.

Discussion agreements received quite different treatments in different jurisdictions[559]. In Australia, Japan, New Zealand and the US, conferences or individual members of conferences were allowed to enter into agreements with non-conference shipping lines, without particular restrictions applying[560]. In Australia, such agreements must be registered, however, they were subject to rein-

556 WTO, supra note 8, p. 20.

557 In most cases, the independent carriers are not interested in joining the conference and giving up their pricing freedom. They are willing however, to join the conference carriers in an agreement which allows for the discussion of rate levels in general, means to control falling rates and capacity within the trade during periods of overcapacity, and mutual agreements on surcharges. Source of information: Freight Transport Association, the UK at: http://www.fta.co.uk/ revisited in August 2006.

558 On trans-Atlantic lines, the Eurocorde Discussion Agreement was created in mid-1980s and later the Trans-Atlantic Agreement (TAA) was established as an enlarged conference. Both of them followed periods of excess capacity and heavy rate discounting, aligned independent lines with conference carriers. TAA also introduced a capacity management program into the Atlantic trades as part of its broader stabilization effort. On trans-Pacific lines, the Transpacific Stabilization Agreement (TSA) was set up in 1989 as a response to rate decline and overcapacity. Source of information: Freight Transport Association, the UK at: http://www.fta.co.uk/ revisited in August 2006.

559 WTO, supra note 8, pp. 19–20.

560 Id. p. 19. See also: Department of Transport and Regional Services, Australia, at: http://www.dotars.gov.au revisited in March 2006.

forced oversight since the 2001 amendment of Section X of the Trade Practices Act. In the US, such agreements were subject to the same procedures as any other form of agreements between carriers[561]. This relatively lenient approach may be explained by the agreements' perceived positive impact on the stability of services and efficient capacity management. In the EU, such agreements did not benefit from the Block Exemption. In the EATA case, a capacity-management program between conference and non-conference lines was prohibited, because it was combined with direct price-fixing[562]. At the beginning of 2000, the Commission launched surprise inspections of shipping companies suspected of fixing prices outside the scope of the conference block exemption. In May 2000, the Commission's FETTCSA Decision came down against an agreement between conference lines and independent operators not to grant discounts on published tariffs[563].

6.2 Selected Multilateral Regulatory Regimes

The changes in the regulatory regime for liner shipping have been brought about by a fundamental ideological change in the global attitude towards international trade. In past decades, many countries emphasized self-sufficiency and the protection of domestic markets in pursuit for economic independence. However, during the most recent decade, there has been a growing consensus that the global economy and international trade are the overwhelming engine for economic growth and development. Many countries have adopted policies to facilitate the liberalization of trade and

561 It is worthy of noting that the OECD in its 1999 discussion paper on the Review of Regulatory Reform recommended the removal of immunity for shipping lines entering into discussion and capacity stabilization agreements. See supra footnote 545, DSTI/DOT/MTC (99) 8 Discussion Document on Regulatory Reform in International Maritime Transport.

562 WTO supra note 8, p. 19.

563 WTO supra note 8, p. 20.

capital flows through multilateral institutions (such as the WTO), regional agreements, bilateral agreements as well as unilateral initiatives[564]. Besides the ideological shift, technological breakthroughs such as containerization, advances in global communications and logistics management, are also important factors in bringing changes in the regulatory regime for liner shipping[565].

Unlike bulk shipping, where issues such as safety and working conditions pose major problem for the regulators, the biggest concern with liner shipping is the potential for abuse of market position and predatory pricing. While most countries provide liner conferences with some degree of antitrust immunity, there has not been uniformity in these policies or in their application, neither has competition policy related to alliances been treated consistently. Furthermore, there is little concerted effort to ensure compatibility between alliance regulation and conference regulation. Lastly, the recent wave of mergers and acquisitions among global carriers has also posed the question of modifying pertinent competition policy so as to be more transnational in nature.

The main objective of regulatory arrangement for international liner shipping is the promotion of efficient, adequate, reliable and competitively-priced services. A threshold question is what market arrangements are most likely to achieve this outcome. Currently, major features of the regulatory regime for liner shipping include[566]:

- From both national and international perspectives, the intervention of governments into liner shipping has been operated under the principle of "allow but constrain";
- As liner conferences' influence has eroded under regulatory and economic pressures, large and loosely-connected agreements have emerged which demand updated and comprehensive regulations.

564 UNESCAP, supra note 540.

565 Id.

566 For features of the regulatory regime, see for example Trevor Heaver, supra footnote 536; UNESCAP, supra note 540.

At the moment, important international/multilateral organizations that deal with the issue of liner shipping include the UNCTAD and the OECD. However, neither of them seems to be the desirable forum to harmonize the anti-trust exemption system for liner shipping on a global scale. From mid-1980s, the significance of the UNCTAD for shipping issues has been much diminished. During its 8th session in 1992, substantive reform was made to the UNCTAD machinery, in which all existing committees other than those on preferences and restrictive practices were suspended, including the Shipping Committee that had been functioning since 1965[567]. Moreover, one of the most significant achievements of the UNCTAD on liner shipping, the 1974 Convention on a Code of Conduct for Liner Conferences, has been largely proven to be a failure. On the OECD side, the proposals and reports of its Secretariat's on the elimination of the anti-trust exemption for liner shipping have not received broad support of the governments. Instead of providing an objective response to the merits of the issues confronting liner shipping, OECD's workshop in this field seems essentially to respond to a perceived demand for the regulatory reform, which has been made in the absence of sufficient convincing analysis.

6.2.1 *The United Nations*

The UN Code of Conduct for Liner Conferences[568] (the Code) was intended as a multilateral cargo-sharing scheme. It represented the first attempt at international level for the regulation of the conference system. The Code, which was first initiated in 1974,

567 See for example, S.P. Jagota, "Developments in the Law of the Sea between 1970 and 1998", Journal of the History of International Law, Brill Academic Publishers, Vol. 2, No. 1/July 2000, pp. 91–119; A. Behnam, "Future of the Shipping Dialogue in UNCTAD", Maritime Policy & Management, Vol. 21, Issue 1 January 1994, pp. 15–27.

568 United Nations, Treaty Series 1983. Also see the website of Admiralty and Maritime Law Guide at: http://www.admiraltylawguide.com revisited in August 2007.

came into force in 1983. It was meant to counter-act the anti-competitive actions of liner conferences and aimed to increase developing countries' share of world shipping tonnage to a more "equitable" level and to increase developing countries' share of income generated by world liner shipping[569]. It also aimed to improve developing countries' balance of payments through substituting domestic production of shipping services for imports. The Code endeavoured to achieve these goals mainly by reserving cargo for national flag shipping lines that may be owned by either the public and/or private sector[570].

In many places of the world, the conference system coexists with a framework of bilateral inter-governmental cargo-sharing agreements that were either the result of historical and colonial links, or were developed to deal with state trading economies. Elsewhere, countries have adopted the Code and signed bilateral agreements to reserve cargo for their national flag ships on either a 40:40:20 or a 50:50 basis. However, in practice, this was confined largely to government-contracted cargo and could not be applied to private cargo due to difficulties in implementing such schemes[571].

In order to meet these objectives, the Code established procedures for relations among conference members, including national flag carrier participation and cargo sharing, relations between conferences and shippers, as well as a conciliation mechanism for dispute settlement[572]. The Code also clearly described and limited the role of governments. It advised that governments have the primary responsibility of recognizing national lines and the right to participate in consultations between shipper organizations and conferences[573].

569 Fink, Mattoo and Neagu, supra note 150, p. 7.

570 OECD supra note 7, pp. 85–88. See also Official Journal of the EU, "Opinion of the European Economic and Social Committee on the White Paper on the review of the Regulation No. 4586/86, applying the EC competition rules to maritime transport", 2005/C157/23, 28.6.2005.

571 WTO, supra note 8, p. 3.

572 OECD supra note 7, p. 85.

573 Id. p. 86.

The cargo sharing formula for liner conferences[574] was stipulated in Article 2 of the Code, under the title of "Participation in Trade". The Code provided a special position for national carriers within conferences and, in particular, to the cargo entitlements of those lines. The Article provided that, "unless otherwise mutually agreed", national shipping lines of the countries at either end of a given trade are entitled to equal rights of participation in the carriage of cargoes generated by their mutual trade and carried by the conference (Article 2 (4) (a)). At the same time, third-country shipping lines, if any, shall have the right to acquire a significant part, such as twenty percent, of the volume of traffic generated by that trade (Article 2 (4)(b)). The so-called 40:40:20 formula was derived from these provisions. The practical significance of the cargo-sharing formula was that national lines at each end of the trade could exact forty percent of the conference trade by simply "not agreeing otherwise".

However, the Code did not regulate non-conference shipping lines nor dealt with individual shipping lines outside conferences[575]. Instead, non-conference shipping was relegated to a Resolution adopted at the same time as the Code, which recognized their existence and allowed them to operate on condition that they adhered to the general principle of free and fair competition on a commercial basis. The Resolution aimed at the preservation of the shippers' option to choose between using conference and non-conference lines, as well as to protect outsiders[576].

574 The definition of a liner conference is provided in chapter I of the Code as: "a group of two or more vessel-operating carriers which provides international liner services for the carriage of cargo on a particular route or routes within specified geographical limits and which has an agreement or arrangement, whatever its nature, within the framework of which they operate under uniform or common freight rates and any other agreed conditions with respect to the provision of liner services". See the legal text of the code supra note 568.

575 OECD supra note 7, p. 86.

576 Id. p. 86.

Despite its wide coverage, the Code actually has only had very limited economic relevance nowadays[577]. It was only effectively implemented between Western Europe and West Africa, which accounted for less than 3 per cent of the world liner trade[578].

6.2.2 *The OECD*

An early effort of the OECD in promoting harmonized shipping policies and free competition was reflected in an initiative in 1987, under the name of the "Common Principles of Shipping Policy for Member Countries"[579]. This non-binding policy is based on elements including[580]:

- The maintenance of open trades and free competitive access to international shipping operations; i.e. Member countries agreed that their shipping policies should be directed to safeguard and promote open liner and bulk trades, and incorporated the concept of not introducing any new measures restricting competitive access[581];
- Coordinated response to external pressure, based on full consultations between Member countries: Member countries agreed to oppose the imposition of regimes which restrict access by commercially operated shipping companies to cargoes which move internationally. However, it was also agreed that before any such action was taken, consultations should be initiated with the country, as well as with governments of other Member countries affected or concerned by the measure[582];

577 Id. p. 87. See also WTO, supra note 8, p. 2.
578 Id. p. 2.
579 OECD Secretariat, "Recommendation of the Council concerning Common Principles of Shipping Policy for Member countries", Council Recommendation [(87)11(Final), 13 February 1987] amended on 28 September 2000 – C (2000)124/Final, available at: http://www.olis.oecd.org revisited in July 2006.
580 OECE supra note 7.
581 Id. p. 84.
582 Id. p. 84.

- Common approach to the application of competition policy to the liner shipping sector: Member countries agreed to prevent anti-competitive agreements and abuse of a dominant position by any commercial party, and to this end paid particular attention to the establishment of guidelines concerning competition policy as applied to liner shipping[583].

The first review of these Common Principles took place in 1998. The Maritime Transport Committee concluded that the Principles served a useful function in underpinning member countries' liberalization of shipping policies. These Principles were reviewed and extended again in late 1999 when the Maritime Transport Committee agreed to a number of new elements to reflect recent developments in the shipping sector. These new items, which were formally adopted by the OECD Council in September 2000 (C(2000)124/FINAL), covered the following points:

- Non-discriminatory treatment as regards the access to and use of maritime auxiliary services. The principle also provided that where these auxiliary services were commercially provided, there should be a free and fair competitive environment as regards their provision[584];
- Non-discriminatory treatment as regards the access to and use of services involving a sea leg in international maritime transport, as well as a free and fair competitive environment in regards to their provision[585];
- Measures relating to the promotion of safety, the protection of the environment and the prevention of substandard shipping[586].

In 1999, the OECD Secretariat circulated a discussion paper with the title of "Discussion Document on Regulatory Reform in International Maritime Transport"[587], in which it recommended that immunity from the application of anti-trust law for common rate

583 Id. p. 84.
584 Id. p. 85.
585 Id. p. 85.
586 Id. p. 85.
587 WTO, supra note 8, p. 16.

fixing by conferences be removed. However, when asked to comment on the discussion document's recommendations, some OECD members, including Finland, Germany, Japan, Korea, the Netherlands and the US, either rejected the proposal or called for further study of its long-term effects on trade and the shipping industry. The US noted that antitrust immunity for price-setting agreements has not inhibited new entrants from competing in the market, nor has the antitrust immunity slowed the pace of technical innovation[588]. Similarly, Japan pointed out that the fundamental goal of regulatory reform should not merely to promote competition, at the same time it must also ensure the stable supply and sound development of ocean-going services which satisfy shippers' demands[589].

A joint workshop involving the liner industry was held in May 2000 to examine the findings of the paper. The result was that ship-owners and some governments under the OECD noted that the current system of immunity was operating well and the liner industry had substantive differences in structure from other industries. Thus the exemption system was necessary to ensure the stability of services to shippers and there was no compelling reason for change[590].

In April 2002, the OECD issued the "Final Report of Competition Policy in Liner Shipping" (the Report)[591], which examined the impacts of common pricing under antitrust exemptions, the impacts of conference, discussion and stabilization agreements on the sector, as well as the potential effects of the removal of antitrust exemptions for liner shipping, in an attempt to determine

588 Id. p. 18.

589 Id. p. 18.

590 See OECD report DSTI/DOT/MTC (2000) 2. Besides, a 2000 World Bank Research Paper under the title of "Trade in international maritime services: how much does policy matter?" raised similar views as the OECD Paper. For conflicting opinions, see: "A review of trade in international maritime services" by the World Shipping Council, May 2001. The paper is available at the website of World Shipping Council: www.worldshipping.org revisited in August 2006.

591 OECD Division of Transport, DSTI/DOT (2002) 2, 16 April 2002. Paper available at: http://www.olis.oecd.org revisited in August 2007.

whether these antitrust exemptions were beneficial or harmful to society at large[592]. Important conclusions drawn from the Report included:

Firstly, the liner shipping industry has changed dramatically since its inception when the principle of conference price-fixing was initiated[593]. The advent of containerization and the arrival of new, strong and efficient independent operators have successively disrupted relatively tight-knit conferences. Most countries have increasingly sought to reduce the power of liner conferences and provide shippers with countervailing powers, which led to a limitation of antitrust exemptions, greater power for shippers and carriers to enter into one-on-one confidential contract negotiations and greater restrictions over the manner in which carriers seek to establish relationships with their competitors[594]. Subsequently, countries have generally chosen to retain some form of antitrust immunity for rate-fixing and/or extended this immunity for rate discussions and capacity agreements among competitors in return for the implementation of more shipper-friendly measures[595].

Moreover, no consensus existed as to liner shipping's impact on competition[596]. It was difficult to address the issue of destructive competition in liner shipping without access to specific cost data from carriers. While many models of liner markets have been developed, no consensus existed as to the most appropriate one for describing the dynamics of liner shipping[597].

Furthermore, liner shipping was now more competitive than at any time before[598]. As conference power weakened, carriers have sought to develop alternative strategies to ensure their ability to deliver regular liner shipping services. New and more flexible inter-carrier relationships have emerged allowing carriers to reduce their costs, widen service scope and increase service quality. Therefore,

592 Id. p. 74.
593 Id. p. 74.
594 Id. p. 74.
595 Id. p. 74.
596 Id. p. 75.
597 Id. p. 75.
598 Id. p. 76.

despite increased competition, many carriers were able to generate financial returns compared to other transport industry service providers. Widespread bankruptcies did not occurr and the industry was not characterized by service instability. More competition in liner shipping, far from leading to less reliable services has led to increases in service innovation and quality.

Based on the above examination, the Report drew the conclusion that anti-trust exemptions for conference price-fixing no longer served their stated purpose and were no longer relevant[599]. Recommendation under the title of "A way out of the impasse" was then put forward with three principles[600]. The first was the principle of freedom to negotiate, that suggested that shippers and carriers should always have the option of freely negotiating rates, surcharges and other terms of carriage on an individual and confidential basis. The second was the principle of freedom to protect Contracts under which carriers and shippers should always be able to contractually protect key terms of negotiated service contracts, including information regarding rates and this confidentiality should be given maximum protection. The third was the principle of freedom to coordinate operations whereby carriers should be able to pursue operational and/or capacity agreements with other carriers as long as these did not confer undue market power to the parties involved.

The Report believed these three principles represented a way of addressing the carrier/shipper impasse since they allowed shippers and carriers to better control what contract information the other parties to their negotiations could share. They were also meant to co-exist with a regulatory regime that continued to extend antitrust exemptions to price-fixing and rate discussions in the liner-shipping sector. However, it might be the case that while under this format the ability of carriers to agree on common rates for customers not covered by individual contracts was unimpaired, their ability to utilize confidential information to set common rates and benchmarks could be limited[601].

599 Id. p. 77.
600 Id. p. 79.
601 Id. p. 80.

6.3 Selected Regional and Domestic Regulatory Systems

Although most countries provide liner conferences with anti-competition exemption, there has been little consistency in the policies or in their application. Likewise, neither has there been a concerted effort to ensure compatibility between different kinds of agreements in liner industry. The consequence is that great divergence exists among countries' national competition laws. For example, the balance of competition policy in the EU and the US is quite different, where in the EU, not only economic goals, but also some other aspects of the society, cultural, political and social goals receive consideration in competition policy[602].

6.3.1 EU Block Exemption System

6.3.1.1 Block Exemption for Liner Conferences: Regulation 4056/86

Regulation 4056/86[603] was adopted in December 1986 for "laying down detailed rules for the application of Articles 85 and 86 of the Treaty to maritime transport", which elaborated the conditions and obligations under which liner conferences operate. Building on the basic spirit of the UN Liner Code Convention, the Regulation demonstrated the EU's positive attitude at that time towards

602 Joseph P. Griffin, "EC/US Antitrust Cooperation Agreement: Impact on Transnational Business", (1993), Law and Policy in International Business, 1051; Diane P. Wood, "The Impossible Dream: Real International Antitrust", (1992), University of Chicago Legal Forum; Eleanor M. Fox, "The End of Antitrust Isolationism: The Vision of One World", (1992), University of Chicago Legal Forum; WTO, Working Group on the Interaction between Trade and Competition Policy, Communication from Hong Kong, China, "Contribution of Competition Policy to Achieving the Objectives of the WTO", WT/WGTCP/W/118 (May 26, 1999).

603 OJ L 378 31.12.1986. The legal text of the Regulation can be found at EU website: http://ec.europa.eu revisited in May 2006.

the concept of liner conferences. This was clearly reflected in the Preamble:

> Whereas liner conferences have a stabilizing effect, assuring shippers of reliable services; whereas they contribute generally to providing adequate efficient scheduled maritime transport services and give fair consideration to the interests of users; whereas such results cannot be obtained without the co-operation that shipping companies promote within conferences in relation to rates and, where appropriate, availability of capacity or allocation of cargo for shipment, and income; whereas in most cases conferences continue to be subject to effective competition...[604]

Some of the main elements of the Regulation include[605]:

- It applies to international maritime transport services to or from a Community port.
- The Regulation specifically excludes tramp vessel services.
- Any regulation of bulk shipping is left to national authorities and courts.
- A group exemption is enacted for agreements, decisions and concerted practices of all or part of the members of one or more liner conferences which operate on the basis of common or uniform rates and also engage in one or more joint activities such as scheduling of sailing and the regulation of the carrying capacity offered by the member lines[606].

Regulation 4056/86 is complemented by Commission Regulation 823/2000, which provides for a block exemption for liner shipping consortia, the other main form of co-operation between liner shipping operators.

The most distinctive feature of Regulation 823/2000 is the group exemption that Article 3 contains in respect of horizontal price fixing by liner shipping conferences[607]. Exemption is also granted

604 Id.

605 Id. More information of the Regulation is available at the Eur-lex of the EU website, where the official documents of the EU can be searched, under: http://europa.eu.int accessed in February 2002 and revisited in August 2005.

606 Id.

607 Id. Article 3 "Exemption for agreements between carriers concerning the operation of scheduled maritime transport services".

to other activities if one or more of these are carried on by the members of liner conferences in addition to fixing prices and conditions of carriage for maritime transport services. The other activities include:

- the coordination of shipping time-tables, sailing dates or dates of calls;
- the determination of the frequency of sailing or calls;
- the co-ordination or allocation of sailings or calls among members of the conferences;
- the regulation of the carrying capacity offered by each member; and,
- the allocation of cargo or revenue among members[608].

Some scholars argue that the block exemption in the Regulation is both exceptional and the most generous in Community competition law, especially because it is unlimited in time and it allows price-fixing between competitors of a sort that is normally regarded as a serious kind of restrictive practice[609]. In accordance with general principles[610] and influenced by the broad scope of the group exemption, the Commission has sought to interpret Article 3 in a narrow way. The general approach is deemed to be endorsed by the Court of First Instance in the CEWAL case[611]

The Commission's approach applying the competition rules to liner conference agreements has two basic principles. Firstly, ex-

608 Id.

609 See for example, Felix Dinger, supra note 531, p. 11.

610 See Case C-70/93, BMW v ALD (1995) ECR I-3439, at paragraph 28 and Case C-266/93, Bundeskartellamt v Volkswagen and VAG, (1995) ECR I-3477, at paragraph 33: "...having regard to the general principle prohibiting anti-competitive agreements laid down in Article 85 (1) of the Treaty, provisions in a block exemption which derogate from that principle cannot be interpreted widely and cannot be construed in such a way as to extend the effects of the regulation beyond what is necessary to protect the interests which they are intended to safeguard".

611 Joined cases T-24-26/93 and T-28/93, Compagnie maritime belge transports SA and Compagnie maritime belge SA, Dafra-Lines A/S, Deutsche Afrika-Linien GmbH & Co. and Nedlloyd Lijnen BV v Commission, ECR (1996) II-1201.

ternal exemption is an essential factor for the granting of the block exemption and competition should not be eliminated on the trade or trades served by a conference. Secondly, the block exemption for conferences is an exception from the basic prohibition of cartel agreements contained in Article 81 (1) and like other exceptions from a general rule, it shall be interpreted strictly. Therefore, the exemption in Regulation 4056/86 applies only to the maritime activities of liner conferences that fall within its terms and cannot apply to other restrictive agreements between shipping companies[612].

Article 4 of the Regulation provides that the exemption contained in Article 3 is conditional upon the fact that differentiated rates and conditions of carriage that disadvantage ports, transport users or carriers must be economically justified[613]. The Regulation is based on the assumption that discrimination without economic justification causes detriment, both to the completion of the internal market and to particular ports and regions. Moreover, Article 4 contains an express severance clause providing that, if it can be served; only that part of any agreement or decision not complying with the non-discrimination provision shall automatically be void pursuant to Article 81 (2) of the Treaty. It remains unclear whether such severance applies also to other non-exempt behaviours.

The Commission holds the view that the group exemption in the Regulation does not allow ship-owners jointly to fix prices for the inland leg of a multi-modal transport operation, such as a movement from factory to port. Such price-fixing by conferences is deemed unlawful and remains punishable if the Commission is not notified[614].

If the Commission believes that the group exemption does not extend to agreements fixing prices for inland transport, then any such agreements must benefit from an individual exemption under Article 81 (3) of the Regulation. Inland price fixing should be demonstrated as indispensable to the improvement in services or in

612 Felix Dinger, supra note 531.
613 Supra note 603, Article 4 "Condition attaching to exemption".
614 Supra note 603, Article 5 "Obligations attaching to exemption".

order to bring about price reduction. The mere fact that ship-owners are offering door-to-door services, or the fact that they wish to fix prices for door-to-door services to prevent price competition, is not sufficient to qualify for exemption.[615] In order to assess applications for exemption from inland price fixing, a committee was established by the Commission with the name of the Multi-modal Group. In December 1997, the Final Report of the Multi-modal Group was issued[616]. It concluded that there was no reason to grant an exemption to collective inland price fixing by conferences.

The justification for the block exemption for liner conference agreements is given in the 8th recital of the preamble to Regulation 4056/86, which states:

> Whereas provision should be made for block exemption of liner conferences; whereas liner conferences have a stabilizing effect, assuring shippers of reliable services; whereas they contribute generally to providing adequate efficient scheduled maritime transport services and give fair consideration to the interests of users; whereas such results cannot be obtained without the cooperation that shipping companies promote within conferences in relation to rates and, where appropriate, availability of capacity or allocation of cargo for shipment, and income; whereas in most cases conferences continue to be subject to effective competition from both non-conference scheduled services and, in certain circumstances, from tramp services and from other modes of transport; whereas the mobility of fleets, which is a characteristic feature of the structure of availability in the shipping field, subjects conferences to constant competition which they are unable as a rule to eliminate as far as a substantial proportion of the shipping services in question is concerned.[617]

The Regulation assumed that price-fixing and supply regulation within conferences led to stability of freight rates, which in turn assured shippers of reliable scheduled maritime transport services.

615 Mensching, J., "Liner Shipping: Examining the Development and Impact of European Legislation", European Commission Competition Directorate-General, Speech given at Containerization International, 3rd Annual Conference "Global 2000", London, 22 March, 2000.

616 Office for Official Publication of the European Communities, 1998; ISBN 92-828-2934-0.

617 Supra note 603.

6.3.1.2 Block Exemption for Liner Consortia and Mergers

Commission Regulation 870/95[618] was adopted in April 1995 with the purpose of

> clarifying the conditions to be met by the consortia in order to benefit from the block exemption and to promote technical and economic progress by facilitating and encouraging greater utilization of containers and more efficient use of vessel capacity[619].

Article 1 and Recitals 1 to 5 of the Regulation give a broad definition of consortia ranging from the highly integrated to those agreements where co-operation is minimal, sometimes referred to as technical agreements, the purpose of which is to include agreements that cover vessels, equipment and terminal rationalization[620]. Article 1 of the Regulation defines a consortium as:

> An agreement between two or more vessel-operating carriers which provide international liner shipping services exclusively for the carriage of cargo, chiefly by container, relating to a particular trade and the object of which is to bring about co-operation in the joint operation of a maritime transport service, which improves the service which would be offered individually by each of its members in the absence of the consortium, in order to rationalize their operations by means of technical, operational and/or commercial arrangements, with the exception of price-fixing.[621]

618 Commission Regulation 870/95 on the application of Article 85 (3) of the Treaty to certain categories of agreements, decisions and concerted practices between liner shipping companies (consortia) pursuant to Council Regulation 479/92. The full text of the Regulation is available at: http://ec.europa.eu revisited in August 2007. For comments on this regulation, see Eric Van Ginderachter and Serge Durande, "EC Regulation 870/95: The Consortia Block Exemption", European Transport Law Vol. XXXVI No. 2-1996, pp. 241–264.

619 Working paper of DGIV (Directorate General): "Report on Commission Regulation No. 870/95, Liner Shipping Consortia", Brussels, 28 January 1999, p. 9. Paper available at: http://ec.europa.eu revisited in August 2007.

620 Id. p. 9.

621 Id. p. 9.

The DGIV Working Paper notes that one of the most important issues in the Regulation includes a maximum trade share calculation. A consortium that has a trade share higher than 50 per cent will not benefit from the group exemption, but which, upon notification of the Commission, may be granted individual exemption if certain conditions are fulfilled. By contrast, a consortium with a trade share of below 30 per cent (or 35 per cent depending on whether it operates within a conference) will automatically benefit from the group exemption. For a consortium holding a market share of between 30 (or 35) per cent and 50 per cent, a more simplified opposition procedure is available under which the group qualifies for exemption unless the Commission objects within six months of its notification[622]

The DGIV Working Paper further points out that there exist a number of issues concerning the relationship between Regulation 4056/86 and Regulation 870/95, in particular regarding the circumstances under which liner shipping companies can benefit from both block exemptions. There are questions concerning the choice of regulation under which agreements should be notified and the consequence of such a choice[623]. Recital 8 to Regulation 870/95 states that the block exemption applies to both consortia operating within and outside a conference except in respect of price-fixing of freight rates. A consortium operating within a conference can apply for exemption under Regulation 4056/86, while a consortium operating outside a conference which wishes to fix rates, but fails to fulfill the conditions for the block exemption contained in Regulation 4056/86, must apply for an individual exemption (Recital 9). It is believed that such an arrangement avoids the possibility that consortia operating outside a conference are disadvantaged compared to those consortia operating within a conference[624].

622 Id. p. 11. The notification period may be extended if the Commission considers the notification to be incomplete and decides to start to run again once the missing information is supplied.

623 Id. p. 12.

624 Id. p. 12.

In addition, one of the conditions attached to the exemption under Article 9 of Regulation 870/95 is the obligation to hold consultations with shippers and transport users. The DGIV Working Paper has clarified that these consultations are restricted to those issues relating directly to the consortium service[625].

In April 2000, the EC adopted Regulation (EEC) No 823/2000[626] renewing the block exemption for liner shipping consortia embodied in Commission Regulation (EEC) No 870/95, the five years' validity of which expired on 25 April 2000. The Commission's favourable attitude towards consortia is mainly due to the cooperative nature of this kind of arrangement. Liner consortia have contributed to the improvement of productivity and the quality of liner transport services by rationalizing the activities of member companies and achieving economies of scale[627].

Besides extending the block exemption for a further five years, Regulation 823/2000 provides that the block exemption also applies to consortia operating in more than one trade[628], and that the market share thresholds are required to be met in respect of each market in which such a consortium operates[629]. The most important change that Regulation 823/2000 makes to the block exemption compared with Regulation 870/95 is the use of market share thresholds instead of trade share thresholds, which is the usual indication of market power used in competition legislation. The reason for adopting trade share criteria in the previous regulation was that the shipping companies had assumed that market shares would be difficult to calculate, while later it was shown that it was quite possible for shipping companies to provide market shares[630].

625 Id. p. 12.

626 O J L 100, 20. 4. 2000, pp. 24–30. Full text is available at: http://ec.europa.eu revisited in May 2006.

627 DG Competition Consultation Document on the Renewal of Commission Regulation No. 823/3000, Consortia Block Exemption, available at: http://ec.europa.eu revisited in August 2007, p. 1.

628 Supra note 626, text of the Regulation, Article 1 on scope of the Regulation.

629 Supra note 626, text of the Regulation, Articles 6 on conditions relating to market share and 7 on opposition procedure.

630 DG Document supra note 627, p. 3.

According to the Regulation, in order to qualify for the exemption provided, a consortium must possess for each market in which it operates a market share of under 30 per cent (calculated by reference to the volume of goods carried) when it operates within a conference and under 35 per cent when it operates outside a conference. The exemption shall continue to apply if this market share is exceeded during any period of two consecutive calendar years by not more than one tenth. Where the above limits are exceeded, the exemption shall continue to apply for a period of six months following the end of the calendar year during which it is exceeded[631]. Moreover, the exemption provided in the Regulation shall also apply to a consortium whose market share for any market in which it operates exceeds the limits laid down above, but does not exceed 50 percent, providing that the agreements in question are notified to the Commission in accordance with the provisions of Commission Regulation (EC) No 2843/98 and that the Commission does not oppose such exemption within a period of six months[632].

6.3.1.3 Purported Merits of the Block Exemption System

The EU's block exemption system for liner shipping provides exemptions that are strictly limited and subject to legal oversight. The system serves the interest of shippers, since the liner services are better able to cope with severe and sudden imbalances in trade flows and with intense seasonal fluctuations[633]. This in turn helps to prevent price fluctuations and helps liner operators to commit to the long term investments that are required to operate their high value assets such as ships, containers and logistics infrastructure.

631 Supra note 626, text of the Regulation, Article 6 on conditions relating to market share.

632 Supra note 626, text of the Regulation, Article 7 on opposition procedure.

633 Peter Marlow and Rawindaran Nair, "Liner Shipping and information exchange – a European Perspective", Transport and Shipping Research Group, Logistics and Operations Management Section, Cardiff Business School, Cardiff University, UK, p. 5.

Commissioned by the Competition Directorate General of the EC, an international team of maritime economists associated with Erasmus University in Rotterdam, analyzed the economic issues related to liner conference in 2003[634]. The findings indicate that liner conferences do not operate as price-fixing cartels, and that, under the block exemption system, they play a complex role as platforms to discuss prices and the related cost levels. While the presence of liner conferences can cause prices to decline, these declines will be relatively stable since each player in the market has access to conference pricing information[635]. Liner shipping conferences that have limited authority to control membership pricing or service frequency have virtually no ability to collectively raise rates. On the contrary, they may foster more competition in the market as a whole. An observation could be made that, liner shipping conferences have little market power and, in fact, compared to a classical cartel situation, may actually heighten competition among both members and independent operators[636].

Based on their research for the EC, the team recommended that the appropriate way forward was to ensure a regulatory policy for liner shipping that maintains a limited antitrust exemption for liner shipping companies that wish to form conferences or trade agreements, while at the same time ensuring that conditions are in place to safeguard the longevity, sustainability and success of liner shipping operational alliances[637].

634 Id. p. 6. Erasmus Universiteit Rotterdam. Final report prepared for European Commission, Competition DG Services/Transport, Rotterdam, 12 November 2003.

635 Id. p. 6.

636 Id. p. 6.

637 Id. p. 6.

6.3.2 US Antitrust Immunity System for Liner Shipping

6.3.2.1 Pre-1984 Regime

The Alexander Committee Report of 1914

The US has a very long history of antitrust laws, economic analysis of the relevant product market, entry barriers and efficiencies that have all played a central role in many antitrust investigations by government agencies and courts alike[638]. On most occasions, the analysis of antitrust law focuses on economic efficiency and consumer welfare in terms of non-restriction of output and prices. The US courts regard that the priority of antitrust law is to promote economic efficiency, to keep markets competitive and to protect the competitive process[639]. According to the US Supreme Court, the US competition policies and antitrust laws have been based on the premise

> that the unrestrained interaction of competitive forces will yield the best allocation of our economic resources, the lowest prices, the highest quality and the greatest material progress, while at the same time, providing an environment conductive to the preservation of our democratic political and social institutions[640].

Right back in 1789, the US was active in this area, when the first act of the first Congress imposed a protective tariff on imported goods and allowed a 10 per cent reduction on goods imported on US ships. Moreover, a heavier port tonnage tax was also levied on

638 See for example, Rudolf J. R. Peritz, *Competition Policy in America, 1888–1892: History, Rhetoric, Law,* New York: Oxford University Press, 1996. More information on the antitrust law history of US is available from the website of American Antitrust Institute at: http://www.antitrustinstitute.org revisited in May 2006.

639 WTO, Working Group on the Interaction between Trade and Competition Policy, Communication from the United States, WT/WGTCP/W/35, Oct. 1, 1997.

640 Northern Pac. Ry. v. United States, 356 U. S. 1, 4 (1958) Accord NCAA v. Bd. of Regents of University of Oklahoma, 468 US 85, 104 n. 27 (1984).

foreign built and owned ships and only ships built in the US could be registered under the American flag[641].

The Alexander Committee Report of 1914 was issued by the House Merchant Marine and Fisheries Committee of the US Congress under the chairmanship of Joshua Alexander[642]. The Committee concluded that, while it would be undesirable to allow completely free and open competition in the shipping market, which might lead to instability and uncertainty, conferences should still be brought under a measure of governmental control. This recommendation was later enacted in the 1916 US Shipping Act, which was the first time that conferences in the US trades were brought under regulations. It was also at that time that conferences in the US were given immunity from process under US antitrust laws.

Shipping Act of 1916

In 1916, the US Shipping Act was enacted, which illustrated an early attempt to impose economic regulation on the maritime industry. It also marked as a turning point for liner conferences, as it was the first occasion that a governmental authority was empowered to intervene in commercial decisions as well as service conditions of conferences[643]. The new legislation brought conferences under the regulatory control of the Interstate Commerce Commission (the Commission)[644] in respect of the rates of freight and terms

641 DA Irwin, "The Early Trade Policy Experience of the United States, 1789–1820", Department of Economics, University of Virginia, 2002. Paper available at: http://www.virginia.edu revisited in August 2007.

642 The Alexander Report was submitted in 1914 to the 63rd Congress and a bill to carry out its recommendations was introduced but not passed. H.R. 17328, 63d Cong., 2d Sess. In the following Congress substantially the same bill was reintroduced, H.R. 15455, 64th Cong., 1st Sess., and became the Shipping Act of 1916. Source of information: http://caselaw.lp.findlaw.com revisited in August 2006.

643 Claude A. Thompson, "Shipping Act of 1916: The Effect of Section 15 on the Sherman Anti-trust Law", Michigan Law Review, Vol. 22, No. 2 (Dec. 1923), pp. 107–117.

644 Later, the regulation of liner shipping in the US trades was handed to the Federal Maritime Board and then to the FMC which holds the responsibili-

of contracts. The Commission was particularly authorized to disapprove agreements filed if they were found to be discriminatory or detrimental to the commerce of the United States. Moreover, the Commission was given the ability to investigate complaints if any rates were unfair. If it assumed proper, it may disapprove the rate, however it was not entitled to set new ones[645].

The 1916 Act also featured rebating in favour of one shipper, the prohibition of discrimination favouring one port as against another, the charging of equal rates on all shippers irrespective of their size, the prohibition of fighting ships[646], and the making unlawful of the deferred rebate system in regard to outbound shipments[647].

The Bonner Amendments of 1961

In 1961, the Bonner amendments (named after the Congressman who chaired the House special sub-committee on Merchant Marine and Fisheries) were enacted[648]. According to the preamble, the amendments aimed at "authorizing common carriers and conferences thereof serving the foreign commerce of the US, to enter into effective and fair dual rate contracts with shippers and con-

---

ties today, though in different terms. Source of information: American Law Sources Online, at: http://www.lawsource.com revisited in August 2006.

645 "Rate Regulation in Ocean Shipping", Harvard Law Review, Vol. 78, No. 3 (Jan. 1965), pp. 635–654.

646 Fighting ships were supposed to drive away non-conference competition. They were put on the berth by conference lines in opposition to outsider lines, and they charged rates sufficiently below those of the competitors, in order to drive them away for lack of cargo.

647 At that time, the deferred rebate system was only used in relation to inward shipments to the US, with outward ones unlawful. As a later stage however, the US put both inwards and outwards shipments under its applicable law, included those activities completely outside the US while had some effect within its shores, under the excuse of "effects doctrine". Source of information: American Law Sources Online, at: http://www.lawsource.com revisited in August 2006.

648 James S. Gordon, "Shipping Regulation and the Federal Maritime Commission: Part I", The University of Chicago Law Review, Vol. 37, No. 1 (autumn 1969), pp. 90–158.

signees and for other purposes"[649]. They required that the conferences to and from the US be "open" to all qualified operators, a requirement that became known as the open conference system. Besides confirming some of the previous principles in the legislations (e.g., the deferred rebate system should not be used), the amendments provided the FMC with wider and stricter government powers, some of which were considered offensive by ship-owners and governments of other countries[650]. It was against this background that the 1960s saw a trend of rapid and intensive involvement of many governments, in the rule-making procedures applying to liner conferences, with the aim of protecting their ship-owners and traders. Many defensive pieces of legislation and formal agreements emerged during this period[651].

649 Id.

650 Examples of such regulations include: (a) Agreements between conference lines and their shippers not only had to be approved by the FMC, but had to be in a standard form laid down by it. This probably would result in the situation that the agreements of this nature between two persons outside the US and subject to their own national laws must be bound by the FMC-prescribed form. (b) The FMC was authorized to ensure that freight rates to and from the US be fair and non-discriminatory, and not detrimental to the commerce of the US. This requirement of controlling both outward rates and inward rates could be detrimental to the trade of other countries, who are entitled to control their own export rates. Source of information: American Law Sources Online, at: http://www.lawsource.com revisited in August 2006.

651 Examples include: (a) The minute on the exchange of shipping information of 1964, negotiated through the OECD, in which the ship-owners agreed to give a small amount of information sought by the FMC for the governments to collate and aggregate; (b) The enactment of the "Shipping Contracts and Commercial Documents Act" 1964 by the British government, in order to secure Her Majesty's jurisdiction against encroachment by certain foreign requirements in respect of the carriage of goods or passengers by sea, and in respect of the production of documents and furnishing information, under which directions were issued to forbid certain conference lines from providing information to FMC when they were asked by FMC to do so, on grounds that the disclosure would not be in Britain's public interest. Source of information: American Law Sources Online, at: http://www.lawsource.com revisited in August 2006.

6.3.2.2 Ocean Shipping Reform Act 1998

The pre-1984 regime for regulating liner shipping was generalized as interventionist, under which the FMC played a deciding role in monitoring shipping agreements and anti-competitive practices. The 1984 Shipping Act[652] reduced the level of government intervention in liner shipping. Under this Act, ship-owners kept the power to form open conferences and shippers were allowed to form associations to protect themselves from exploitation by conferences possessing market power.

By giving the authority the power to approve inter-modal conference agreements and new forms of contracts with shippers, this Act helps to clarify the anti-trust position of lines and sets up a new approach for the establishment of joint ventures and other methods of rationalization. Under the Act, conferences are allowed to quote a through rate. However they are not allowed to negotiate the inland rate, which can only be done by individual lines. Moreover, conferences are required to permit any conference member to take independent action on any rate or service, after which that new level or agreed item becomes available to other shippers as well. The Act also allows the authorization of service contracts with individual shippers or shippers' associations, subject to the filing of their essential terms, which would then also become available to other shippers in similar situation[653].

The Ocean Shipping Reform Act 1998[654] (the OSRA, effective May 1, 1999) amended the Shipping Act 1984 and was expected to lead to increased competition in the ocean transport industry

652 Legal text of the Act is available at the website of Maritime Administration, Department of Transport, US: http://www.marad.dot.gov/publications revisited in May 2006.

653 Richard E. Neel, Carl W. Wooding and Jerry H. Padgett, "Proposed Ocean Shipping Reform Act's likely effects on conferences and rates", International Advances in Economic Research, Vol. 2, No. 4/November 1996, pp. 477–483.

654 Legal text of the Act is available at the website of Maritime Administration, Department of Transport, US: http://www.marad.dot.gov/publications revisited in May 2006.

by providing more flexibility for shippers, carriers and government regulators[655]. It introduced significant changes to the regulatory regime in the US although there were also substantial levels of continuity. For instance, like the 1984 Shipping Act, the OSRA applies to common carriers, ocean freight forwarders and marine terminal operators. Both conference agreements and non-conference co-operative agreements are regulated under the OSRA[656].

There are a number of important points of difference between the two Acts.

- In the first place, the OSRA allows members of conferences and other forms of agreement to negotiate confidential individual service contracts with shippers and their associations, a right that also applies to unaffiliated shippers, previously not allowed to enter into such contracts;
- Secondly, the OSRA eliminates the obligation of ocean common carriers and conferences to file their tariffs with the FMC and to seek for approve, although tariffs still need to be made public in electronic form;
- Thirdly, while contracts still have to be filed with the FMC, the disclosure of detailed freight rates negotiated with individual customers is no longer needed under the OSRA;
- Fourthly, the OSRA authorizes the FMC to take action against owners, operators, agents or masters of foreign vessels who exercise anti-competitive pricing practices;
- Finally, under the OSRA, carriers are permitted to undertake joint negotiations with railroads, trucking companies and airlines for the inland transportation component of inter-modal services[657].

655 Cargo Systems, "the Future of the Container Shipping Industry", London: Cargo Systems, 1999, p. 20.

656 The following types of agreement between non-conference lines are subject to the OSRA: agreement to discuss rates and conditions of services; agreements to pool or apportion revenue, earnings or losses; agreements to regulate sailings or the volume of cargo carried; agreements to engage in exclusive, preferential or co-operative working arrangements; agreements to regulate the use of service contracts.

657 Neel, Wooding and Padgett, supra note 653.

On moving from the Shipping Act of 1984 to the OSRA, the regulation increased the requirements for conferences to allow member lines greater freedom to price independently. In the 1984 Act, this was to set rates independently on notice. In the OSRA, this was extended by requiring conferences to allow shippers and carriers to sign confidential contracts independently[658], which has resulted in the cessation of a number of conference agreements.

The OSRA provides for an orderly transition to a more deregulated ocean-shipping environment. It gives shippers and common carriers greater choice and flexibility in entering into contractual relationships with shippers for ocean transportation and inter-modal services[659]. The most significant contribution of the OSRA, according to FMC, is the right of members of ocean carrier agreements to negotiate and enter into service contracts with one or more shippers independent of the agreement. This helps to reduce the expense of the tariff filing system and privatize the function of publishing tariff information, while maintaining current enforcement and common carriage principles with regard to tariff shipments.[660] At the same time, it protects US exporters from disclosure to their foreign competitors of their contractual relationships with common carriers and proprietary business information, including targeted markets. Furthermore, the OSRA reforms the licensing and bonding requirements for ocean freight forwarders and the NVOCCs, and consolidates the definitions of those two entities under the term "ocean transportation intermediary". It also strengthens the provisions of the 1984 Act, the Foreign Shipping Practices Act of 1988 and section 19 of the Merchant Marine Act, 1920 which prohibited unfair foreign shipping

658 This requirement brings US law in accord with the view of the EU Competition Directorate that prohibition by conferences of individual service contracts was contrary to EC Regulation 4056/86.

659 US Federal Maritime Commission, "The Impact of the Ocean Shipping Reform Act of 1998", September 2001, p. 8. Information can also be found in: US Federal Maritime Commission, "The Ocean Shipping Reform Act: An Interim Status Report", June 2000.

660 WTO background paper, supra note 8, p. 17.

practices in order to provide greater protection from certain discriminatory actions[661].

Under the OSRA, common carriers may enter into agreements to discuss, fix or regulate transport rates, including through-rates. Conferences and groups of ocean carriers are permitted to negotiate inland haulage rates or services with rail and trucking operators. Conferences are asked to open to new members, allowing lines to withdraw without penalty and to take independent action on any tariff rate or service item after giving not more than five days' notice. Some important regulating provisions of the OSRA include:

Service contracts

The 1984 Act provided the specific statutory authority for vessel-operating common carriers and conferences to enter into service contracts with shippers and shippers' associations[662]. Service contracts stipulated the terms and conditions whereby the shipper commited to a certain volume of cargo over a fixed time period in exchange for the carrier's commitment to charge a certain rate and provide a defined level of service. According to the FMC Interim Report, one of the attractions of shipping under service contracts is the ability of the parties to negotiate and tailor contracts to meet their specific shipping needs[663].

Under the OSRA, the statutory authority to allow service contracting by all agreements between carriers instead of just between conferences has been expanded. Any agreement setting mandatory rules or requirements that may obstruct the right of their members to enter into individual service contracts is prohibited. In addition, the OSRA has enhanced the confidentiality of service contracts between shippers and ocean common carriers. Although service contracts are still required to be filed with the FMC as before, fewer essential items are filed as public information now. The rates are not longer publicly filed and the only terms made

661 Id. pp. 8–10.
662 FMC Interim Report on OSRA, supra note 659, p. 17.
663 Id. p. 17.

public are the origin and destination port ranges, the commodity or commodities involved, the minimum volume or portion and the duration of the contract[664].

The parties to a contract are permitted to agree on provisions for keeping all, or a portion of, the contract confidential from their competitors. Shippers do have the option of entering into service contracts individually, through a shippers' association or through a group of unrelated shippers, and contracts may be negotiated for a portion of a shipper's cargo as opposed to a fixed quantity. Moreover, the authority to offer joint service contracts has been expanded from conferences alone to any agreement among ocean common carriers[665].

Agreements

The OSRA has maintained antitrust immunity for the concerted carrier actions under agreements, while limiting the permissible activities to which such immunity applies. Under the OSRA, agreements may no longer limit or prohibit service contracting by their members. Agreements are also prohibited which require members to disclose their service contract negotiations or the details of any contracts into which they have entered[666]. An agreement may publish guidelines applicable to members' individual contracting practices, but the guidelines shall be voluntary and non-enforceable by the agreement and filed confidentially with the Commission.

Tariffs

One of the most important changes concerning tariff in the OSRA is that the requirement for carriers to file their tariffs with FMC has been eliminated. Instead, carriers are allowed to develop and utilize their own electronic systems for notifying the public of the prices and practices applicable to their various shipping services[667]. The

664 Id. p. 18. See also FMC 2001 Report, supra note 659, pp. 2–3.
665 Id. p. 19.
666 Id. pp. 25–26.
667 Id. pp. 38–39.

public must be provided with access to information on tariffs, although a reasonable charge may be made for such access. The FMC is authorized to prescribe requirements for the accessibility and accuracy of carriers' automated tariff systems. Since the OSRA came into effect, the FMC has conducted several audits to examine tariff accessibility which found different strengths and weaknesses of the tariff system. Moreover, the OSRA also rules that marine terminal operators may make schedules of rates, regulations and practices including any limitations of liability publicly available[668].

Ocean transportation intermediaries

The OSRA applied a new term to define both freight forwarders and the NVOCCs, ocean transportation intermediaries (OTIs). It requires that all OTIs in the US obtain a license[669], and it authorized the FMC to reevaluate the amount of financial information required of these entities and to set up an alternative procedure for pursuing a claim against an OTI[670].

Given the importance of the US economy to world trade, and given also that the OSRA will deregulate tariffs and service contracting practices in US foreign shipping lanes, the new Act will have a substantial impact on the international liner shipping industry. The OSRA is believed to have brought about the following changes[671]:

- There will be a tendency for conferences to be replaced by discussion agreements;
- Freight rates will initially fall as carriers seek to secure cargo volumes under individual contracts. As this in turn will lead to an intensification of the financial pressure on carriers;
- Larger shippers will secure freight rate advantages over smaller shippers;

668 Id. p. 39.
669 Id. p. 34.
670 Id. p. 34.
671 World Shipping Council, "The Ocean Shipping Reform Act of 1998: Achieving Success", paper available at the website of World Shipping Council: www.worldshipping.org revisited in August 2007.

- Smaller shippers will react by pooling cargo volumes and forming shipper associations;
- Carriers will use IT as a marketing and pricing tool, although initially the value-added component of IT capability may have to be given away in negotiations with shippers;
- The OSRA will be the catalyst in raising innovative carriers above the lowest common denominator pricing mentality that has dominated the market; and
- Successful carriers will establish long-term contractual relationships with major clients across global trade lanes, thus becoming an integral part of the global supply chain and guaranteeing future cargoes.

Since the passage of the OSRA, discussion agreements have tended to replace conference agreements as the primary vehicle for concerted carrier activity. The FMC notes that, as of mid-2000, there was only one conference operating in the major east-west trade, the TACA. The majority of the remaining conference agreements relating to the US are in the Latin American trades[672].

The majority of carrier agreements filed since the passage of the OSRA are operational agreements, most of which include vessel-sharing arrangements. The FMC argues that the continued filing of such agreements indicates that carriers are still making use of antitrust immunity to rationalize service and lower their costs[673]. The FMC notes that the use of service contracts has grown substantially since they were first authorized by the 1984 Act. The FMC's examination of 408 contracts entered into by the top 13 ocean carriers operating in the US foreign trades suggests that most post-OSRA service contracts are individual rather than group contracts, stemming from one-to-one negotiation between shippers and carriers[674].

672 FMC, supra note 659, p. 28.

673 Id., p. 29.

674 Id. p. 30. The FMC emphasizes that the contracts reviewed did not constitute a random statistical sample. The FMC notes also that because the OSRA was enacted in May, during one of the heaviest periods of contract renewal, most shipper-carrier contracts in 1999 varied little from traditional contracts. The flexibility introduced by the OSRA became apparent in the new contracts negotiated in 2000.

There have been few contracts between shippers and conferences in this period. The majority of contracts which involve only one trade lane and a one-year contract appears to remain the industry standard. While many of the contracts contain no confidentiality provisions, the use of confidentiality provisions varies greatly among carriers. For some carriers, confidentiality provisions are a standard part of contracts, while other carriers include confidentiality provisions only when requested by a shipper[675].

The OSRA has provided a predictable, competitive and relatively successful regulatory system that is compatible with the laws of the US's trading partners. At the same time, the OSRA is trying to make the liner shipping industry more market-driven with conferences giving way to more relaxed types of agreements[676]. As the FMC noted in its Interim Status Report:

> Shippers are negotiating one-on-one with carriers for contract terms. The number of conferences is declining, leaving discussion agreements – which are prohibited from imposing binding commitments on their members – as the primary means for carriers to exercise their antitrust immunity with regard to rate levels. Indications are that rates and services increasingly are being driven by market forces[677].

The US regulators hold the view that whatever forms they may take, carrier agreements are necessary for providing stable and reliable international liner services, that antitrust immunity for price setting agreements has not inhibited new entrants from competing in the market, and that antitrust immunity has not slowed the pace of technical innovation[678].

675 Id. p. 32.
676 World Shipping Council, supra note 671.
677 FMC Interim Report, supra note 659, p. ii.
678 Id. See also APEC: Transparency Exercise Questionnaire, 2000, available at APEC website: http://www.apec-tptwg.org.cn visited in August 2006.

Part Three

Jurisdiction and Dispute Settlement

7 Dispute Settlement Mechanisms under the WTO and the LOS Convention

7.1 The Dispute Settlement Mechanism under the WTO

7.1.1 Dispute Settlement Provisions under the GATS

The dispute settlement regulations of the GATS are contained in Articles XXII and XXIII of the Agreement[679]. Two types of complaints are allowed in the GATS: the violation complaint and the non-violation complaint[680]. For a violation complaint, Article XXIII: 1 of the GATS provides that if a member country considers that another country has failed to carry out its obligations under the GATS, it may have recourse to the Dispute Settlement Understanding (DSU). Because the GATS does not apply nullification or impairment as a requirement in addition to the failure to carry out obligations, Article 3.8 of the DSU is of no relevance to complaints brought under the GATS[681]. On the other hand, similar to the approach of the GATT 94 for non-violation complaint, a member country can allege nullification or impairment of a benefit that it could reasonably expect, in order to accrue to it under a specific commitment of another Member in the absence of a conflict with the provisions of the GATS[682].

New legal problems have been raised in the dispute settlement proceedings of the GATS, which are brought about by the broader coverage of the GATS, the different modalities of international

679 These provisions are contained in Annex 1B of the WTO Agreement.

680 WTO, dispute settlement system training module: chapter 4 – legal basis for a dispute, available at WTO website: http://www.wto.org revisited in August 2007.

681 Id.

682 Id.

trade in services, the complex system of market access commitments (Article XVI), national treatment commitments (Article XVII), additional commitments (Article XVIII) and the sectoral focus of the "progressive liberalization" pursuant to Part IV of the GATS[683]. Due to the integrated nature of the WTO dispute settlement system, the dispute settlement procedures in the DSU apply also to services disputes[684]. Some special provisions have been made on dispute settlement procedures in the GATS, such as[685]:

- The GATS Council or the DSB may, at the request of a member, consult with any member(s) in respect of any matter for which it has not been possible to find a satisfactory solution through consultation under Article XXII: 1;
- A number of provisions regulate specific conflicts of jurisdiction between the GATS and other sectoral or bilateral agreements on international services and related matters. Thus, according to Article XXII: 3, a "Member may not invoke Article XVII, either under this Article or Article XXIII, with respect to a measure of another Member that falls within the scope of an international agreement between them relating to the avoidance of double taxation";
- Article XXIII: 1 of the GATS permits violation complaints in case of "failure to carry out obligations or specific commitments under this Agreement" without reference to the traditional GATT concept of "nullification or impairment of treaty benefits";
- Article XXI of the GATS on "Modification of Schedules provides for arbitration if agreement is not reached between the modifying Member and any affected Member before the end of the period provided for negotiations...Any affected Mem-

683 Ernst-Ulrich Petersmann, *The GATT/WTO Dispute Settlement System*, Martinus Nijhoff, 1997, p. 210.

684 Article XXII: 1 of the GATS: "Each Member shall accord sympathetic consideration to, and shall afford adequate opportunity for, consultation regarding such representations as may be made by any other Member with respect to any matter affecting the operation of this Agreement. The Dispute Settlement Understanding (DSU) shall apply to such consultations".

685 Ernst-Ulrich Petersmann, supra note 683, pp. 210–211.

ber that wishes to enforce a right that it may have to compensation must participate in the arbitration";
- Article 22 of the DSU includes special rules on compensation and suspension of concessions in the field of the GATS.

All GATS rules including individual cases involving individual service providers and their acquired rights are applicable under the GATS dispute settlement system. Presently there is no formal requirement for prior exhaustion of local remedies, which was opposed in the GATS negotiations because of a fear that it would unnecessarily restrict governments in bringing cases before the GATS dispute settlement system.

The GATS dispute settlement was invoked for the first time in September 1995 in a WTO dispute settlement proceed in the context of complaints by Guatemala, Honduras, Mexico and the US and joined later by Ecuador, against the EC regime for the importation, sale and distribution of bananas[686]. The complaints argued that the EC importation restrictions and licensing regulations for bananas were not only inconsistent with Articles I, III and XI of GATT 1994 and Articles 1 and 3 of the WTO Agreement on Import Licensing Procedures, but also with Articles II, XVI and XVII of the GATS, in so far as they restricted the EC market access commitments and national treatment commitments for the marketing and distribution of bananas[687].

In June 1996, a violation complaint, as well as a non-violation complaint within the meaning of Article XXIII: 3 of the GATS, were raised by the US when it requested consultation with Japan pursuant to Article 4 of the DSU regarding measures affecting distribution services, applied by the government of Japan in connection with the Law Pertaining to Adjustment of Business Activities of the Retail Industry for Large Scale Retail Stores, and related legislation, regulations and administrative measures[688].

686 Ernst-Ulrich Petersmann, supra note 683, p. 212. See also Salas, M. and Jackson, J.H., "Procedural Overview of the WTO EC – banana dispute", Journal of International Economic Law 2000 3(1), pp. 145–166.

687 Id. Ernst-Ulrich Petersmann, p. 212.

688 Id. Ernst-Ulrich Petersmann, p. 213.

7.1.2 The Dispute Settlement Understanding and the Merit of the WTO's Jurisprudence

Unlike its predecessor in the 1947 GATT system, the present DSU is not a collection of ad hoc agreements, panel reports and understandings of the parties[689]. Instead, the current dispute settlement procedures enjoy the advantage of being a permanent and standing procedure. The decisions of the WTO Appellate Body are final unless disapproved by consensus within the Dispute Settlement Body (DSB)[690]. By contrast, under the 1947 GATT system, decisions were not final unless the GATT Council, consisting of all Contracting Parties, approved them by consensus.

The WTO's jurisprudence is of value not only to international trade law, but also to public international law as a whole. The decisions of the panels and the Appellate Body have dealt extensively with the law of treaties, environmental law, human rights and State responsibility[691]. In particular, some important principles have significant value to international law. Firstly, the Vienna Convention on Law of Treaties (the VCLT) represents the codification of customary international law and is therefore binding on all States. This principle is reflected in the Appellate Body Report, Japan – Taxes on Alcoholic Beverages, complaints by the EC (Section D, WT/DS.8/AB/R). In this case the Appellate Body also noted that the general rules of treaty interpretation contained in Articles 31 and 32 of the VCLT have "attained the status of a rule of customary or general international law"[692].

Moreover, treaties should be interpreted in good faith and in accordance with the ordinary meaning of terms in pertinent provisions, keeping in view the object, purposes, and the overall text

689 James Cameron and Kevin R. Gray, "Principles of International Law in the WTO Dispute Settlement Body", 50 International Law & Comparative Law Quarterly, 248, 248 (2001).

690 P. 950. Pemmaraju Sreenivasa Rao, "Multiple International Judicial Forums: A Reflection of the Growing Strength of International Law or Its Fragmentation?", Michigan Journal of International Law, Vol. 25–929, Summer 2004, pp. 929–961.

691 Id. p. 951.

692 Id. pp. 950–951.

of the treaty. This is reflected in the Appellate Body Report, United States – Import Prohibition of Certain Shrimp and Shrimp Products (paragraph 114, WT/DS58/AB/R). In addition, as illustrated in the Appellate Body Report on Canada – Certain Measures Concerning Periodicals (WT/DS31/AB/R), given the various cross-references in each of the agreements to other WTO agreements, the interpretation of any one of the agreements must achieve harmony with the terms of the other agreements[693].

Furthermore, it is also established that *travaux préparatoires* is to be regarded as only a supplementary tool of interpretation in cases where the ordinary meaning of the provision does not resolve the problem of interpretation or confirm a textual interpretation[694]. This principle can be found in cases such as European Communities – Measures Affecting the Importation of Certain Poultry Products (paragraph 83, Appellate Body Report, WT/DS69/AB/R).

The following chart illustrates the overview of the dispute settlement process under the DSU[695]:

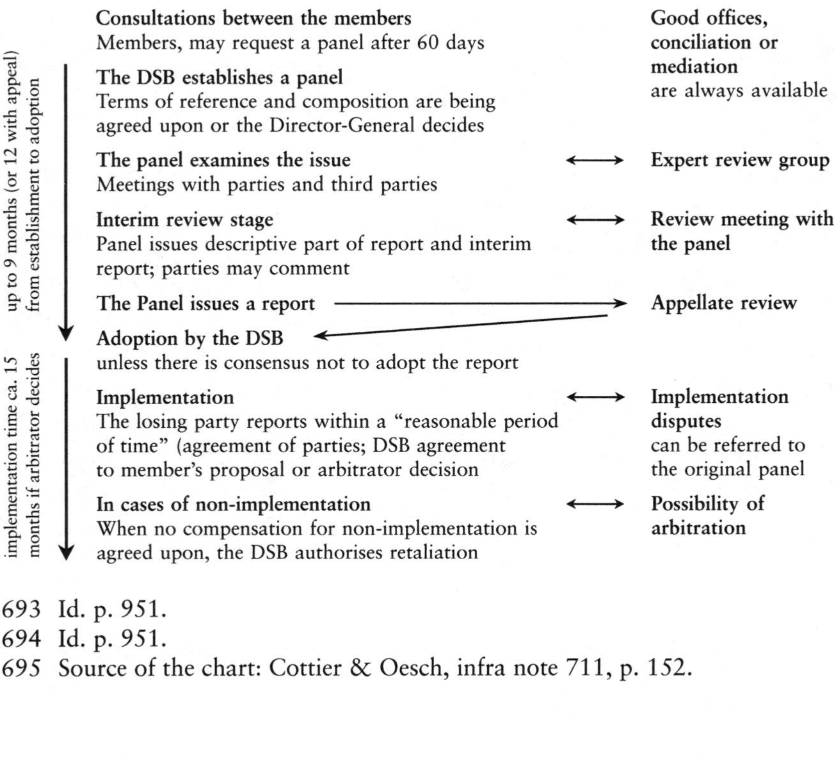

693 Id. p. 951.
694 Id. p. 951.
695 Source of the chart: Cottier & Oesch, infra note 711, p. 152.

One of the major features of the DSU is that it reaffirms that Members shall not themselves determine violations or decide on retaliation, but shall make use of the dispute settlement rules and procedures of the DSU. In addition, several other features make the GATT/WTO dispute settlement system different from traditional modes of international adjudication[696], such as its non-exhaustion of local remedies, limited third-party intervention, tight time schedules, interim review followed by recommendations and decisions.

Although the WTO dispute settlement system is in the process of improvement, compared to the dispute settlement mechanisms in other international institutions, it enjoys a number of priorities. This is the case in contrast to that of the adjudication of the LOS Convention, which will be discussed later in this Chapter. The WTO dispute settlement system has become a preferred dispute settlement forum of member countries, due to the power of the sanction in the WTO dispute settlement system and its potential to impact directly on the economic interests of disputants.

7.1.3 The Relationship between the WTO Law and Other Fields of International Law

As referred to earlier in this work, Article XX of the GATT provides an exception to substantive GATT obligations, allowing Members to adopt and enforce measures for a range of purposes, including the protection of human, animal or plant life or health[697]; the protection of national treasures or artistic, historic or archaeological value[698]; and the conservation of exhaustible natural resources[699]. Such measures may be taken subject to the requirement that they are not applied in a manner which would constitute a means of arbitrary or unjustifiable discrimination between countries where the same conditions prevail. Article XX is a critical

696 Cottier & Oesch infra note 711, pp. 154–156.
697 Paragraph (b).
698 Paragraph (f).
699 Paragraph (g).

provision in analyzing the relationship between the WTO law and other fields of international law. Although it does not refer to other agreements, such agreements come into play where Members take measures listed in Article XX pursuant to their obligations under them.

The relationship between the WTO law and the broader realm of international law has been an uncertain one[700]. As McRae put it, the GATT law was "not perceived as part of the mainstream of international law"[701]. However, unlike the GATT jurisprudence, the WTO jurisprudence has attracted significant interest in the broader realm of international law. The DSU and other WTO agreements establish links between the WTO law and other fields of

700 Mark Jennings, "The WTO and International Law: Mapping the Relationship", WTO law and international law, ANZSIL (the Australian and New Zealand Society of International Law) Conference 2004, p. 3.
For other writings on WTO law on dispute settlement, see for example: World Trade Forum 2002 – Dispute Settlement and Decision Making in the Multilateral Trading System: Current Operation and Options for Reform, available at the website of World Trade Institute, Bern, Switzerland at: www.wti.org revisited in August 2006; Giorgio Sacerdoti, (book review), The WTO Dispute Settlement System: 1995–2003 (Studies in Transnational Economic Law, volume 18), edited by Federico Ortino and Ernst-Ulrich Petersmann, The Hague: Kluwer Law International, 2004, Journal of International Economic Law 2006 9: 1025–1027; Craig VanGrasstek and Pierre Sauvé, "The Consistency of WTO Rules: Can the Single Undertaking Be Squared with Variable Geometry?" Journal of International Economic Law 2006 9: 837–864; Yuka Fukunaga, "Securing Compliance Through the WTO Dispute Settlement System: Implementation of DSB Recommendations", Journal of International Economic Law 2006 9: 383–426; Chad P. Bown and Bernard M. Hoekman, "WTO Dispute Settlement and the Missing Developing Country Cases: Engaging the Private Sector", Journal of International Economic Law 2005 8: 861–890; Ernst-Ulrich Petersmann, "Addressing Institutional Challenges to the WTO in the New Millennium: A Longer-Term Perspective", Journal of International Economic Law 2005 8: 647–665; Thomas Cottier, "The WTO Dispute Settlement System: New Horizons", in: The American Society of International Law (ed). *The Challenge of Non-State Actors*, Proceedings of the 92nd Annual Meeting, Washington, D.C., 1998, pp. 86–91.

701 Donald M. McRae, "The WTO in International Law: Tradition Continued or New Frontier", Journal of International Economic Law 2000; 3: pp. 27–41.

international law. Article 3.2 of the DSU clarifies that the WTO dispute settlement mechanism serves to preserve the rights and obligations of Members under the covered agreements and to clarify the existing provisions of those agreements in accordance with customary rules of interpretation of public international law. Recommendations and rulings of the DSB cannot add to or diminish the rights and obligations provided in the covered agreements[702].

The reference to "the customary rules of interpretation of public international law" is of particular importance. The WTO Appellate Body recognized that Articles 31 and 32 of the Vienna Convention on the Law of Treaties have attained the status of customary rules of interpretation[703]. In doing so, the Appellate Body cited judgments by judicial bodies such as the International Court of Justice in Libya v. Chad[704].

Article 31.3 (c) of the Vienna Convention requires "any relevant rules of international law applicable in the relations between the parties" to be taken into account, together with the context, in interpreting a treaty[705]. The Appellate Body has also had recourse to some general principles of interpretation such as the principle of effective interpretation, stating in its Report in US – Gasoline that: "One of the corollaries of the 'general rule of interpretation' in the Vienna Convention is that interpretation must give meaning and effect to all the terms of a treaty. An interpreter is not free to adopt a reading that would result in reducing whole clauses or paragraphs of a treaty to redundancy or inutility[706]." In support of its statement, the Appellate Body again cited, amongst other sources, the ICJ judgment in Libya v Chad[707].

702 Paragraph 2 of Article 3 on "General Provisions".

703 See WTO Appellate Body Report, *US – Gasoline*, WT/DS2/AB/R, p.17 and Appellate Body Report, *Japan – Taxes on Alcoholic Beverages*, WT/DS8/AB/R, WT/DS10/AB/R, WT/DS11/AB/R, p. 10.

704 The territorial dispute case between Libya and Chad is available from the website of ICJ at: http://www.icj-cij.org revisited in July 2006.

705 Joost Pauwelyn, *The Nature of WTO Obligations,* Jean Monnet Working Paper No. 1/02 (2002).

706 WTO Appellate Body Report, *US – Gasoline*, p. 23.

707 Id.

In addition, the WTO agreements incorporate by reference parts of a range of other agreements. In some cases, the relevant WTO provision should be interpreted as requiring obligations in other agreements to be enforced as WTO obligations[708]. Furthermore, there are circumstances where an obligation from an outside agreement "is explicitly referenced to define or delimit an obligation whose focus is within a WTO agreement"[709]. This may happen when, pursuant to Article IX of the Marrakesh Agreement, Members adopt a waiver "which will then refer to an outside treaty (or set of obligations) to justify or explain the purpose, object and scope of the WTO waiver"[710].

In their case book *International Trade Regulation, Law and Policy in the WTO, The European Union and Switzerland*[711], Thomas Cottier and Matthias Oesch have referred to the works of Joost Pauwelyn on the relationship between WTO law and other sources of international law, in which Pauwelyn elaborated his point of view that the applicable law before panels and the Appellate Body extends to all international law. Cottier and Oesch argued in favour of this theory which "allows to adjudicate WTO disputes on the basis of other international agreements as well as general principles of law and custom"[712].

708 Joost Pauwelyn, supra note 705.

709 WTO Appellate Body Report, supra note 706, p. 112.

710 Id, p. 113.

711 Thomas Cottier & Matthias Oesch, *International Trade Regulation, Law and Policy in the WTO, the European Union and Switzerland, Cases, Materials and Comments*, Staempfli Publishers Ltd. Berne, Cameron May Ltd. London, 2005, pp. 115–116.

712 Id, p. 115. For Joost Pauwelyn's detailed illustration on this issue, see Joost Pauwelyn, "The Role of Public International Law in the WTO: How Far Can We Go?", The American Journal of International Law, Vol. 95 (2001) pp. 535, 577–78.
For other writings of Joost Pauwelyn on dispute settlement in WTO, see for example: *Conflict of Norms in Public International Law, How WTO Law Relates to Other Rules of International Law* (Cambridge University Press, 2003); "The Nature of WTO Obligations", Jean Monnet Working Paper No. 1/02 (2002). "The Jurisdiction of the WTO", in Proceedings of the 98th Annual Meeting of the American Society of International Law 135–138 (2004); "WTO Dispute Settlement: Of Sovereign Interests, Private Rights,

Detailed illustrations on the relationship of the WTO law and other branches of public international law are made by Cottier and Oesch in their case book, in which they examine this issue from the perspectives of the issue of jurisdiction, the WTO law and Multilateral Environmental Agreements, the WTO law and human rights, together with contractual to constitutional law. What is particularly thought-provoking is the discussion about the possibility of building a strong relationship between other branches of public international law and the WTO legal framework within the limited jurisdiction of panels and the Appellate Body. The authors clearly examine the potential conflicts of interfacing the WTO law and other international agreements. Based on this examination, the authors recommended:

> Interfacing WTO law and other international agreements does not remain without potential conflicts. It does not take a legal mind to detect constellations in which it seems impossible to bring WTO law, at least at first sight, into compliance with other international agreements. Such constellations may happen, for instance, in the field of the protection of the environment. There are many MEAs which make use, and rightly so, of trade instruments. In essence, these agreements often authorize national or regional governments to impose import restrictions in a field of particular goods. ...[713]
>
> General principles of law and principles of international law, we are reminded by panels and the Appellate Body, are valid for the WTO and form the basis of the relations between and among WTO Members. The Appellate Body clearly stated: "The chapeau of Article XX (of the GATT 1947) is, in fact, but one expression of the principle of good faith. This principle, at once a general principle of law and a general principle of international law, controls the exercise of rights by states" (US – Shrimps). Therefore, besides interpreting international agreements and domestic and regional law, the panels and the Appellate Body may be faced also with the question whether an invoked principle has attained the status of customary international law or that of a general principle of law as recognized by major legal system....[714]

---

and Public Goods", in *International Public Goods and Transfer of Technology Under a Globalized Intellectual Property Regime 817–830 (Keith E. Maskus & Jerome H. Reichman eds., 2005)*; "Expert Advice in WTO Dispute Settlement", in *Trade and Human Health and Safety* 235–256 (George A. Bermann & Petros C. Mavroidis eds., 2006).

713 Cottier and Oesch, supra note 711, pp. 515–516.

714 Id.

> ...From a practical point of view, there will be constellations in which it will be necessary to rule as to whether an invoked principle has attained the status of customary international law or whether it is to be qualified as a general principle of law. Such a decision by a panel or Appellate Body then will not only bind the parties to the dispute. It will consequently become part of the WTO law and, moreover, have implications for the broader field of international law. The situation is not different from other major fields of international law, such as the law of the sea. And it is not different from other courts of international law, in particular the International Court of Justice, or regular or ad hoc courts of arbitration the findings of which add to the rich body of international law precedents[715].

The importance of the WTO dispute settlement system has been described as a "new frontier" of international law[716]. The WTO provides a mechanism for the settlement of disputes arising out of the application of the WTO Agreements, which, although not unique in some respects[717], is considered noteworthy in the sense that the dispute settlement system is obligatory for all WTO Members and its decisions are both final and binding[718]. Furthermore, the WTO dispute settlement mechanism does more than resolve individual disputes. It provides a basis for the development of international trade law through judicial decision-making. It has become a forum for developing the process of international dispute settlement, both procedural and substantive, as well as creating an opportunity for the application and refinement of concepts and doctrines of international law[719].

Therefore, the interpretation of the WTO agreements is an active, law-creating process[720]. The application of GATT Article XX

715 Id.

716 See for example, Donald M. McRae, "the WTO in International Law: Tradition Continued or New Frontier?", supra note 701. See also WTO, *A Handbook on the WTO Dispute Settlement System*, Cambridge University Press, 2004, pp. 2–3.

717 WTO, id.

718 Id. Apart from questions of compliance, there is no recourse after a panel or Appellate Body report has been adopted by the DSU. Non-compliance with an adopted report can lead to retaliation in accordance with Article 22 of the DSU.

719 Id.

720 Joost Pauwelyn, supra note 705.

has highlighted the cross-over between international trade law with other branches of international law, in particular the overlap between trade and environment. While this overlapping is important in considering the relationship between international trade law and international law, the substantive issues relating to these two fields comprise only part of the contribution that is currently being made to the development of the international law through the operation of the WTO dispute settlement process[721].

7.1.4 Withdrawal of Concessions – the WTO Term of Sanction

The most important application of a liability rule in the WTO system is pursuant to the DSU, which governs claims by one member nation when another member has violated its obligations. Article 21(3) of the DSU provides that a member has a reasonable period of time to bring its policies into conformity with its obligations after it has been found to have violated them[722]. Article 22(1) then states that compensation or a suspension of concessions may result if compliance has not been achieved within a reasonable period of time[723]. The first step in the process is a negotiation over compensation, in effect to determine whether the case can be

721 Id.

722 See DSU, Art. 21 (3) "At a DSB meeting held within 30 days after the date of adoption of the panel or Appellate Body report, the Member concerned shall inform the DSB of its intentions in respect of implementation of the recommendations and rulings of the DSB. If it is impracticable to comply immediately with the recommendations and rulings, the Member concerned shall have a reasonable period of time in which to do so...".

723 Id. Article 22 (1) "Compensation and the suspension of concessions or other obligations are temporary measures available in the event that the recommendations and rulings are not implemented within a reasonable period of time. However, neither compensation nor the suspension of concessions or other obligations is preferred to full implementation of a recommendation to bring a measure into conformity with the covered agreements. Compensation is voluntary and, if granted, shall be consistent with the covered agreements".

"settled"[724]. Should those negotiations fail, the aggrieved party (or parties) can propose a suspension of concessions, which must be substantially equivalent to the ongoing harm that they suffer from the violation[725]. An arbitration procedure can be resorted to examine the substantial equivalence question if the member faced with such a suspension of concessions objects that the suspension is excessive[726].

Suspension of concessions is regarded as the WTO term for countermeasure[727]. Its key features include the requirement that the concessions must be "equivalent to the level of nullification or impairment" (Art. 22.4 DSU) and are seen as an interim measure pending implementation of the report, since "full implementation of a recommendation to bring a measure into conformity with the covered agreements" is always preferred (Art. 22.1 DSU). Suspension of concessions is regarded as the *ultima ratio* to guarantee that legality has been respected in the WTO[728].

Withdrawal of concessions is one of the most influential tools of the WTO law compared to other instruments in international law,

724 Id. Article 22 (2) "If the Member concerned fails to bring the measure found to be inconsistent with a covered agreement into compliance therewith or otherwise comply with the recommendations and rulings within the reasonable period of time determined pursuant to paragraph 3 of Article 21, such Member shall, if so requested, and no later than the expiry of the reasonable period of time, enter into negotiations with any party having invoked the dispute settlement procedures, with a view to developing mutually acceptable compensation. If no satisfactory compensation has been agreed within 20 days after the date of expiry of the reasonable period of time, any party having invoked the dispute settlement procedures may request authorization from the DSB to suspend the application to the Member concerned of concessions or other obligations under the covered agreements".

725 Id. Article 22 (4) "The level of the suspension of concessions or other obligations authorized by the DSB shall be equivalent to the level of the nullification or impairment".

726 Id. Article 22 (6–7).

727 Horn Henrik & Mavroidis Petros C. "Remedies in the WTO Dispute Settlement System and Developing Country Interests", pp. 20–21, World Bank, April 1999, p. 18. Paper available at: http://www.econ-law.se revisited in August 2007.

728 Id. p. 18.

in particular the adjudication of LOS Convention. In their above mentioned case book *International Trade Regulation, Law and Policy in the WTO, The European Union and Switzerland*[729], Cottier and Oesch discuss in detail how this method worked effectively in major cases such as EC – Bananas, but failed in other politically sensitive cases such as EC – Hormones. They also point out that the main deficiencies of withdrawing concessions consist of allocating retaliatory powers according to market size. This method is useful only for large market such as the US and the EU. The withdrawal of concessions by medium and small markets usually does not offer the necessary incentives for larger market to comply. The authors put forward several proposals for reforming this method. One of them suggests leaving the purely bilateral relationship of retaliation and allowing for multilateralization of sanctions within the system. Another proposal consists of allowing equally affected countries to join the action upon adoption of a report by the DSB and to suspend concessions as determined in arbitration. They believe this would help to create a more level playing field in the marketplace as well as in terms of reducing the discrepancies in political power[730].

In October 2002, nine developing countries made a joint proposal to the DSB on the severe difficulties that they were encountered with concerning the suspension of concessions[731]. In their proposal, they pointed out that developing countries had participated in as many as 149 disputes (out of 262) either as complainants or defendants. They raised 47 complaints against developed country Members and 37 between themselves[732]. However, securing compliance from the defaulting Member proved to be a difficult task and in many disputes the developing countries may be left with no option other than to seek recourse to suspension of concessions and other obligations under the provisions of Article 22. However

729 Cottier & Oesch supra note 711, pp. 188–193.

730 Cottier & Oesch supra note 711, p. 193.

731 WTO Dispute Settlement Body Special Session, Negotiations on the Dispute Settlement Understanding, "Proposals on DSU by Cuba, Honduras, India, Indonesia, Malaysia, Pakistan, Sri Lanka, Tanzania and Zimbabwe", TN/DS/W/19, 9 October 2002.

732 Id. p. 1.

they believed that the significant imbalance in the trade between developed and developing countries placed severe constraints on the ability of developing countries to exercise their rights under Article 22. The economic cost of withdrawal of concessions in the goods sector would have a greater adverse impact on the aggrieved developing country Member than on the defaulting developed country Member and would only further deepen the imbalance in their trade relations already seriously impacted by the nullification and impairment of benefits[733].

In their joint proposal, these developing countries proposed that an aggrieved developing-country Member should be permitted to seek authorization to suspend concessions and other obligations in sectors of their choice. They should not be required to go through the process of proving that, (1) it was not "practicable or effective" to suspend concession in the same sector or agreement where the violation was found; and (2) the "circumstances were serious enough" to seek suspension of concessions under the agreements other than those in which violation was found exist. This burden of proving was quite onerous as Ecuador's experience in *Bananas* dispute showed[734].

Horn and Mavroidis quoted in their paper of other scholars' studies on this subject. For example, Maggie Giovanni suggested similar proposals for reforming this method by highlighting the multilateral character of the dispute settlement system[735]. She argued that the benchmark was not the absence of a system of dispute settlement, but a situation in which countries had to enforce their agreements unilaterally[736]. A basic idea was that the dispute settlement system provided for third country participation in punishment of illegalities. If there were "power imbalances" in the

733 Id. p. 1.

734 Id. p. 2.

735 Horn & Mavroidis, supra note 727, p. 23. For other works of Giovanni on this subject, see Giovanni Maggie, "The Role of Multilateral Institutions in International Cooperation", The American Economic Review, Vol. 89, No. 1 (March 1999), pp. 199–214. See also: Robert Z. Lawrence, "Rulemaking Amidst Growing Diversity: A Club-of-Clubs Approach to WTO Reform and New Issue Selection", Journal of International Economic Law 2006 9: 823–835.

736 Horn & Mavroidis, id. p. 23.

sense that countries stood to lose differently from going back to the Prisoners' Dilemma situation, then countries could contribute relatively more to the punishment of those responsible for illegalities which they stood less to lose from punishing[737]. Hence, certain countries could be seen as having particular "advantages" in the penalties of certain other countries. If the agreement permitted countries to redistribute the responsibility for penalties so that they were delivered by those who could undertake them at relatively low expense, then the system may impose punishments against defectors more effectively, thus facilitating the liberalization process, for developing countries in particular[738].

Other scholars have argued that the withdrawals of concessions within the WTO agreement were narrow in scope[739]. They pointed out that the withdrawal of concessions was normally intended to be undertaken by the Complainant alone. While this was natural with regard to the prevention of further losses for the complainant, it restricted the effectiveness of the withdrawal with regard to the purpose of inducing the Respondent to change his behaviour and to deter unlawful acts[740].

Moreover, it has been argued that the DSU not only ruled out explicit countermeasures by third parties, it also failed to provide the complainant with any means to enforce the ruling alone[741]. Furthermore it was not seen as providing any financial support to a complainant that undertook costly countermeasures. Finally, it was pointed out that the DSU allowed the complainant only to take countermeasures that were equivalent to the level of nullification or impairment, which was referred to in Art. 22.4 of the DSU. There was still no case law with regard to the interpretation of "equivalent", nor was there room for punitive damages in the WTO legal system. The DSU thus did not allow for countermeasures that were strong enough to be deterrent by themselves[742].

737 Id. p. 23.
738 Id. p. 23.
739 Id. p. 21.
740 Id. p. 21.
741 Id. p. 21.
742 Id. p. 22.

7.2 The Dispute Settlement Mechanism under the LOS Convention

Unlike withdrawal of concessions under the DSB of the WTO, the dispute settlement mechanism under the LOS Convention does not provide for specific sanction instruments. This partially results in the fact that the conflict resolving capability of LOS is not as effective as that of the WTO. This section discusses the dispute settlement arrangement under the LOS Convention and the ITLOS. By describing how the ITLOS and the ICJ manage to prevent the overlapping between their jurisdictions through explicit regulation in their Rules, the discussion raises the question as to whether this may shed light to the jurisdictional ambiguity between the ITLOS and the WTO panels and Appellate Body.

7.2.1 Part XV of the LOS Convention

The dispute settlement mechanism in Part XV of the 1982 LOS Convention was drafted to allow maximum flexibility for the State parties in their choice of dispute settlement procedures[743]. The primary obligation of the parties under this Part is to resolve their disputes by peaceful means[744]. States are free to choose whatever

743 Howard Schiffman, "The Dispute Settlement Mechanism of UNCLOS: A Potentially Important Apparatus for Marine Wildlife Management", Journal of International Wildlife Law and Policy, pp. 293–306 (1998), p. 1. For more writings on the dispute settlement system under 1982 LOS Convention, see for example Jonathan I. Charney, "The Implication of Expanding International Dispute Settlement System: The 1982 Convention on the Law of the Sea", The American Journal of International Law, Vol. 90, No. 1(January 1996), pp. 69–75.

744 Id. Schiffman, p. 3. Article 279 of the Convention, under the title of "Obligation to settle disputes by peaceful means" Not only is the requirement of peaceful dispute settlement the first provision of Part XV, but Article 279 also refers to the obligation of peaceful dispute settlement set forth in the UN Charter.

means they wish to resolve disputes arising under the Convention[745]. Only when they are unable to resolve a conflict by their own means is it necessary to invoke the compulsory and binding machinery of Section 2 of Part XV[746]. Similarly, where State parties have agreed separately to submit a LOS dispute to a binding procedure that will apply in line of Part XV, unless the parties agree otherwise[747]. The Convention requires that when a dispute arises the parties shall proceed expeditiously to an exchange of views regarding its settlement by negotiation or other peaceful means[748].

Some scholars argued that the third party dispute settlement mechanism of conciliation is of special interest in the protection of the marine environment[749], where it is specifically mentioned as a means of settlement that a party may invite without entailing a binding decision[750]. In fact, it is the only method of third party settlement specifically referred to in Section 1 (General Provisions) of Part XV. In disputes involving the conservation, management, determination and allocation of living resources in an EEZ, Article 297 (Limitations on Applicability of Section 2) requires conciliation upon the demand of any party to the dispute, where no settlement has been reached under Section 1[751]. Moreover, some disputes concerning marine scientific research may also be submitted to conciliation at the request of either party and subject to certain rights of the coastal states[752].

745 Article 280: Settlement of disputes by any peaceful means chosen by the parties.

746 Article 281: Procedure where no settlement has been reached by the parties.

747 Article 282: Obligations under general, regional or bilateral agreements.

748 Article 283 (1) The obligation to exchange views is not limited to the pre-dispute settlement phase. On the contrary, it is extended to those cases where a method of dispute settlement has failed and, additionally, where it has been successful and the question of implementation remains. Although negotiation is not specifically enumerated in the Convention as a method of dispute settlement, its centrality to modern international dispute settlement is beyond doubt.

749 Schiffman, supra note 743, p. 3.

750 Article 284: Conciliation.

751 Schiffman, supra note 743, p. 3.

752 Article 297 (2) (b). Also see id. p. 3.

Scholars such as Howard Schiffman, argued that one of the innovations of the LOS Convention is the regulation of binding dispute settlement for the peaceful resolution of maritime controversies between and among States[753], which is elaborated in Section 2 of Part XV[754]. Where States are unable to resolve disputes by methods of their own choosing, any party to the dispute that is a party to the LOS Convention may submit the matter to a court or tribunal having jurisdiction under Section 2[755]. Article 288 endorses the court or tribunal listed in Section 2 with jurisdiction over any dispute concerning the interpretation or application of the Convention properly submitted to it. Such court or tribunal has jurisdiction over any dispute concerning the interpretation or application of an international agreement related to the purposes of the LOS Convention[756].

Article 287 of the LOS Convention states that member states are free to choose by written declaration one or more methods of dispute settlement enumerated in Section 2, when signing, ratifying or acceding to the Convention, or at any time thereafter. Paragraph (1) of this Article contains a list of choices for the states, which include:

a) the International Tribunal for the Law of the Sea established in accordance with Annex VI[757];
b) the International Court of Justice[758];
c) an arbitral tribunal constituted in accordance with Annex VII[759], and
d) a special arbitral tribunal constituted in accordance with Annex VIII for one or more of the specified categories[760].

Where the parties to a dispute have accepted the same procedure, it must be utilized unless they agree otherwise[761]. If no choice is

753 Id. p. 4.
754 Part XV, Section 2: "Compulsory Procedures Entailing Binding Decisions".
755 Article 286: Application of procedures under this section.
756 Article 288 (2). Also see Schiffman, supra note 743, p. 4.
757 Article 287 (1) (a).
758 Article 287 (1) (b).
759 Article 287 (1) (c).
760 Article 287 (1) (d).
761 Article 287 (4).

designated by written declaration, that State is deemed to have accepted arbitration[762]. Similarly, if two States have both designated methods of dispute settlement under Article 287, but have not accepted the same method, then their dispute may only be submitted to arbitration[763].

According to Article 290, when it considers it appropriate under the circumstance, a court or tribunal may prescribe provisional measures pending the final decision to preserve the respective rights of the parties or to prevent serious harm to the marine environment[764]. This may be undertaken through the special arbitration, whose scope of activities is defined in Annex VIII of the LOS Convention. The categories of disputes that may be referred to special arbitration include: fisheries, protection and preservation of the marine environment, marine scientific research, navigation which includes pollution from vessels and by dumping. The fact that navigation-related disputes are included in the powers of the special arbitral tribunal indicates that Article 290 has close relevance to maritime transport services, which is particularly the case where a coastal state tries to avoid a binding settlement through the limitation of this Article.

7.2.2 *International Tribunal for the Law of the Sea*

The International Tribunal for the Law of the Sea (the ITLOS) is an independent judicial body established by the UN LOS Convention with the purpose to adjudicate dispute arising out of the interpretation and application of the Convention[765]. The initial consideration in creating the ITLOS was the need for a sole forum to settle all disputes concerning the interpretation and application of the new concept of the common heritage of mankind, and thus

762 Article 287 (3).
763 Article 287 (5).
764 Article 290: Provisional measures.
765 International Tribunal for the Law of the Sea, General Information – Overview, at the website of ITLOS: http://www.itlos.org revisited in July 2006.

help a progressive development of the law governing the international seabed area and its resources[766].

The ITLOS has been functioning since October 1996 and has given rise to some very important decisions, which generally involved the prompt release of detained vessels and crews, fishery management in the EEZ, flags of convenience, hot pursuit and espousal of claims relating to crew members not of the nationality of the applicant State and the issuance of provisional measures[767].

The decisions of the ITLOS have opened up the family of international tribunals[768]. As Alan Boyle noted, the LOS Convention deals with "much that had been in dispute, much that is new and much that remains unresolved, it inevitably represents a complex balance of interests, and contains many inherently uncertain or ambiguous articles"[769]. The jurisdiction of the ITLOS over contentious cases includes the following aspects[770]:

- *Jurisdiction over disputes concerning the interpretation or application of the Convention.* It has jurisdiction over any dispute that is submitted to it in accordance with Part XV of the LOS Convention concerning the interpretation or application of the Convention and the Agreement relating to the Implementation of Article XI of the Convention. With the consent of the parties to the dispute, any dispute belonging to the categories referred to in Articles 297 (Limitations on applicability of section 2) and 298 (Optional exceptions to applicability of section 2) of the Convention may be submitted to it[771].

766 Rao, supra note 690, p. 949.

767 Shabtai Rosenne, "The Case-Law of the ITLOS (1997–2001): An Overview", in Current Marine Environmental Issues and the International Tribunal for the Law of the Sea 127, 127–28 (Myron H. Nordquist & John N. Moore, eds., 2001).

768 Rao, supra note 690, p. 947.

769 Alan E. Boyle, "Dispute Settlement and the Law of the Sea Convention: Problems of Fragmentation and Jurisdiction", 46 Int'l & Comparative Law Quarterly 37, 50 1997.

770 International Tribunal for the Law of the Sea, Proceedings and Judgments – Competence, available at the Tribunal website: http://www.itlos.org revisited in July 2006.

771 Id.

- *Jurisdiction over disputes concerning the interpretation or application of other agreements.* Article 288 of the LOS Convention stipulates that the ITLOS has jurisdiction over any dispute concerning the interpretation or application of an international agreement related to the purposes of the Convention which is submitted to it in accordance with the agreement. This has been reaffirmed in Articles 21 and 22 of its Statute[772].
- *Jurisdiction of the Seabed Dispute Chamber.* Article 187 of the LOS Convention confirms that the Seabed Disputes Chamber has jurisdiction over disputes with respect to activities in the Area. Disputes concerning the interpretation or application of a contract referred to in Article 187, subparagraph (c) (i) of the Convention are required to be submitted, at the request of a party, to binding commercial arbitration, unless the parties otherwise agree[773].
- *Provisional measure.* Under Article 290 of the LOS Convention, if a dispute has been duly submitted to the ITLOS, and if it considers that "prima facie" it has jurisdiction under Part XV or Part XI, section 5, of the Convention, it may prescribe any provisional measures which it considers appropriate under the circumstances to preserve the respective rights of the parties to the dispute or to prevent serious harm to the marine environment, pending the final decision. This jurisdiction is reaffirmed in Article 25 of its Statute[774].
- *Prompt release of vessels and crews.* Article 292 of the LOS Convention grants the ITLOS the jurisdiction to consider an application for the prompt release of a detained vessel or its

772 Under Article 21 of the Statute, the jurisdiction of the Tribunal includes all matters specifically provided for in any agreement, other than the Convention, which confers jurisdiction on the Tribunal. Under Article 22 of the Statute, any disputes concerning the interpretation or application of a treaty or convention already in force and relating to the subject-matter covered by the Convention may, if all the Parties to such agreement agree, shall be submitted to the Tribunal in accordance with the agreement.

773 Id. ITLOS supra note 770.

774 Id.

crew. Under this Article, if one state party detained a vessel flying the flag of another state party, and it is alleged that the detaining state has not complied with the provisions of the LOS Convention for the prompt release of the vessel or its crew upon the posting of a reasonable bond or other financial security, then within ten days from the time of the detention, the question of release from detention may be submitted to the ITLOS[775].

The other feature of the jurisdiction is that the ITLOS is open to disputes involving not only States, but also individuals, corporations, State enterprises and international organizations[776]. When disputes arise between private persons and the authority established to regulate the international seabed area, the ITLOS is the place to resort to, because the ICJ could not be awarded jurisdiction over such disputes due to the existing limitations in its Statute[777].

7.3 The Jurisdictions of the DSU, the ITLOS and the ICJ

7.3.1 A Comparison of the DSU and the ICJ

There are some jurisdictional similarities and differences between the DSU of the WTO and the ICJ. The decisions of the panels or the Appellate Body, similar to the decisions of the ICJ, do not have formal precedent value for later cases[778]. Nevertheless, they are followed or relied upon unless a good cause exists to depart from them. The pattern of decision-making in the DSU is also similar to the ICJ in promoting judicial economy without rejecting the need

775 Id.
776 Rao, supra note 690, p. 949.
777 Id. p. 949.
778 Id. p. 953.

to be flexible and active in settling and clarifying the ambiguities in the WTO Agreements[779].

Unlike the position of the ICJ, which has a prominent role in the progressive development of international law without the need for adoption by the UN, the DSU does not have the power of judicial legislation that changes the rights and obligations of the parties to the WTO. Nor does it have the role of authoritatively interpreting the GATT 1994. This is the function of the Ministerial Conference and the General Council, where decisions are adopted by a two-thirds majority[780].

There are also differences between the DSU and the ICJ in procedural matters, such as third party intervention in the settlement of disputes[781]. In the case of the ICJ, although third parties can intervene in the case before the court if they can convince the court that they have an interest of a legal nature that is likely to be affected by the decision, in practice the ICJ rarely allows third party intervention. By contrast, the DSU seems more liberal on the issue of third party intervention in a case. Article 10 and Appendix 3 of the DSU permit third parties the opportunity to make written submissions or oral submissions[782]. For example, in the EC – Banana case, there were six parties representing 15 States and 20 third parties. The Appellate Body confirmed that a State could seek the establishment of a panel, even if it did not have a legal interest or could not show an actual trade impact[783]. It also states that the interest in ensuring free international trade in goods and services, as well as the interest in clearly determining rights and obligations under the WTO Agreement, provide sufficient grounds to pursue WTO dispute settlement mechanism[784].

779 Id. p. 954.
780 Id. p. 953.
781 Id. p. 954.
782 Id. p. 954.
783 WTO Appellate Body, European Communities – Regime for the Importation, Sale and Distribution of Bananas, WT/DS27/AB/R, AB-1997-3 (adopted Sept. 9, 1997).
784 Id.

7.3.2 The ITLOS and the ICJ

Prior to its creation, although most scholars reached consensus on the value of ITLOS in resolving disputes concerning the exploration and exploitation of the international seabed area, questions were raised on the problem of multiple judicial forums at the international level. Judge Oda noted in 1995:

> The creation of a court of judicature in parallel with the International Court of Justice, which has been in existence for many years as the principal judicial organ of the United Nations, will prove to have been a great mistake. One should not lose sight of the fact that the law of the sea always has been, and always will be, an integral part of international law as a whole. The law of the sea must be interpreted in the light of the uniform development of jurisprudence within the international community and must not be dealt with in a fragmentary manner...If the development of the law of the sea were to be separated from the general rules of international law and placed under the jurisdiction of a separate judicial authority, this could lead to the destruction of the very foundation of international law.[785]

Although the merit of the ITLOS was later proved, the potential for its jurisdiction to overlap that of the ICJ still exists. The possible conflicts of jurisdiction and jurisprudence between the ITLOS and the ICJ are particularly brought about by the proliferation of international courts and tribunals within the international system that has no unified judiciary[786]. As the Appeals Chambers of the International Criminal Tribunal for the Former Yugoslavia puts it, "in international law every tribunal is a self-contained system unless otherwise provided"[787]. Therefore, there are no general rules by which questions of coordination and conflict could be resorted to[788].

785 Shigeru Oda, "Dispute Settlement Prospects in the Law of the Sea", 44 Int'l & Comp. L.Q. 863, 864 (1995).

786 Tullio Treves, "Conflicts between the International Tribunal for the Law of the Sea and the International Court of Justice", International Law and Politics, vol. 31: 809, pp. 809–821, February 2004, p. 809.

787 Id. p. 809.

788 Id. p. 809.

The jurisdiction of the ITLOS and the ICJ may encompass cases concerning the interpretation or application of the 1982 LOS Convention[789]. In the negotiation leading to the special agreement, the problem of forum shopping may appear. When a case is submitted by application, theoretically the disputing party that takes the initiative has the advantage of choosing the forum it prefers. However in practice, Article 282 of the LOS Convention serves as a mechanism that aims to preclude forum shopping and the possibilities of overlapping litispendence between the two judicial institutions[790]. This Article stipulates that:

> If the states parties that are parties to a dispute concerning the interpretation or application of this Convention have agreed, through a general, regional or bilateral agreement or otherwise, that such dispute shall, at the request of any party to the dispute, be submitted to a procedure that entails a binding decision, that procedure shall apply in lien of the procedures provided for in this Part, unless the parties to the dispute otherwise agree.

The implication of this Article is that the acceptance by all parties to a dispute of the Court's compulsory jurisdiction, under Article 36, paragraph 2 of the Statute of the ICJ, should be considered "the agreement" mentioned this Article[791]. In practice, possible conflicts of jurisdiction between the ICJ and the ITLOS may occur in a complex dispute, where some aspects may come under the jurisdiction of the ICJ, and others under the jurisdiction of the ITLOS. When this occurs, each court would be competent to rule on different questions. This may end up a difficult situation where both of them hear the case in parallel or in sequence[792].

It seems more practical for the parties involved to try and concentrate the whole of their dispute before one court or tribunal, and to grant competence over the entire case to the one court or

789 Articles 279 and 286 of the Convention specify that the provisions on the settlement of disputes of the Convention refer to disputes concerning the interpretation and application of the Convention.

790 Tullio Treves, supra note 786, p. 811.

791 Id. p. 812.

792 Id. p. 816.

tribunal that has been chosen[793]. In both the Rule of the Court (Article 38) under the ICJ and the Rule of the Tribunal (Article 54) under the ITLOS, there exist the forum prorogatum clauses, which establish similar regulation[794]. For example the Rules of the Tribunal for the ITLOS states that

> when the Applicant State proposes to found the jurisdiction of the Tribunal upon consent thereto yet to be given or manifested by the State against which such application is made, the application shall be transmitted to that State. It shall not however be entered in the List of cases, nor any action be taken in the proceedings, unless and until the State against which such application is made consents to the jurisdiction of the Tribunal for the purpose of the case.[795]

Therefore, the Parties may concentrate their case before the court or tribunal either by their acquiescence, by the above forum prorogatum clause, or by both.

The Spain – Canada Fisheries Dispute is often cited as an example to illustrate the jurisdiction relation between the ICJ and the ITLOS[796]. In 1995, Canadian authorities arrested the Spanish fishing vessel Estai slightly seaward of Canada's EEZ in response to the Estai's pursuit of turbot stocks which straddled Canadian waters and the EEZ[797]. Still pending before the ICJ, the dispute was not brought under Part XV of LOS Convention, but rather under the optional clause of Article 36 (2) of the ICJ Statute[798].

793 Id. p. 816.

794 Id. p. 816.

795 Paragraph 5, Article 54, Rules of the Tribunal, ITLOS/8, 27 April 2005.

796 Schiffman, supra note 743, pp. 7–8. Fisheries Jurisdiction (Spain v. Canada), available at the website of International Court of Justice: www.icj-cij.org revisited in June 2007.

797 Id. p. 7. Application of the Kingdom of Spain (Spain v. Canada), 1995 ICJ Application (filed March 25, 1995) For further discussion of the problem of straddling fish stocks, and the legal and policy issues raised by the Spain-Canada dispute, see William T. Abel, "Fishing for an International Norm to Govern Straddling Stocks: The Canada-Spain Dispute of 1995", 27 University of Miami Inter-American Law Review, 553 (1996).

798 Id. p. 7. 1995 Application of the Kingdom of Spain (Spain v. Canada) Article 36 (2) of the Statute of the ICJ provides that: the states parties to the

For States that are parties to the LOS Convention, disputes similar to Spain – Canada one may be addressed within the applicable machinery of Part XV[799]. As a straddling stocks dispute involving the rights of a coastal State, compulsory and binding settlement may not be available. However even if a binding procedure is unavailable, Part XV may provide a formula for successful resolutions of these types of disputes. The availability of conciliation as a non-binding method may generate proposals that can facilitate a negotiated settlement[800].

Future disputes like that between Spain and Canada may highlight the issues of forum shopping between the ICJ, the ITLOS, arbitration and special arbitration[801]. A State may choose the ITLOS or special arbitration where there are highly technical issues in a dispute. Similarly, a State might choose the ICJ where the issue to be decided has wider implications for general international law[802].

---

present Statute may at any time declare that they recognize as compulsory ipso facto and without special agreement, in relation to any other state accepting the same obligation, the jurisdiction of the Court in all legal disputes concerning:

a) The interpretation of a treaty;
b) Any question of international law;
c) The existence of any fact which, if established, would constitute a breach of an international obligation;
d) The nature or extent of the reparation to be made for the breach of an international obligation.

799 Id. p. 8.

800 Id. p. 8.

801 Id. pp. 8–9. See also Alan E. Boyle, "Further development of the Law of the sea convention: mechanisms for change", 54 (3) International and Comparative Law Quarterly (2005).

802 Id. p. 9. See also Malcolm N. Shaw, "The International Court of Justice: A Practical Perspective", 46 International & Comparative Law Quarterly 831, 834 (1997).

7.4 The Analogy between Private International Law in Assessing Jurisdiction and Choice of Forum

7.4.1 Forum Shopping among International Institutions

The contemporary governance of international trade is characterized by complex and overlapping institutionalization[803]. One of the consequences of this situation is the proliferation of "forum shopping", which refers to the strategic selection of favourable venues from among a plural menu of alternatives. The increasingly complicated institutionalization of the international system has expanded the range of alternatives confronting factors as they seek to reach agreements, resolve disputes and govern the interactions of parties involved[804].

Generally speaking, the choice of forums is determined by two sets of interactive factors. On the supply side, opportunities for forum shopping are defined by the existence of overlapping institutional alternatives. As the number of alternatives increases, the likelihood of forum shopping also increases. On the demand side, incentives for forum shopping arise with the consequential differentiation of alternative venues. The greater the differentiation of alternatives in terms of the consequences they produce, such as the binding effects and outcomes for plaintiffs and defendants, the greater the likelihood of forum shopping[805]. The outcome of forum shopping is generally seen as negative, because it undermines the rule of law and decreases the effectiveness and efficiency of international organization's dispute settlement competency.

803 Joseph Jupille, "Trading Rules: Forum Shopping Within and Among International Institutions", University of Colorado at Boulder, June 2006.

804 Id.

805 Id.

7.4.2 *The Theory of "Most Substantive Link" in Private International Law*

Different countries have different laws, and conflicts may arise when more than one country may have jurisdiction and more than one law can be applied. Under this circumstance, private international laws have been designed to eliminate these conflicts by indicating which court should have jurisdiction and which of the "conflicting laws" shall be applied. This is mainly concerned with disputes between individuals arising out of contracts, torts, marriages, wills and other private law matters. It usually involves the three basic elements, namely, the questions of jurisdiction, choice of law, recognition and enforcement of foreign judgments.

An important procedure in private international law is the choice of law in ascertaining which law has the closest relevance to either the parties or the cause of action. There could be a range of choices as to the appropriate law that might apply to the dispute in question and the court has to seek guidance from a variety of connecting factors. Some of the most frequently used connecting factors include "lex fori" (the law of the forum), "lex patriae" (the law of the nationality), "lex loci contractus" (the law of the place where the contract was made) and "lex situs" (the law of the place where the property is situated).

The increasing global legal factors of economic freedom, non-discrimination and the rule of law in the WTO and other branches of international law have not only stimulated the growing protection of individual rights and access to domestic courts, but also encouraged direct access by private citizens to international dispute settlement bodies, including the LOS Convention. Under these circumstances, it may be feasible to facilitate the settlement of trade-related international disputes by borrowing some procedural practices from private laws, such as the choice of law rules in private international law.

When a dispute arises which involves several branches of international law, and more than one international judicial institution may be resorted to, what can be done is to classify the different degrees of relevance of all the relevant laws with this particular case. In other words, which subject of law is most substantially linked to the cause of action in this case and contributes to the triggering of the disputes, and which ones are of secondary relevance or importance. Once this sequence is identified, it will help to determine the gravity of the law, as well as indicating which international institution is the most appropriate to hear the case. It should be noted that not every trade-*related* dispute is trade-*triggered*.

One of the criteria for determining which branch of law is the most relevant connecting factor in a particular case is to consider in the case that particular element was not triggered, whether or not other relevant elements in the case would not become subjects of dispute. The EU – Chilean swordfish case is studied as an example of assessing jurisdiction and the choice of forums.

7.4.3 The EU – Chilean Swordfish Case

7.4.3.1 The Case

Swordfish are a highly migratory species that cross the jurisdictional boundaries of many states and the high seas[806]. Chile has long argued that South Pacific swordfish stocks were seriously depleted due to over-fishing by commercial long-line vessels. Reliable stock assessments for these fish did not exist but 1990s catch data indicated that swordfish had been fished above a maximum sustainable yield for some time. Chilean Fisheries Law has since made provisions to conserve depleted stocks[807].

This dispute began in 1991 when Chile banned EU fleets from port landing and processing swordfish caught both inside and

806 European Communities, "Report to the Trade Barriers Regulation Committee, TBR Proceedings concerning Chilean Practices affecting transit of Swordfish in Chilean Ports", March 1999, p. 8. Paper is available at EC website: http://trade.ec.europa.eu/ revisited in July 2006.

807 More information about Chilean Fisheries Law can be found in Orrego Vicuña F., *The Changing International Law of High Seas Fisheries,* Cambridge University Press, 1999.

outside of its EEZ, on the basis that they disregarded the conservation standards laid out in Article 165 of "*Chilean Fisheries Law*"[808]. Chile argued that the EU was in violation of the "*United Nations agreement on Straddling Fish Stocks and Highly Migratory Fish Stocks*". In addition, Chile had also justified the restriction on the basis of Article 23 (3) of this agreement, which allows states to prohibit landings where capture has compromised the effectiveness of multilateral conservation measures. Although at the time of the dispute, Chile had not ratified this agreement, it was a member of CPPS (Permanent Commission for the South Pacific) and therefore did endorse such measures[809].

Chile's main purpose was to pressurize foreign fishing vessels beyond its EEZ and to pursue fishing activities in a more responsible and transparently regulated manner. There was a great deal of support from international environmental organizations such as World Wildlife Foundation due to the conservational motivation behind Chile's actions[810].

The EU on the other hand, argued that the restrictions enforced by Chile were in violation of Article V of the GATT that related to providing freedom of transit for goods through the territory of each contracting party on their way to or from other contracting parties, as well as *Article XI* that related to prohibiting quantitative restrictions on imports or exports, subject to some exceptions for imports of agricultural or fisheries products. The EU also argued that the Chilean restrictions had reduced competition for Chilean fishing vessels and thus incurred losses for the EU fleet. It should be noted that at that point there was disagreement about why this dispute arose, both sides shared the same objective of preserving the swordfish population with minimum impact on trade and achieving sustainable development of fish resources[811].

Both parties recognized the need for co-operation on data collection relating to fisheries resources in the international waters of

808 EC Report, supra note 806.
809 Id.
810 Id.
811 Id.

the Southeast Pacific. Meetings took place in 1995 and 1998 respectively where data was exchanged, but no agreement was made on the status of swordfish stocks, and neither meeting made any progress towards settling the dispute. In addition to these meetings, Chile and the EU carried out bilateral consultations in an attempt to settle the issue. However, a lack of success motivated each party to take their cases to higher bodies for settlement[812].

The EU, arguing that the dispute was about trade issues, chose to bring the case before the WTO panel in April 2000. Chile, however, argued that it was an environmental conflict with regard to multilateral conservation agreements (protection of trans-boundary and migratory fish stocks) and therefore invited the EU to engage in a formal dispute settlement process under the ITLOS. While both parties believed these settlement processes were necessary to safeguard their rights and actions, Chile and the EU continued to explore alternative avenues to achieve settlement through negotiations in order to avoid the need for either the WTO or the ITLOS panels.

In January 2001, the two sides managed to reach a compromise and settled the swordfish dispute. This agreement was made through bilateral negotiation and both parties suspended proceedings with the WTO and the ITLOS panels[813]. The agreement provided limited access for EU fishing boats and bilateral and multilateral scientific and technical co-operation in order to achieve the conservation of swordfish stocks[814]. Under the agreement, Chile would allow four EU vessels to land a total of 1,000 metric tons of

812 Id.

813 For the progress of the case under ITLOS, see the Orders and Press Releases of "the Special Chamber of ITLOS constituted to deal with 'the Case concerning the Conservation and Sustainable Exploitation of Swordfish Stocks in the South-Eastern Pacific Ocean (Chile/European Community)', Proceedings and Judgements of Case No. 7" at ITLOS website: http://www.itlos.org revisited in July 2006.

814 For more information on the settling of this dispute, see relevant readings of the International Centre for Trade and Sustainable Development (ICTSD), at its website: www.ictsd.org visited in September 2002 and revisited in August 2006.

swordfish at three designated Chilean ports, while at the same time, similar restrictions existed for Chilean vessels. A program of intensive data collection would take place to enable a joint EU – Chilean evaluation of South Pacific swordfish stocks. Meetings would be resumed between the EU and Chile within the framework of a Bilateral Scientific and Technical Commission (BSTC) in which both parties would work towards the establishment of a multilateral framework for the conservation and management of swordfish in the South-eastern Pacific.

The BSTC met four times during 2001 and 2004[815]. Multilateral International Consultations aiming to establish multilateral co-operation in the South – East Pacific were held in May and July 2002, with the participation of coastal states and limited participation of other fishing states (the EC, Chile, Colombia, Ecuador, Japan and Peru). Further multilateral consultations took place in March 2004 in Brussels with a positive outcome. In May 2004, the Chilean Government adopted Decree 123 relating to access to Chilean ports by foreign fishing vessels. Following concerns expressed by the Commission on the implications of this new piece of legislation for the EC vessels and their rights under the 2001 Arrangement, the Ambassador of Venezuela to the EU indicated that Decree 123 would not affect the rights of EC vessels operating under the 2001 Arrangement[816].

At the last BSTC meeting held in Santiago in October 2004, delegations from the two sides noted that there had been some progress in two of the three elements of the 2001 Arrangement, namely the bilateral exchange of scientific and technical information and the development of multilateral co-operation among participants in the Pacific swordfish fisheries. The delegations agreed that the exchange of scientific information was functioning well. The EC concerns on the provisions of the Decree 123 were again

815 Marcos Orellana, "The EU and Chile Suspended the Swordfish Case Proceedings at the WTO and the International Tribunal of the Law of the Sea", ASIL Insights, February 2001. The paper is available at ASIL website: www.asil.org revisited in August 2006.

816 Id.

raised at the EU-Chile Association Committee which was held in Chile in December 2004. On this occasion, Chile indicated that access to Chilean ports for logistic operations by the EC vessels whose main activity was the fishing of swordfish would not be restricted under the new Decree. This was subsequently confirmed in a Note Verbal by the Chilean Mission to the EU received in February 2005[817].

7.4.3.2 The Potential Problem of Forum Shopping

With two jurisdictional forums (the WTO and the ITLOS) hearing the swordfish case, the potential for contradictory or incompatible decisions was increased. The overlap between different branches of international law relevant to this discussion – international environmental law, the law of the sea and international trade law highlights the potential for forum shopping[818].

In 1996, the Committee for Trade and Environment (the CTE) under the WTO recommended that members resolve disputes on trade measures taken pursuant to a MEA through the dispute settlement mechanisms available under the MEA. In its 1999 Trade Barriers Regulation Committee Report (the TBR), the EC expressed its support for this recommendation by stating that:

> It is the Community's policy to apply, in a first instance, to dispute settlement bodies under the auspices of a MEA rather than revert to the WTO proceedings under the DSU. The political aim is to avoid the undermining and weakening the credibility and effectiveness of the MEAs by allowing them to be bypassed or even circumvented via the WTO route.[819]

Despite the fact that both Chile and the EC are party to the LOS Convention, the EC was reluctant to take the dispute through that procedure, instead insisting that it be taken to the WTO, despite Chile expressing a preference to solve this dispute within the LOS Convention. The TBR of the EC believed that the dispute was

817 Id.
818 Marcos Orellana, supra note 815.
819 Supra note 806.

mainly a jurisdictional one revolving around Chile's interpretation of its Exclusive Economic Zone, and not an environmental issue. At the same time, a positive judgment in favour of the EC could be enforced under the WTO through the possibility of imposing retaliation measures, with tighter time limits to solving the dispute.

The TBR noted that while a positive ruling by the LOS Arbitrators would ease the burden of making a case later at the WTO, it would not provide a practical solution because, unlike GATT Article V, the LOS Convention could not obligate parties to allow free access to their ports. The WTO was recommended because it would be difficult to justify the choice of a dispute settlement procedure to the complainant because, even if successful, the decision would have no consequences in terms of removal of the impugned trade barrier.

The EC outlined the problems with the relationship between MEAs and the WTO in the trade and environment debate, and pointed out that although the LOS Convention has a powerful compulsory and binding dispute settlement system compared to most other MEAs, it cannot grant the EC the desired remedy. The LOS Convention cannot decide on a dispute within the strict time limits of the WTO and cannot allow retaliation if there is non-compliance.

There is concern that if the EC chooses to bring a case to the WTO that undermines the LOS Convention, other WTO Members who are not as supportive of clarifying the MEA relationship, may follow suit and ignore the recommendation of the CTE[820]. The problem of forum shopping and jurisdiction overlapping will be further discussed in the following section, where the Swordfish Case will be referred to as an example of the possibility of direct relevance for private laws in international dispute settlement.

820 Supra note 806.

7.4.3.3 The Most Substantive Link: Environmental, Jurisdictional or Trade Related?

In the EU – Chilean dispute on transit of swordfish in Chilean ports, the two parties invoked the dispute settlement mechanisms of the WTO and the LOS Convention respectively, leading to the result that two jurisdictional forums were hearing the same case and could have come to contradictory or at least incompatible decisions. In this instance, the two parties held divergent views on the nature of the conflict, namely, whether its genesis was jurisdictional, environmental, or trade-related. If jurisdictional and/or environmental problems prove to be pre-dominant in the dispute, the LOS Convention or other MEA may be the procedure to which to resort to. Alternatively, if it is mainly a trade-provoked and trade-dominated conflict, the WTO proceedings under the DSU seem to be a more appropriate forum for discussion. The three areas of choice associated with the case are discussed below.

As to the jurisdictional dispute concerning Chile's interpretation of its Exclusive Economic Zone, besides the LOS regulations over the regime of the EEZ in Part V and rules on the conservation and management of the living resources of the high seas in Part VII, a delicate compromise was reached in the text of the "1995 UN Agreement on the Conservation and Management of Straddling Fish Stocks and Highly Migratory Fish Stocks" (in force as from 11 December 2001), which distinguishes clearly between straddling stocks and highly migratory species. The agreement illustrates the fundamental principle established in the LOS Convention for States to co-operate in ensuring conservation and promotion of the optimum utilization of fisheries resources both within and beyond the EEZ. Neither the fact that this agreement was not yet in force at the time of the case, nor that Chile refused to sign the agreement, necessitates the re-opening and re-discussing of this difficult issue in the ITLOS.

From an environmental viewpoint, the central issue is to examine whether the Chilean refusal to allow access to port for the purpose of transhipment as a sanction for the violation of national conservation measures, can be seen as in conformity with the environmental exemptions under Article XX of GATT 1994, whose paragraphs (b) and (g) in conjunction with its chapeau, offers general exceptions that may be applicable to the present case[821].

Paragraph (b) suggests that Chile did not exhaust all options reasonably available to it in pursuing its protection objectives through measures consistent with the GATT, which include a negotiated solution between the two parties before taking any unilateral sanction[822]. Indeed, the need for a multilateral approach for trade measures related to conservation policies is echoed by many other international bodies and agreements outside the WTO, such as the 1992 Rio Declaration[823], Agenda 21[824], the 1992 Convention on Biological Diversity[825] and the 1995 FAO Code for Responsible Fisheries[826].

Paragraph (g) is composed of three cumulative criteria, and the failure to abide with any one of them would bar the measure from being exempted under the whole Article XX. Analysis of the case indicates that the Chilean actions failed to satisfy the first criterion of the paragraph, which requires the measure be aimed at the conservation of "exhaustible natural resources". According to the interpretation of the Appellate Body on this paragraph in the US Shrimp case, the term "exhaustible resources" shall be interpreted strictly and only be applied for species specifically mentioned in internationally agreed conventions, such as the Convention on International Trade in Endangered Species of Wild Fauna and

821 Supra note 806.

822 Id.

823 UN Environment Programme (UNEP), Rio Declaration on Environment and Development, available at the website of UNEP: www.unep.org revisited in August 2007.

824 Agenda 21 is a comprehensive plan of action being taken globally, nationally and locally by organizations of the UN and governments in every area in which human impacts on the environment. It is available at the website of UN Department of Economic and Social Affairs, http://www.un.org revisited in August 2007.

825 Legal text of the Convention is available at the website of Convention on Biological Diversity: http://www.cbd.int revisited in August 2007.

826 The Code is available at FAO website: http://www.fao.org revisited in August 2007.

Flora[827]. In fact, swordfish is not classified as endangered or protected species in this Convention or other pertinent conventions, nor is there sufficient evidence for its over-fishing in the disputed area[828].

Finally, the examining of the chapeau of Article XX demonstrates that the unilateral measures of Chile constitute unjustifiable discrimination between members of the WTO and run contrary to the requirements of the chapeau[829].

The jurisdictional problem of harnessing highly migratory marine species has already been brought under the regime of relatively uniform and multilaterally agreed agreements. This not only renders it unnecessary to repeat the same discussion in the ITLOS, but also downgrades the jurisdiction-concerned element to secondary importance in this case, which cannot be classified as the most substantial linking factor to the cause of action. Moreover, the analysis of the substantive and procedural applicability of Article XX makes it clear that the so-called environmental consideration invoked by Chilean authorities is untenable and cannot be justified under this Article. This inference is logical and self-evident and hopefully will not be further contented by the parties concerned. Thus, although both jurisdiction and environment problems are relevant elements in this case and deserve consideration, neither of them amounts to the most substantial linkage. It can therefore be concluded that the ITLOS is not the appropriate court for settling this dispute.

This observation gives rise to the key question as to whether Chile is justified in suspending its MFN obligations concerning freedom of transit and access to port.

The EC Report to the Trade Barriers Regulation Committee concerning Chilean practices affecting transit of swordfish in Chilean ports (March 1999) holds the view that the main source of international law applicable to the regime of access to port is the LOS Convention[830]. This work does not subscribe to such a view.

827 EC Report, supra note 806.
828 Id.
829 Id.
830 Id.

The Report bases this judgment on Article 11 of the Convention, which reads:

> For the purpose of delimiting the territorial sea, the outermost permanent harbour works which form an integral part of the harbour system are regarded as forming part of the coast. Off-shore installations and artificial islands shall not be considered as permanent harbour works.

It may be justified to say that this provision integrates internal waters to state territory and submits port regime to national law, in other words, it clarifies the legal status of ports and empowers port states to regulate ports as part of their sovereignty.

However, this work finds it somehow circular to infer from this provision that the LOS Convention has in this way established a general principle for the right of access to port, or set up explicit rules on the possible conditions or extent that foreign vessels may acquire freedom of access. The point is, while the LOS Convention advocates and encourages innocent passage in various maritime zones, it also manages to balance this right by strengthening port state's jurisdictional right and supervision on port access requirements for foreign vessels. These standards and disciplines have later been further strengthened through a series of IMO conventions.

Part Four

Conclusions

8 Summary

Ever since the beginnings of international law, the law of the sea has been of paramount importance for international trade. The regime of the high seas and access to ports were issues of prime importance, shaping international trade relations over time. However, the law of the sea and international trade regulation, in particular under the GATT since World War II, emerged as two very distinct areas of law, hardly interfacing with each other. The same holds true for maritime law, entailing regulation of commerce. The GATT and the WTO emerged in parallel to the LOS Convention, both areas amounting to perhaps the broadest efforts in international treaty making since the 1970s. The relationship of trade regulation and the law of the sea however, has hardly been explored. Unlike environmental law or human rights law, it is one of the linkages which still needs exploration in greater depth.

The inclusion of services into the WTO law has rendered this relationship of great importance in the future rounds of trade negotiations, as maritime transport services are brought under the umbrella of the WTO agreements. It will be only a matter of time until the current exclusion of it under special exemptions be reviewed in future negotiations.

This work studies the interfacing relationship between the law of the sea and international trade law. The merit of this work lies in that it undertakes, for the first time, a comprehensive study on the commonalities and mutual integration between public international law and international trade law. Issues which were traditionally restricted to the realm of public law, for example the right of port access, were seldom brought under a systematic discussion in line with subjects in trade law areas such as competition laws. Moreover, few previous studies was conducted on the convergence and divergence between major principles in customary international law such as those on sovereignty rights on port access, and key principles in trade law such as transparency and non-discrimination in trade.

Furthermore, the scarcity of cross-section study between the law of the sea and international trade law has aggravated the proliferation of forum shopping, which was highlighted by the jurisdictional perplexity such as in the decade-long Swordfish Case.

The methodology of this work, together with the highly complex and sensitive nature of the issues involved, renders it difficult for the current work to explore this relationship in an exhaustive manner. Instead, this work seeks to provide the background and a normative basis for addressing some of the key issues, which will help to pave way for further studies in coming years.

9 Main Recommendations

9.1 Port Access – Strengthening the WTO Principles to Facilitate Access to Ports

While there is a widespread practice of permitting access to maritime ports, this seems to be insufficient to overcome the basic presumption that a state has the right to exercise exclusive control over its internal waters. The 1923 Ports Convention and many bilateral agreements confirm this right in large measures. However, their application is limited because the clauses involved are broader, narrower, or lack uniformity.

The adoption of the LOS Convention and the recognition of an expanding role for the port state has made it necessary to reconsider the adoption of an international instrument to regulate entry to maritime ports and determine the circumstances under which access may be denied[831]. One recommendation by the UNCTAD is worth noting, in which it suggested that consideration should be given to the adoption of international standards concerning the clearance, access and stay of merchant vessels in foreign ports[832].

831 During the UNCLOS III, the cautious approach was adopted of awaiting the outcome of the Conference before any initiative might be taken. Despite the fact that the LOS Convention is a comprehensive document, quite a few relevant points were left open to negotiation or interpretation by the Parties.

832 UNCTAD Report 136 recommended that the following measures must be taken in order to facilitate the development of ocean-borne trade: (a) maritime ports should be open to foreign merchant vessels for a lawful purpose; (b) adoption of international standards concerning conditions and procedures governing access; (c) determination of the circumstances under which access may be denied.

Despite the fact that the WTO principles are aiming at ensuring the smooth and non-discriminatory flow of trade across borders, some key articles (e.g. GATT Articles V, VIII, XX and XXI) and associate agreements (e.g. the SPS and TBT Agreements), suffer from the lack of transparency, uniformity and certainty. This situation has hampered the effective use of port and auxiliary services.

This work suggests that transparency should be enhanced in the relevant WTO requirements, procedures and charges[833]. As discussed in Part I of this work, the principle of transparency is one of the fundamental principles to guarantee the fair and efficient implementation of government policies and legislations. The three transparency requirements under the GATS Article VI (licensing requirements, technical standards, qualification requirements) are all relevant to the access and use of port facilities. The publication and notification of detailed and updated information relevant to import is crucial for foreign governments and business to be better informed of different levels of rules and implementation practices in the host country.

Moreover, it is proposed in this work that key terminology should be clarified in order to reduce perceived uncertainty and avoid loopholes. Examples include the definition of "goods" (including baggage) in GATT Article V, paragraph 1, as well as the definition of "public interest" and "national security" in the Exception Articles (GATT Articles XX & XXI)[834]. The ambiguity in these concepts is a major source of conflicts in practice. At the same time, documentation, data requirements and procedures applied to port access and transport in transit should also be simplified and standardized[835]. As cited in Chapter 4 of this work, a number of relevant country proposals have already been submitted to the WTO in relation to GATT Article VIII, including pre-arrival processing of transit documents, the use of commercially available information and risk management.

833 See for example, WTO report TN/TF/W/35, supra note 425, pp. 2–3.
834 Id. p. 3.
835 Id. p. 2.

Furthermore, this work recommends that another important field for future work is to encourage bilateral and regional collaboration and consultation on the facilitation of port access. As noted by a number of WTO Members, in many cases solutions to transit problems can be best solved through regional collaboration, since it is at the regional level that unnecessary hindrances to transit are largely experienced[836]. Consideration should be given to providing guidance on the main elements of regional transit as well as their proper implementation and improvement of regional co-operation on transit. WTO Members can also envisage provisions to take account of international standards and instruments, particularly when drawing up bilateral or regional instruments[837]. This work argues that the EU – Chilean Swordfish Case discussed in Part III is a prime example of resolving disputes on port access through bilateral consultation and co-operation.

9.2 Access to Cargo in Coastal Shipping – Enhancing Domestic and International Consultation and Cooperation

Cabotage is a complex issue in maritime transport which is interwoven with national policies on immigration, ship registration, domestic labour, safety, security and fiscal measures. It seems difficult to come to a uniform conclusion on whether cabotage protection should be abolished, maintained or deregulated. To some extent, this is a case-by-case issue, depending on the variances among countries in respect of social backgrounds, geographical locations, legal frameworks and governmental policies. It has been argued in many writings that the provision of protection to a par-

836 Id.
837 Id. p. 3.

ticular industry should not result in negative externalities[838]. At the same time, the benefits of protectionism should be weighed against the costs of providing protection, which include higher costs and taxes paid by the benefactors of the industry being protected.

The proponents of protectionism therefore need to ensure that policies towards protectionism do not result in such pitfalls and give a false sense of progress and comfort. It is necessary to review the relevance and the effectiveness of cabotage policies with a view to opening up particular sectors if such a move would make a positive overall contribution to the maritime transport sector[839].

It is important that countries examining their coastal shipping policies and ensure that their regulatory arrangements take into account the full range of factors relevant to the particular coastal shipping task and options available. Regardless of its particular position on cabotage, a government needs to conduct periodical reviews of related policies in respect of their social and economic benefit and achieving better balance between the two.

This work argues that governments should encourage consultation and cooperation on cabotage issue on bilateral, regional and multilateral levels. This is an important means to obtain certain level of transparency in respect of a country's cabotage policy. In addition, it is also a necessary step towards discussing the issue in a wider scope, and paving the way to bring the issue into relevant international forums, such as the WTO, in some future stage. Appropriate international consultation and cooperation may also lead to relevant agreements between countries, most probably on reciprocal basis, resulting in the application of beneficial cabotage policies to each other[840]. As far as WTO negotiations on maritime transport services are concerned, governments' cooperative initiatives also makes it possible to bring the issue to the WTO negotiation table in some future stage, when countries could agree upon

838 For example, Nazery Khalid, "Proposal for a National Maritime Transport Masterplan", Maritime Institute of Malaysia, August 2004, p. 6.

839 Id. p. 6.

840 For the benefits of reciprocity, see Mattoo, supra note 154, pp. 24–26.

certain commitments on cabotage policies, in exchange for some kind of preferential treatment on other sections of maritime transport services from other member countries.

The establishment of sustainable coastal shipping policy demands significant knowledge and experience. This work argues that a government needs to have a clear understanding of the country's cabotage policy in particular from economic perspectives. In respect of the legal framework of cabotage, governments should supervise the development of the market and continuously monitor the quality of services provided. Governments must be able to forecast demand and direct supply based on market conditions, to confirm that the level of service demanded by the public is being offered. Through the coordination of port infrastructure and land connections, governments should be able to direct the supply of coastal shipping services where they are needed, following the principles of sustainable development, through fair and equal development and protection of the environment

These initiatives would help to update governments' information and knowledge regarding their cabotage law and policy. They would also facilitate the harmonization of the issue among countries and pave the way for possible international regulation of this issue in some future stage.

9.3 Access to Cargo in Coastal Shipping – Clarification of WTO Principles on Security Exceptions

The WTO principles do not directly apply to coastal shipping due to the fact that it is excluded from negotiations on maritime transport services. However, the protection of coastal shipping through cabotage is gaining increasing attention as an impediment to the further liberalization of maritime transport services. This work notes that governments and shipping industry are conducting works on national and regional levels to review and update legislations and policies on cabotage[841]. As a result, a number of WTO rules that have relevance to cabotage may be strengthened in order to facilitate the work of national governments and enhance regional cooperation on this issue. Apart from the principle of transparency which was discussed in Part I of this work, the other is the principle of security exceptions, which is frequently resorted to for maintaining a cabotage system.

GATT Article XXI regulates security exceptions, which provides that nothing in the GATT shall be construed to require any contracting party to furnish any information the disclosure of which it considers contrary to its essential security interests, or to prevent any contracting party from taking any action which it considers necessary for the protection of its essential security interests, or to prevent any contracting party from taking any action in pursuance of its obligations under the United Nations Charter for the maintenance of international peace and security.

This work argues that one of the controversial issues of this Article is the ambiguity on who is in a position to determine whether or not trade-restricting measures are *necessary* for the protection of the invoking Member's essential security (pursuant to paragraph (b))[842]. While case laws establish that the invoking Member has authority to determine the necessity[843], this inter-

841 For example, Australian government and shipping industry have reviewed the coastal shipping policy since 2003. From government's side, see Richard Webb, "Coastal Shipping: An Overview", Parliament of Australia, Research Paper No. 12, 2003–04, May 2004, available at the Parliament's website: www.aph.gov.au revisited in August 2006; from industry's side, see Australian Shipowners Association, "Independent Review of Australian Shipping", September 2003, available at its website: www.asa.com.au revisited in August 2006.

842 For similar argument see also Kiyoun Sohn and Taek Dong Yeo, "Does the international trade help to enhance national security?", paper available at: http://faculty.washington.edu/karyiu/confer/sea05/papers/sohn_yeo.pdf revisited in August 2007.

843 Regarding the case by the Czechoslovakia against the US export control measure in 1949, it was ruled that every country must have the last resort on questions relating to its own security. See Jackson, John H., William J. Davey and Alan O. Sykes, Jr., 2002, *Legal Problems of International Economic Relations* (4th ed.), St. Paul, MN: West Group, p. 1046.

pretation of self-judging authority has itself become another matter for argument[844].

The principle of general exception is also reflected in GATS Article XIVbis on security exceptions and the Agreement on TBT. In addition, Article XXII: 1 of Government Procurement Agreement allows national security exceptions, which provides that nothing in the Agreement shall be construed to prevent any Party from taking any action or not disclosing any information which it considers necessary for the protection of its essential security interests relating to the procurement of indispensable matters for national security or for national defence purposes.

This work proposes that in order to minimize the negative effect of national security on international trade, it is important to define more precisely the concept of national security for the purpose of trade measures[845]. Under many circumstances the GATT/WTO trade disputes was triggered by the absence of precise definitions of key terms such as "essential security interests[846]". This work argues that it is important to develop a more precise and workable definition so that the abusive use of national security provisions could be discouraged[847]. Some writings also suggested that the negotiating history of the WTO Subsidies Agreement may provide a useful guide in which subsidy agreement provides the definition of a subsidy and three categories of subsidies which require different invoking conditions and different remedies[848].

Moreover, this work suggests that the determination of necessity in GATT Article XXI and GATS Article XIVbis should be further clarified. As discussed in Chapter 3 of this work, although these two provisions provide that trade-restricting actions shall be necessary for the protection of a Member's essential security interests, they do not specify criteria for determination of necessity. This lack of criteria has become one frequent trigger of trade dis-

844 Supra note 842, p. 8.
845 Id. p. 20.
846 Id. p. 20.
847 Id. p. 21.
848 See for example, id. p. 21.

putes in the WTO. Therefore this work holds the view that there is a need to develop necessity criteria which are applicable to national security measures. Several provisions of the WTO Agreements include necessity requirements, such as Article XX of GATT, Article 2.1 of SPS, Article 5.1 and Article VI:4 of GATS. They may provide useful guidance for the clarification of the national security conception[849].

9.4 Access to Cargo in International Shipping – whether the Exemption System Should be Repealed or not

This work notes that the purported value of the anti-competition exemption (antitrust immunity) system for liner shipping is determined by the fact that liner shipping is a global industry whose operations are simultaneously subject to the laws and regulations of more than one countries[850]. The national competition policies of different countries are greatly diversified and some countries do not have specific regulation on liner shipping at all. Under such circumstances, the most practical means of maintaining an efficient ocean transport system and minimizing possible conflicts between national regulatory regimes seems to be that the liner industry be regulated with a certain degree of limited anti-competition exemption accompanied by reasonable government oversight.

Moreover, the liner shipping market seems to be inherently unstable, and needs flexibility to deal with the endemic volatility of prices and demand[851]. The market is also faced with the introduc-

849 Id. p. 22.

850 See also World Shipping Council supra note 671.

851 See the website of US Federal Maritime Commission www.fmc.gov/speeches for a speech of the Chairman of the US Federal Maritime Commission delivered in March 2001 before the 4th Annual Conference of Containerization International. Visited in June 2002 and revisited in August 2005.

tion of larger ships, unbalanced and seasonally fluctuating in trade flows, together with the influence of non-commercial factors such as national prestige and security. Although other industries may share some of the features of the liner industry, the combined impact of these features could force the industry into a chronic cycle of market instability and imbalanced international trade flows. Under such circumstances, certain degree of anti-competition exemption seems to be necessary to form a certain level of protection and prevent over-adjustments in the international market. The exemption has also made it possible for carriers to team up and share larger and more efficient vessels, terminals and other assets.

This work identifies that the value of the exemption system is illustrated when carriers establish agreements that involve a co-operative sharing of operating assets such as ships and equipment, which contribute to efficiency and the reduction of operating costs. They also allow shipping lines to expand their service networks, optimize capital investment and reduce business risks. The other form of cooperation, multi-trade alliance, offers an alternative to greater industry concentration through merger and acquisition. Such alliances demonstrate the clear benefit of the anti-competition exemption system that allows carriers to undertake detailed discussion to establish, operate and revise their agreements[852]. According to the World Shipping Council, carriers have been joining with other carriers in capacity sharing agreements and entering into new trades under the anti-competition system, a trend especially noticeable from mid-1990s[853].

852 FMC supra note 659, pp. 29–30.

853 Examples include: APL entered the US-Northern Europe trade, and the US-Mediterranean trade, the US-Central America trade, the US-South America trade, a number of intra-Asia trades, the Asia-Middle East trade, and the Asia-Mediterranean trade; COSCO, Evergreen, the Malaysia International Shipping Corporation and the K Line in February 2001 announced a joint entry into the Northern Europe-Indian Subcontinent trade; Evergreen entered the US East Coast-North Europe trade, the US Gulf Coast-North Europe trade, the US-Mediterranean trade, and the all water Asia-US East Coast trade; NYK entered the Canada-North Europe trade, the US-North Europe trade, the US-West Coast of South America trade, the Korea-Middle East trade and a number of intra-Asia trades; P. & O. Nedlloyd entered the

At the same time, the value of this trend is demonstrated when carriers establish trade-lane agreements with conferences and discussion agreements, which is mainly due to the evolution of traditional liner conferences into less rigid organizations, which either provide for confidential and independent carrier contracting, or provide a forum for members to discuss trade. The benefits of trade-lane agreements include:

- engaging in collecting, exchanging and discussing market information;
- developing and proposing standardized surcharges such as bunker charges, currency adjustment charges and terminal handling charges;
- discussing and proposing common approaches to pricing to the extent permitted by law, such as common tariffs, recommended prices, proposals for general rate increases and peak season charges; and
- conducting dialogues with national shippers' councils and government agencies[854].

The existence of shipping conferences and other forms of cooperative and/or collusive activity in liner shipping has implications for technical, allocative and dynamic efficiency[855]. It seems that for many countries, the perceived benefits of technical efficiency and rate stability continue to outweigh any disbenefits that may flow from reduced competition[856].

This work observes that notwithstanding the presence of conferences, it is clear that the growing number of independent lines enhances the contestability of liner markets. A market is regarded

---

trans-Pacific trade, the Asia-US East Coast trade, the Europe-Canada trade, the US East Coast – East Coast of South America trade, the US Gulf Coast-East Coast of South America trade, the Mexico-Europe trade, the Mexico-Asia trade and the Mercosul trade. Source of information: World Shipping Council, Industry Information, http://worldshipping.org/ind.html revisited in August 2006.

854 FMC supra note 659, pp. 30–31.

855 OECD, "Competition Policy in Liner Shipping", DSTI/DOT(2002)2, p. 40.

856 OECD Maritime Transport Committee: Annual Report 1999.

as contestable when excess profits encourage entry on a scale sufficient to lower prices and in time erode profit levels. Liner shipping is not perfectly contestable since loyalty agreements and entry and exit costs may allow short run monopoly profits to accrue to a conference[857]. However, the presence of independent lines demonstrates that there is a degree of contestability sufficient to prevent a perfect monopoly outcome. Independent lines are no longer minor players in global container scene. Other major operators, such as China Shipping Group, are expanding rapidly outside of the conference system[858].

Under the present market circumstances, this work holds the view that it seems still premature to repeal the existing anti-competition exemption system and replace it with certain new regulatory instrument. The present exemption system can be characterized as limited and well-regulated exemption with reasonable safeguards from the government. On one hand, it operates in accordance with the nature of the shipping markets as discussed above while on the other hand, it has been subject to active oversight by the governmental regulatory agencies that have considerable authority to investigate and apply remedial measures[859]. This work argues that the regulated and limited nature of the existing exemption system for liner shipping is capable of ensuring competition and the healthy operation of the market[860]. This work also

857 UNESCAP, supra note 540.

858 Id. UNESCAP.

859 World Shipping Council, supra note 671, p. 20.

860 For instance, FMC of the US has ruled that the following activities are prohibited for liner shipping: operating under an agreement that has been rejected, disapproved or cancelled by the FMC; operating under an agreement without observing to the terms filed and reviewed by the FMC; engaging in unjust or unfair practices; retaliating against any shipper; restricting members of an agreements from entering into individual, confidential service contracts with the shippers; requiring a member of an agreement to disclose the terms of its individual service contracts; driving competitors out of a trade; unreasonably refusing to deal or negotiate; engaging in predatory practices; offering or paying deferred rebates; allocating shippers, etc. Source of information: the website of FMC at: http://www.fmc.gov/ revisited in August 2005.

believes that under the current global market circumstance, the key issue is not whether such exemption system should be repealed altogether, but rather, how to convert it into a more effective multilateral regulatory mechanism, preferably under the WTO.

At the same time, this work argues that further work needs to be done in order to set up a more effective multilateral regulatory and monitoring mechanism for liner shipping, preferably within the framework of the WTO. This is because countries and regions have different social backgrounds and legislative bases, leading to the problem that the different antitrust systems in different countries and regions do not run harmoniously with each other in many aspects. This has caused both substantive and procedural conflicts for the global liner shipping industry, which in turn, has hampered the fair and smooth operation of international trade. The next step should be the strengthening of the regulation of these immunity systems under a multilateral/international framework.

9.5 Access to Cargo in International Shipping – Possibility of Addressing Liner Shipping Issues in the WTO

It is identified in this work that principles with respect to anti-competitive activities in private business are reflected in the GATS provisions. The GATS also imposes obligations applicable to specific service sectors for which a member has made a market access commitment. Article I:1 of the GATS provides that "this Agreement applies to measures by Member affecting trade in services". Article I:3 further defines "measures by Members to include measures taken by non-governmental bodies in the exercise of powers delegated by central, regional or local governments or authorities".

With respect to general obligations and disciplines binding on all members regardless of market access commitments, Article VII (Recognition) encourages the mutual recognition of licenses and certificates issued by other members and gives full credit to other members' pertinent licenses and certificates. This Article is designed to prevent the use of licensing and certification as a barrier to market access for foreign service-suppliers. Moreover, bilateral, plurilateral and multilateral mutual recognition agreements are also encouraged, provided that other WTO members are given adequate opportunity to become parties to such agreements[861]. Members are required to notify the Council for Trade in Services of any new recognition measures or agreements or any existing ones that they have in place[862]. Wherever appropriate, recognition is expected to be based on multilaterally agreed upon criteria[863].

Article VIII of the GATS on Monopolies and Exclusive Service Suppliers obligates members to ensure that any monopoly service supplier in its territory, whether public or private, does not act in a manner inconsistent with the GATS Article II on MFN requirement and does not discriminate against foreign firms in the provision of services. Article VIII further requires that in service sectors covered in a member's schedule of commitments, members ensure that when a monopoly supplier (as well as an exclusive service supplier whose rights are granted by the government) competes in the supply of a service outside the scope of its monopoly rights, it does not abuse its monopoly position by acting in a manner inconsistent with that member's commitments on national treatment and market access for foreign service suppliers. This Article also obligates members to consult with each other regarding restrictive

861 On May 29, 1997, the Council for Trade in Services adopted "Guidelines for Mutual Recognition Agreements or Arrangements in the Accountancy Sector". The text is available from WTO website at www.wto.org revisited in August 2006.

862 Article VII: 4. For example, on Feb. 10, 1997, the US filed notification under GATS Article VII: 4 regarding mutual recognition agreements with Canada on certifications, accreditations and educational equivalency for architects, and with Australia, Hong Kong, Ireland, New Zealand, South Africa and the UK for engineers. See Notification Pursuant to Article VII:4 of the General Agreement on Trade in Services, United States, Architecture, S/C/N/52 (1997); Notification Pursuant to Article VII: 4 of the General Agreement on Trade in Services, United States, Engineering, S/C/N/53 (1997).

863 GATS Article VII: 5.

business practices of certain incumbent service suppliers[864]. However, the narrow definition of the term "monopoly supplier" in Article XXVIII (h) of the GATS severely limits the coverage of the obligations under Article VIII[865].

Moreover, Article IX of the GATS on Business Practices provides that certain business practices of service suppliers, other than the practices mentioned in Article VIII may restrain competition and thereby restrict trade in services. Members are therefore encouraged to enter into consultation with other members with a view to eliminating such restrictive business practices. The Article also imposes a duty to cooperate by providing non-confidential information of relevance to the matter in issue[866].

864 According to Article VIII:

1. Each member shall ensure that any monopoly supplier of a service in its territory does not, in the supply of the monopoly service in the relevant market, act in a manner inconsistent with that member's obligations under Article II on the MFN commitment and specific commitments such as market access;
2. Where a member's monopoly supplier competes, either directly or through an affiliated company, in the supply of a service outside the scope of its monopoly rights and which is subject to that member's specific commitments, the member shall ensure that such a supplier does not abuse its monopoly position to act in its territory in a manner inconsistent with such commitments.

865 Article XXVIII (h) provides that: "monopoly supplier of a service" means any person, public or private, which in the relevant market of the territory of a Member is authorized or established formally or in effect by that Member as the sole supplier of that service.

866 Article IX provides that:

1. Members recognize that certain business practices of service suppliers, other than those falling under Article VIII, may restrain competition and thereby restrict trade in services.
2. Each Member shall, at the request of any other Member, enter into consultations with a view to eliminating practices referred to in paragraph 1. The Member addressed shall accord full and sympathetic consideration to such a request and shall cooperate through the supply of publicly available non-confidential information of relevance to the matter in question. The Member addressed shall also provide other information available to the requesting Member, subject to its domestic law and to the conclusion of satisfactory agreement concerning the safeguarding of its confidentiality by the requesting Member.

This work argues that the main avenue to address liner shipping under the WTO/GATS system should be by means of specific commitments under market access and national treatment, which could be brought about by sectoral negotiations. One of the options is to set up sectoral agreement on the exemption system for international liner shipping[867]. Similar suggestion was put forward under the pro-competitive principles in the Reference Paper on Basic Telecommunication[868], which aims to control restrictive business practices and abuse through the dominant position of services suppliers[869]. Although the Reference Paper's impact on market access, national treatment and development of national regulatory framework has not yet been fully analyzed, this work argues that its regulation could be relevant to other sectors representing essential facilities for delivery of other services, such as international liner shipping services. Its provisions on control of abuse of dominant position could be developed further to strengthen the provisions of Articles VIII and IX on a generic basis[870].

In addition, it is the recommendation of this work that the effectiveness of relevant GATS provisions needs to be strengthened to ensure control of abuse of dominant position through addressing specific private sector restrictive practices and establishing a notification requirement for restrictive business practices[871]. Moreover, to tackle the abuse of dominant position of service suppliers from developed countries, as well as the operators of distribution channels and information networks, regulation needs to

867 Mattoo, supra note 154, p. 18.

868 The Reference Paper was originally put forth by the United States and was adopted by countries without any real negotiation. Most of its provisions were already covered by the Annex on Basic Telecommunications and therefore this partly facilitated its adoption. See Mattoo, id., p. 29.

869 Id. p. 18. Pro-competitive principles are directed both at regulatory practices of governments to ensure good governance and least trade restrictiveness and at private operators' practices to prevent anti-competitive behaviour and abuse of dominant position.

870 Id.

871 Mattoo, supra note 154, p. 17.

be made to ensure effective access for developing countries suppliers of such facilities[872].

As discussed in Part I of this work, the fundamental principles of the WTO, in particular those on non-discrimination and transparency, should be enhanced in the relevant GATS provisions on restrictive business practices. For liner shipping which is largely shielded under the anti-competition exemption system, the degree of regulatory transparency is particularly important to enable both the customers and service-providers to obtain the necessary information for the compliance of policy and the evaluation of their benefits and costs.

Furthermore, this work suggests that during the process of reinforcing the WTO fundamental principles, flexibility needs to be permitted especially for developing countries, many of which suffer from the lack of well-developed competition legislation. Given the diversity in stages and patterns of economic development among Members, with regard to the relevance of exceptions or exemptions from national competition laws, sufficient flexibility should be incorporated in any possible framework to make it workable among all WTO Members[873]. This work also shares the view that a multilateral framework on competition should provide for the possibility of appropriate exemptions or exclusions in two aspects. Firstly, small and medium-sized enterprises may be provided with greater flexibility under national competition laws than other firms. Secondly, sensitive economic sectors may be provided with higher degree of exemption or exclusion in order to safeguard national interests[874]. Such exemption or exclusion, however, must be subject to appropriate transparency procedures, so that firms trading with a Member or investing in a Member's economy are fully informed of their situation[875].

872 Id. p. 17.
873 For similar argument see for example WTO Secretariat, Report (2002) of the Working Group on the Interaction between Trade and Competition Policy to the General Council, WT/WGTCP/6 9 December 2002.
874 Id.
875 Id.

Bibliography

Abbott, K.W., "The Uruguay Round and Dispute Resolution: Building a Private-Interests System of Justice", *Columbia Business Law Review*, 1992.

Abel, W.T., "Fishing for an International Norm to Govern Straddling Stocks: The Canada-Spain Dispute of 1995", 27 *University of Miami Inter-American Law Review* 553, 1996.

Adlung, R., "Services Negotiations in the Doha Round: Lost in Flexibility?", 9 *Journal of International Economic Law*, 2006.

Akehurst, M., *A Modern Introduction to International Law*, London, 1982.

Alexandrowicz, C.H., *An Introduction to the History of the Law of Nations in the East Indies*, Oxford, 1967.

Anand, R.P., *The Law of the Sea: Caracas and Beyond,* Atlantic Highlands, New Jersey, 1980.

Anand, R.P., "Maritime Practice in South-East Asia until 1600 A.D. and the Modern Law of the Sea", 30 *The International and Comparative Law Quarterly* 2, 1981

Anand, R.P., *Origin and Development of the Law of the Sea, History of International Law Revisited*, The Hague, 1983.

Anderson, A.D.M., "Seeking Common Ground: Canada-U.S. Trade Dispute Settlement Policies in the Nineties", Boulder, Colorado, 1995.

Anderson, R.D. & Jenny, F., "The Current Proposals for WTO Negotiations on Competition Policy: Background and Overview." Paper presented to the Conference Board 2003 Conference on Antitrust Issues in Today's Economy. March 18–19, 2003.

Argiroffo, A., "Flags of Convenience and Substandard Vessels", 110 *International Labor Review*, 1974.

Arnold, J.R., "The Oilseeds Dispute and the Validity of Unilateralism in a Multilateral Context", 30 *Stanford Journal of International Law*, 1994.

Arup, C., *The New World Trade Organization Agreements: Globalizing Law Through Services and Intellectual Property*, Cambridge Studies in Law and Society. New York, 2000.

Baker, S., *First Steps in International Law*, London: Kegal Paul, Trench Trubner and Co., 1899.

Bardin, A., "Coastal State's Jurisdiction over Foreign Vessels", 14 *Pace International Law Review*, 2002.

Bax, N., Williamson, A., Aguero, M., Gonzales, E., & Geeves, W., "Marine Invasive Alien Species: A Threat to Global Biodiversity", 27 *Marine Policy*, 2003.

Baxter, R.R., *The Law of International Waterways*, Cambridge, Massachusetts, 1964.

Bederman, D.J., "Marine Preservation Law: Old Challenges, New Trends", 8 *Widener Law Symposium Journal*, 2002.

Beesley, J.A., "The Arctic Pollution Prevention Act: Canada's Perspective", 1 *Syracuse Journal of International Law* 226, 1973.

Bekker, P.H.F., "Land and Maritime Boundary between Cameroon and Nigeria (Cameroon v. Nigeria; Equatorial Guinea Intervening)", 97 *American Journal of International Law*, 2003.

Behnam, A., "Future of the Shipping Dialogue in UNCTAD", 2 *Maritime Policy & Management* 1, January 1994.

Bhagwati, J.N., "Splintering and Disembodiment of Services and Developing Nations", *The World Economy* 7, June 1984.

Blackhurst, R., "Reforming WTO Decision Making: Lessons from Singapore and Seattle", in: Deutsch, K. & Speyer, B. (eds.), *The WTO Millennium Round: Freer Trade in the Twenty-First Century*, London, 2001.

Blanco-Bazán, A., "IMO Interface with the Law of the Sea Convention", January 2000, available at the website of IMO: <http://www.imo.org/Circulars> revisited in July 2006.

Bliss, J.C., "GATT Dispute Settlement Reform in the Uruguay Round: Problems and Prospects", *Stanford Journal of International Law* 23, 1987.

Bown, C.P. & Hoekman, B.M., "WTO Dispute Settlement and the Missing Developing Country Cases: Engaging the Private Sector", 8 *Journal of International Economic Law*, 2005.

Boyle, A.E., "Dispute Settlement and the Law of the Sea Convention: Problems of Fragmentation and Jurisdiction", 46 *International & Comparative Law Quarterly* 37, 50, 1997.

Boyle, Alan E., "Further Development of the Law of the Sea Convention: Mechanisms for Change", 54 (3) *International and Comparative Law Quarterly*, 2005.

Bradley, A.J., *Implementing the Results of GATT Panel Proceedings: an Area for Uruguay Round Consideration. The New GATT Round of Multilateral Trade Negotiations*, 2nd ed., The Netherlands, 1991.

Briggs, H.W., *The Law of Nations (Cases, Documents and Notes)*, New York, 1952.

Brittan, L., "European Objectives for Services Worldwide: How the WTO Can Help", speech, 2 June 1998, Brussels, available at: <http://GATS-info.eu.int/GATS-info/gnews.pl?NEWS=ccc>, accessed 1 November 2000.

Brooks, M.R. & Button, K.J., "The Determinants of Shipping Rates: A North Atlantic Case Study", 1 *Transport Logistics* 1, 1996.

Brooks, M.R., *Sea Change in Liner Shipping: Regulation and managerial Decision-making in a Global Industry*, Amsterdam, 2000.

Brooks, M.R., "The Jones Act under NAFTA and its Effects on the Canadian Shipbuilding Industry", research paper for the Atlantic Institute for Market Studies (AIMS), September 2006.

Brown, D., Deardorff, A.V. & Stern, R.M., "Modelling Multilateral Trade Liberalization in Services", research paper for the Third International Conference on the Asia-Pacific Economy, "International Trade in Services", Brisbane, Australia, July 12–13, 1995.

Brown, E.D., *The International Law of the Sea*, Dartmouth, 1994.

Brownlie, I., *Principles of Public International Law*, 3rd ed., Oxford, 1979.

Buglass, L.J., *Marine Insurance and General Average in the United States*, 3rd ed., Centreville, Maryland, 1991.

Burke, K.M. & Deleo, D.A., "Innocent Passage in the United Nations Convention on the Law of the Sea", 9 *Yale Journal of World Public Order* 389, 1983.

Burke, W.T., Legatski, R. & Woodhead, W.W., "National and International Law Enforcement in the Ocean", Washington Sea Grant Publication, *International Marine Studies,* Washington, Seattle/London, 1977.

Burke, W.T., "Exclusive Fisheries Zones and Freedom of Navigation", 20 *San Diego Law Review*, 1983.

Busch, M.L. & Reinhardt, E., "Testing International Trade Law: Empirical Studies of GATT/WTO Dispute Settlement", in: Kennedy, D.L.M & Southwick, J.D. (eds.), *Political Economy of International Trade Law: Essays in Honor of Robert E. Hudec*, Cambridge, 2002.

Busch, M.L., "Democracy, Consultation, and the Paneling of Disputes under GATT", 44 *Journal of Conflict Resolution*, 2000.

Buzan, B., "Negotiating by Consensus: Developments in Technique at the United Nations Conference on the Law of the Sea", 75 *American Journal of International Law*, 1981.

Cady, J.R., *Southeast Asia: Its Historical Development*, New York, 1964.

Caflisch, L.C., "Landlocked States and Their Access to and from the Sea", 49 *British Yearbook of International Law* 71, 1978.

Carstensen, N.C., "A Re-internationalization of Dispute Settlement in the Law of the Sea", 62 (1/2) *Zeitschrift für Ausländisches Öffentliches Recht und Völkerrecht*, 2002.

Cavana, R.Y., "Policy Issues Relating to Coastal and International Shipping in New Zealand", GSBGM Working Paper Series 2/95, Victoria University of Wellington, 1995.

Centre for Studies and Research of the Hague Academy of International Law, "Rights and Duties of Riparian States of International Rivers", Dordrecht, 1991.

Charney, J. & Lewis, A.M., 1, *International Maritime Boundaries*, Dordrecht, 1993.

Charney, J.I., "The Implication of Expanding International Dispute Settlement System: The 1982 Convention on the Law of the Sea", 90 *The American Journal of International Law*, January 1996.

Charteris, A.H., "The Legal Position of Merchantmen in Foreign Ports and National Waters", 1 *British Year Book of International Law*, 1920.

Chircop, A.E. & Linden, O., *Places of Refuge for Ships: Emerging Environmental Concerns of a Maritime Custom*, Dordrecht, 2006.

Chung, K.C. & Tsutsumi, T., "Port State Control", Transportation, Water and Urban Development Department, World Bank, May 1994.

Churchill, R., "The Role of IMO in Combating Marine Pollution", in: Cusine, D.J. & Grand, J.P. (eds), *The Impact of Marine Pollution*, London, 1980.

Churchill, R. & Lowe, A.V., *The Law of the Sea*, 2nd ed., Manchester, 1988.

Churchill, R. & Lowe, A.V., *The Law of the Sea*, 3rd ed., Manchester, 1999.

Churchill, R., "The International Tribunal for the Law of the Sea: Survey for 2003", 19 (4) *International Journal of Marine and Coastal Law*, 2004.

Churchill, R., "Dispute settlement under UN Convention on the Law of the Sea: survey for 2004", 21 (1) *International Journal of Marine & Coastal Law*, 2006.

Clarke, R.L., "An Analysis of the International Ocean Shipping Conference System", 36 *Transportation Journal* 4, 1997.

Clyde, P.S. & Reitzes, J.D., "The Effectiveness of Collusion under Antitrust Immunity: The Case of Liner Shipping Conferences", United States Federal Trade Commission Bureau of Economics Staff Report, December 1995.

Colombos, D.J., *The International Law of the Sea*, 6th ed., London, 1967.

Cormack, D., *Response to Marine Oil Pollution: Review and Assessment*, Berlin, 1999.

Cottier, T. & Krista, N.S., "Non-Violation Complaints in the WTO/GATT Dispute Settlement: Past, Present and Future", in: Petersmann, E.-U. (ed.), *International Trade Law and the GATT/WTO Dispute Settlement System*, The Hague/London/Boston, 1997.

Cottier, T., "Emerging Doctrines of Good Governance: The Impact of the WTO and China's Accession", in: Abbott, F.M. (ed.), *China in the World Trading System: Defining the Principles of Engagement*, The Hague/London/Boston, 1998.

Cottier, T., "The WTO Dispute Settlement System: New Horizons", in: The American Society of International Law (ed.). *The Challenge of Non-State Actors*, Proceedings of the 92nd Annual Meeting, Washington, D.C., April 1–4, 1998.

Cottier, T. & Krista, N.S., "Good Faith and the Protection of Legitimate Expectations in the WTO", in: Bronckers, M. & Quick, R. (eds.). *New Directions in International Economic Law: Essays in Honor of John H. Jackson*, The Hague/London/Boston, 2000.

Cottier, T., "Limits to International Trade: The Constitutional Challenge", ASIL, Proceedings of the 94th annual Meeting, Washington, 2000.

Cottier, T., Mavroidis, P.C. & Blatter, P. (eds.), *Regulatory Barriers and the Principle of Non-Discrimination in World Trade Law*, Ann Arbor, Michigan, 2000.

Cottier, T. & Oesch, M., "WTO Law, Precedents and Legal Changes", 3 *Turku Law Journal*, 2001.

Cottier, T., "Trade and Human Rights: A Relationship to Discover", *Journal of International Economic Law* 5, 2002.

Cottier, T. & Satoko, T., "The Balance of Power in WTO Decision-Making: Towards Weighted Voting in Legislative Response", *Aussenwirtschaft* 5, 2003.

Cottier, T. & Mavroidis, P.C., "Concluding Remarks", in: Cottier, T. & Mavroidis Petros C. (eds.), *The Role of the Judge in International Trade Regulation,* Ann Arbor, Michigan, 2003.

Cottier, T., "The WTO Permanent Panel Body: A Bridge Too Far?", 6 *Journal of International Economic Law* 1, (March), 2003.

Cottier, T., "The Legal Framework for Free Trade Areas & Customs Unions in WTO Law", in: Godel, M. & Gage, J. (eds.). *Multilateralism and Bilateralism After Cancún. Challenges and Opportunities of Regionalism,* Bern, 2004.

Cottier, T. & Oesch, M., *International Trade Regulation, Law and Policy in the WTO, the European Union and Switzerland, Cases, Materials and Comments*, Bern, 2005.

Cottier, T., "From Progressive Liberalization to Progressive Regulation in WTO Law", 9 *Journal of International Economic Law*, 2006.

Crafts, N., "Steam as a General Purpose Technology: A Growth Accounting Perspective", *The Economic Journal* 114 (495), 2004.

Cullinane, K. & Khana, M., "Economies of Scale in Large Containerships: Optimal Size and Geographical Implications", 8 *Journal of Transport Geography* 3, 2000.

Cundick, R.P., "International Straits: the Regime of Access", 5 *Georgia Journal of International and Comparative Law* 107, 1975.

Daniels, P.D., *Service Industries: A Geographical Appraisal*, Oxford, 1985.

Davies, J.E., "Destructive Competition and Market Unsustainability in the Liner Shipping Industry", 17 *International Journal of Transport Economics* 3, 1990.

Davies, J., Pirrong, C., Sjostrom, W. & Yarrow, G., "Stability and Related Problems in Liner Shipping: An Economic Overview", Paper submitted in September 1995 to the Court of First Instance of the European Communities in Case T-395/94, 1995.

Degan, V.D., "Internal Waters", 17 *Netherlands Yearbook of International Law* 3, 1986.

De La Fayette, L., "Access to ports in international law", 11 *International Journal of Marine and Coastal Law*, 1996.

Delupis, I., "Landlocked States and the law of the sea", 19 *Scandinavian Studies in Law*, 1975.

Derrington, S. & White, M., "Australian Maritime Law Update: 2002", 34 *Journal of Maritime Law and Commerce*, 2003.

De Vattel, E., *The Law of Nations or the Principles of Natural Law Applied to the Conduct and to the Affairs of Nations and Sovereigns,* Charles G. Fenwick, trans. Washington D.C., Carnegie Institute of Washington, 1916 (1758).

DeWinter, R., "Issues of Fairness in the Tuna-Dolphin Cases", available at the website of International Economics Study Center: <http://internationalecon.com> revisited in February 2006.

De Yturriaga, J.A., *Straits Used for International Navigation: A Spanish Perspective*, Dordrecht, 1991.

Dinger, F., "What Shall We Do with the Drunken Sailor? EC Competition Law and Maritime Transport", Basel, 2001.

Djalal, H., "Cost Sharing in the Straits of Malacca and Singapore", paper presented at the 31st Annual Conference of the Law of the Sea Institute, University of Miami, 1998.

Douven, W.J.A.M., Buurman, J.J.G. & Kiswara, W., "Spatial Information for Coastal Zone Management: The Example of the Banten Bay Seagrass Ecosystem, Indonesia.", 46 *Ocean & Coastal Management*, 2003.

Dukgeun, A., "Environmental Disputes in the GATT/WTO: before and after US-Shrimp Case", 20 *Michigan Journal of International Law* 4, 1999.

Dunfee, G.E., "Territorial Status of Deepwater Ports", 15 *San Diego Law Review* 603, 1977–78.

Esser, M., "Conflict Resolution under the General Agreement on Tariffs and Trade: Experience and Reform. Conflict Resolution in International Trade: a Symposium", Friedmann, D. & Mestmäcker, E.-J. (eds.), Baden-Baden, 1993.

European Commission, "Progress towards a Maritime Policy", COM (85) 90 Final, 14 March 1985.

European Commission, "A Common Policy on Safe Seas", COM (93) 55 Final, 24 February 1993.

European Commission, Commission Decision of 19 October 1994 Relating to a Proceeding Pursuant to Article 85 of the EC Treaty (IV/34.446-Trans-Atlantic Agreement), Document 394D0980, Official Journal, L 376, 31 December, 1994.

European Commission, "Towards a New Maritime Strategy", COM (96) 81 Final, 18 March 1996.

European Shippers' Council (ESC), Maritime Regulatory Reform, European Shippers' Council Submission to the OECD Division of Transport Inquiry on Regulatory Reform in Maritime Transport, 10 April, 2001.

Fawcett, J.E.S., "Trade and Finance in International Law", 123 *Recueil des Cours* 215, The Hague, 1968.

Federal Maritime Commission (US), "The Ocean Shipping Reform Act: An Interim Status Report", Washington: Federal Maritime Commission, June 2000.

Feketekuty, G., "Improving the Architecture of the GATS", in: Stephenson, S. (ed.), *Services Trade in Western Hemisphere: Liberalization, Integration and Reform*, Washington D.C., 2001.

Fenn, P.T., "Origins of the Theory of Territorial Waters", 20 *American Journal of International Law*, 1926.

Finger, J.M., "Implementing the Uruguay Round Agreements: Problems for Developing Countries", *Global Trade Policy*, 2001.

Finger, J.M. & Schuler, P., "Implementation of Uruguay Round Commitments: The Development Challenge", *The World Economy* 23, 2000.

Finger, J.M. & Winters, L.A., "Reciprocity", in: Hoekman, B., English, P. & Mattoo, A. (eds.), *Development, Trade and the WTO: A Handbook*, Washington, 2002.

Fink, C., Matoo, A. & Neagru, C., "Trade in International Maritime Services: How Much Does Policy Matter?", World Bank Development Research Group Working Paper No. 2522, 2000.

Fischer, T.C., *The United States, the European Union, and the "Globalization" of World Trade*, Connecticut/London, 2000.

Fitzgerald, B.F., "Port State Jurisdiction and Marine Pollution under UNCLOS III", *Journal of The Maritime Law Association of Australia and New Zealand* 11, 1995.

Fleming, D.K & Hayuth, Y., "Spatial Characteristics of Transportation Hubs: Centrality and Intermediacy" *Journal of Transport Geography* 2, 1994.

Fleming, D.K., "Selected Pages from the History of US Cargo Liner Service", available at: <http://www.sma.washington.edu/faculty/working_papers/Fleming_2001.pdf>, revisited in June 2006.

Footer, M.E., "GATT and the Multilateral Regulation of Banking Services", 27: 2 *International Lawyer* 343, 1993.

Fortuin, H., "The Regime of Navigable Waterways of International Concern and the Statute of Barcelona", 7 *Netherlands International Law Review*, 1960.

Foster, E.G. & Haward, M., "Integrated Management Councils: A Conceptual Model for Ocean Policy Conflict Management in Australia", 46 *Ocean & Coastal Management*, 2003.

Foulke, R.R., *A Treatise on International Law*, Philadelphia, 1920.

Fox, E.M., "The End of Antitrust Isolationism: The Vision of One World", *University of Chicago Legal Forum*, 1992.

Fox, E.M., "Toward World Antitrust and Market Access", 91 *American Journal of International Law*, 1997.

Fox, N.R., "An Oligopoly Model of Ocean Liner Shipping", 9 *Review of Industrial Organization* 3, 1994.

Fox, N.R. & White, L.J., "U.S. Ocean Shipping Policy: Going against the Tide", 553, *Annals of the American Academy of Political and Social Science*, Transport at the Millennium 1997.

Franck, B. & Bunel, J.C., "Contestability, Competition and Regulation, The Case of Liner Shipping", 9 *International Journal of Industrial Organization* 1, 1991.

Francois, J., "Maximizing the Benefits of the TPRM for Developing Countries", in: Hoekman, B. & Martin, W. (eds.), *Developing Countries and the WTO: A Pro-Active Agenda*, Oxford, 2001.

Francois, J.F. & Reinert, K.A., "The Role of Services in the Structure of Production and Trade: Stylized Facts from a Cross-Country Analysis", 2 *Asia-Pacific Economic Review*, May 1996.

Francois, J. & Wooton, I., "Special Section: The New International Trade Agenda and the WTO Trade in International Transport Services: The Role of Competition", 9 *Review of International Economics* 2, 2001.

Fu, K.C. "Current Legal Developments China – A Chinese Perspective on the UNESCO Convention on the Protection of the Underwater Cultural Heritage", 18 *The International Journal of Marine and Coastal Law*, 2003.

Fukunaga, Y., "Securing Compliance Through the WTO Dispute Settlement System: Implementation of DSB Recommendations", *Journal of International Economic Law* 9, 2006.

Galdorisi, G., "The United States and the Law of the Sea, Changing Interests and New Imperatives", 69 *US Navy, Naval War College Review* 4, Autumn 1996.

Galpin, W.F., *A History of England,* New York, 1938.

Garrison, W.L., "Historical Transportation Development", Institute of Transportation Studies, University of California, Berkeley, 2003.

Gaskell, N., "Decision Making and the Legal Committee of the International Maritime Organization", 18 *The International Journal of Marine and Coastal Law*, 2003.

Ginderachter, E.V. & Durande, S., "EC Regulation 870/95: The Consortia Block Exemption", 36 *European Transport Law* 2, 1996.

Giovanni, M., "The Role of Multilateral Institutions in International Cooperation", 89 *The American Economic Review* 1, March 1999.

Glassner, M.I. (ed.), *Bibliography on Land-Locked States, Economic Development and International Law*, 5th rev. ed., Armonk, New York, 2000.

Gordon, J.S., "Shipping Regulation and the Federal Maritime Commission: Part I", 37 *The University of Chicago Law Review* 1, 1969.

Goss, R.O. & Marlow, P.B., "Internationalism, Protectionism and Interventionism in Shipping" in: Gwilliam, K.M. (ed.), *Current Issues in Maritime Economics.* Deventer, 1993.

Gould, E. & Joy, C., "In Whose Service? The Threat Posed by the General Agreement on Trade in Services to Economic Development in the South", World Development Movement, London, December 2000, available at: <http://www.wdm.org.uk>, revisited in March 2001.

Griffin, J.P., "EC/US Antitrust Cooperation Agreement: Impact on Transnational Business", 24 *Law and Policy in International Business* 1051, 1993.

Grotius, H., *De Jure Praedae Commentarius*, vol. I: A translation of the original manuscript of 1604 by Gwladys L. Williams and Walter H. Zeydel, No 22 of the Classics of International Law, edited by James Brown Scott Publication of the Carnigic Endowment for International Peace (Washington), Oxford, 1950.

Grynberg, R., "WTO Fisheries Subsidies Negotiations: Implications for Fisheries Access Arrangements and Sustainable Management", 27 *Marine Policy*, 2003.

Gudmundur, E., *The International Tribunal for the Law of the Sea*, The Hague, 2000.

Hakapää, K., *Marine Pollution in International Law, Material Obligations and Jurisdiction*, Helsinki, 1981.

Hammer, M., Holmlund, C.M. & Almlöv, M.Å., "Social-Ecological Feedback Links for Ecosystem Management: A Case Study of Fisheries in the Central Baltic Sea Archipelago", 46 *Ocean & Coastal Management*, 2003.

Haralambides, H.E., Cheung Tam He, C. & Tsolakis, S.D., "The Future of the Hub-and-Spoke System in Liner Shipping", paper presented at the 16th International Port Logistics Conference, Alexandria, Egypt, 6–8 February 2000.

Hare, J., "Port State Control: Strong Medicine to Cure a Sick Industry", available at: <http://www.uctshiplaw.com/psc2.htm>, viewed in May 2003.

Hart, H.H., *Sea Road to the Indies*, New York, 1950.

Hartridge, D., "Opening Markets for Banking Worldwide: The WTO General Agreement on Trade in Services", speech to international banking seminar, London, 8 January 1997.

Heaver, T., "The Shipping Conferences Exemption Act: Review and Suggestions of Positions Appropriate for the Panel", April 2001, research conducted for the Canada Transportation Act Review, available at: <http://www.reviewcta-examenltc.gc.ca>, revisited in August 2006.

Heng, D.T.S., "Export Commodity and Regional Currency: The Role of the Chinese Copper Coins in the Melaka Straits, 10th to 14th Centuries", 37 *Journal of Southeast Asian Studies*, 2006.

Henkin, L., "Arctic Anti-pollution: Does Canada Make – or Break – International Law", 65 *American Journal of International Law* 131, 1971.

Hertel, T., Hoekman, B. & Martin, W., "Developing Countries and a New Round of WTO Negotiations", World Bank Research Observer, Oxford, the UK, 2001.

Hilf, M., *Settlement of disputes in international economic organizations: comparative analysis and proposals for strengthening the GATT dispute settlement procedures. The new GATT Round of Multilateral Trade Negotiations*, 2nd ed., Deventer, 1991.

Hill, T.P., "On goods and services", *The Review of Income and Wealth* 4, December 1977.

Hirsch, Seev, "Services and Service Intensity in International Trade", 125 *Weltwirtschaftliches Archiv* 45, 1989.

Hoekman, B. & Sauvé, P., "Liberalizing Trade in Services", Discussion Paper No. 243, Washington D.C., 1994.

Hoekman, B. & Braga Carlos A. Primo, "Protection and Trade in Services: A Survey", *Open Economies Review*, Dordrecht, 1997.

Hoekman, B. & Mavroidis, P.C., "WTO Dispute Settlement, Transparency and Surveillance", *The World Economy* 23, 2000.

Hoekman, B., "Strengthening the Global Trade Architecture for Development: the Post Doha Agenda", 1 *World Trade Review* 1, 2002.

Hoffmann, J., "Concentration in Liner Shipping: Its Causes and Impacts for Ports and Shipping Services in Developing Regions", 1998 available at: <www.eclac.cl/english/research/dcitf/lcg2027/contents.htm>, viewed in December 2000.

Hoppe, H., "The Work of the Sub-committee on Flag State Implementation – An Overview" 2000, available at: <www.imo.org>, viewed in October 2001.

Hoppe, H., "Port State Control – an Update on IMO's Work (2000)", available at IMO website: <http://www.imo.org/Circulars>, revisited in July 2006.

Horn, H. & Mavroidis, P.C., "Remedies in the WTO Dispute Settlement System and Developing Country Interests", World Bank, Washington D. C., April 1999.

Hudec, R.E., "Dispute Settlement. Completing the Uruguay Round: a Results-Oriented Approach to the GATT Trade Negotiations" Washington, D.C., 1990.

Hudec, R.E., "The Role of the GATT Secretariat in the Evolution of the WTO Dispute Settlement Procedure", in Bhadwati, J. and Hirsch, M. (eds.), *The Uruguay Round and beyond: Essays in Honor of Arthur Dunkel*", Berlin, 1998.

Hummel, D., "Have International Transportation Costs Declined?", University of Chicago Working Paper, September 1999.

Hyde, C.C., *International Law – Chiefly as Interpreted and Applied by the United States*, Boston, 1922.

Hydeman, L.M. & Berman, W.H., *International Control of Nuclear Maritime Activities*, Ann Arbor, Michigan, 1960.

Ianchovichina, E., Mattoo, A. & Olarreaga, M., "Unrestricted Market Access for Sub-Saharan Africa: How Much is it Worth and Who Pays?" Policy Research Working Paper 2595, World Bank, 2001, available at: <www.worldbank.org/trade>, revisited in August 2005.

IMO, "List of Obligations Undertaken by Governments by Ratifying SOLAS 74, MARPOL 73/78 LL 66, STCW 78 and Protocols Relating Thereto", London, IMO, 1993.

IMO, "International Safety Management Code – Guidelines on Interpretation of the ISM Code", London, IMO, 1994.

Irwin, D.A., "The Early Trade Policy Experience of the United States, 1789–1820", Department of Economics, University of Virginia, 2002.

Jackson, J.H., *International Competition in Services: A Constitutional Framework*. Washington, D.C., 1988.

Jackson, J.H., *The World Trading System, Law and Policy of International Economic Relations*, 2nd ed., the UK, 1997.

Jackson, J.H. & Sykes, A.O., *Implementing the Uruguay Round*, Oxford, 1997.

Jackson, J. H., *The Jurisprudence of GATT & the WTO*, the UK, 2000.
Jackson, J. H., Davey, W. J. & Sykes Jr., A. O., *Legal Problems of International Economic Relations*, 4th ed., St. Paul, Minneapolis, 2002.
Jagota, S. P., "Developments in the Law of the Sea between 1970 and 1998", 2 *Journal of the History of International Law* 1, July 2000.
Jennings, M., "The WTO and International Law: Mapping the Relationship", WTO Law and International Law, ANZSIL (The Australian and New Zealand Society of International Law) Conference, 2004.
Jennings, R. & Watts, A., *Oppenheim's International Law*, 9th ed., London, 1992.
Jessup, P. C., *The Law of Territorial Waters and Maritime Jurisdiction*, New York, 1927.
Jessup, P. C., *Trans-national Law*, New Haven, Connecticut, 1956.
Jessup, P. C., "The United Nations Conference on the Law of the Sea", 55 *Columbia Law Review* 234, 1959.
Jin, A. T. K., "The Sea Transport Industry and the Challenge of State Regulations", UNITAR Conference on the Seas and Security, Hiroshima, Japan, 6–8 March 2002.
Joseph, A., "The Legal Status, Privileges and Immunities of the International Tribunal for the Law of the Sea", 2 *Max Planck Yearbook of United Nations Law*, 1998.
Juda, L., *International Law and Ocean Use Management,* Oxford, 1996.
Kasoulides, G. C., *Port State Control and Jurisdiction*, The Netherlands, 1993.
Kasoulides, G. C., *The Port State Enforcement Regime Through International Organizations*, Dordrecht, 1993.
Kennedy, K. C., *Competition Law and the World Trade Organization: the Limits of Multilateralism*, London, 2001.
Kerwin, J. G., "The Role of United Nations General Assembly Resolutions in Determining Principles of International Law in United States Courts", *Duke Law Journal* 876, 1983.
Keselj, T., "Port State Jurisdiction in Respect of Pollution from Ships: The 1982 United Nations Convention on the Law of the Sea and the Memoranda of Understanding", 30 *Ocean Development & International Law* 2, June 1999.
Khor, M., "WTO 'Singapore Issues': What's at Stake and Why it Matters", TWN Briefings, 2003.
Kindt, J. W., *Marine Pollution and the Law of the Sea*, New York, 1986.
Kintner, E. W., Joelson, M. R. & Vaghi, P. J., "Groping for a Truly International Antitrust Law", *Virginia Journal of International Law*, 1973.
Knudsen, K., "Zero Taxation of World Shipping Industry", 4 *Maritime Policy and Management* 1, 1997.
Kolodkin, A. L., "National Legislation in the Light of UNCLOS and the Practice of the International Tribunal for the Law of the Sea", in Nordquist, M. H. & Moore, J. N. (eds), *Current Marine Environmental Issues and the International Tribunal for the Law of the Sea*, The Hague, 2001.

Kono, M. et al., "Opening Markets in Financial Services and the Role of the GATS", WTO Special Studies, Geneva, 1997.

Kuyper, P.J., "The law of GATT as a special field of international law: ignorance, further refinement or self-contained system of international law?" *Netherlands Yearbook of International Law* 25, 1994.

Kwiatkowska, B., "The Ireland v. United Kingdom (Mox Plant) Case: Applying the Doctrine of Treaty Parallelism" 18 *The International Journal of Marine and Coastal Law*, 2003.

Kwiatkowska, B., "The Southern Bluefin Tuna Arbitral Tribunal Did Get It Right: A Commentary and Reply to the Article by David A. Colson and Dr. Peggy Hoyle." 34 *Ocean Development & International Law*, 2003.

Lauterpacht, E., "Freedom of Transit in International Law", 44 *Transactions of Grotius Society*, 1958–59.

Lawrence, R.Z., "Rulemaking Amidst Growing Diversity: A Club-of-Clubs Approach to WTO Reform and New Issue Selection", *Journal of International Economic Law* 9, 2006.

Leaver, T., Meersman, H., Moglia, F. & Van De Voorde, E., "Do Mergers and Alliances Influence European Shipping and Port Competition?", 27 *Journal of Maritime Policy and Management* 4, 2000.

Legatski, R.A., "Port State Jurisdiction over Vessel-Source Pollution", 2 *Harvard Environmental Law Review* 456, 1977.

Li, J. & Li, D. "The Dotted Line on the Chinese Map of the South China Sea: A Note", 34 *Ocean Development & International Law*, 2003.

London C. & Llamas, M., *EC Law on Protection of the Environment and The Free Movement of goods*, London, 1995.

Long, O., *Law and Its Limitations in the GATT Multilateral Trade System,* London, 1987.

Low, P. & Mattoo, A., "Is There a Better Way? Alternative Approaches to Liberalization Under the GATS" presented at the WTO 2000 Global Conference, Geneva, 1999.

Lowe, A.V., "The Right of Entry into Maritime Ports in International Law", 14 *San Diego Law Review*, 1977.

Maddison, A., "Quantifying and interpreting world development: macromeasurement before and after Colin Clark", 44 *Australian Economic History Review* 1, 2004.

Magee, K. "US Cabotage Laws: Protective or Damaging?" Monterey Institute of International Studies, April 2002, available at: <http://www.commercialdiplomacy.org/pdf/ma_projects/magee.pdf>, revisited in July 2006.

Malone, T.C. "The Coastal Module of the Global Ocean Observing System (GOOS): An Assessment of Current Capabilities to Detect Change", 27 *Marine Policy*, 2003.

Mankabady, S., *The International Maritime Organization – International Shipping Law*, Vol. 1, 2nd ed., Beckenham, 1993.

Marin, P.L. & Sicotte, R., "Exclusive Contracts and Market Power: The Case of Ocean Shipping", Centre for Economic Policy Research discussion paper no. 2828, 1999, available at: <http://econ.ucalgary.ca/fac-files/rs/dp2828.pdf>, viewed in October 2001.

Marlow, P. & Nair, R., "Liner Shipping and Information Exchange – a European Perspective", Transport and Shipping Research Group, Logistics and Operations Management Section, Cardiff Business School, Cardiff University, UK, 2006.

Marsden, W. (ed.), *The Travels of Marco Polo*, New York, 1948.

Mashayekhi, M., "GATS 2000 Negotiations: Options for Developing Countries", South Centre, December 2000.

Mattoo, A., "National Treatment in the GATS: Corner-Stone or Pandora's Box?" *Journal of World Trade* 107, 1997.

Mattoo, A., "Shaping Future GATS Rules for Trade in Services", NBER Conference on Trade in Services, Seoul, June 2000.

Mattoo, A., "MFN and the GATS", in: Cottier, T. and Petros, M. (eds.), *Regulatory Barriers and the Principle of Non-discrimination in World Trade Law*. Ann Arbour, 2000.

Mattoo, A., "Liberalizing Trade in Services", World Bank, 2001, available at: <www.worldbank.org/trade>, viewed in June 2002.

McGuire, G., Schuele, M. & Smith, T., "Restrictiveness of international trade in maritime services", in: Findley, C. & Warren, T., *Impediments to Trade in Services: Measurement and Policy Implications*, London, 2000.

McKay, M.R., "Jones Act is always at Risk in Trade Pact Negotiations", American Maritime Officer, available at: <http://www.amo-union.org>, revisited in July 2006.

McRae, D.M., "The WTO in International Law: Tradition Continued or New Frontier", *Journal of International Economic Law* 3, 2000.

Menachof, D., "Risk management methods for the Liner Shipping Industry: the Response to Customer Service Demands for Simplified Tariffs", 28 *Journal of Maritime Policy and Management* 2, 1996.

Mengozzi, P. "The Marrakesh DSU and its implications on the international and European level. The Uruguay Round Results: a European lawyers' perspective". Brussels, 1995.

Mensching, J., "Liner Shipping: Examining the Development and Impact of European Legislation", European Commission Competition Directorate-General, Speech given at Containerization International, 3rd Annual Conference "Global 2000", London, 22 March, 2000.

Messerlin, P. & Zarrouk, J., "Trade Facilitation: Technical Regulations and Customs Procedures", *World Economy* 23, 2000.

Midoro, R. & Pitto, A., "A Critical Evaluation of Strategic Alliances in Liner Shipping", 27 *Journal of Maritime Policy and Management* 1, 2000.

Mills, P. & Tayham, S., "ISM: the Legal Implications", Lloyd's List Maritime Asia, Parliament 47, April 1997.

Molenaar, H.J. & Van de Voorde, E. (eds.), "Competition Policy in Liner Shipping: Proceedings of a Conference", February 1994, Antwerp, Belgium, International Association of Maritime Economists, 1994.

Montero, L. & Francisco, J., "Open Registers: Past, Present and Future", 27 *Marine Policy*, 2003.

Munster, M., "Confidentiality in Service Contracting under the Ocean Shipping Reform Act of 1998", Williams, Mullen, Clarke & Dobbins, Attorneys and Counselors at Law, 2000, available at: <http://www.wmcd.com/articles/maritime/reform.html>, revisited in May 2006.

Murray, C.F., "Any Port in a Storm? The Right of Entry for Reasons of Forece Majeure or Distress in the Wake of the Erika and the Castor", 63 *Ohio State Law Journal* 1465, 2002.

Nambiar, O.K., *Our Seafaring in the Indian Ocean*, Bangalore, 1975.

Nazery, K., "Proposal for a National Maritime Transport Masterplan", Maritime Institute of Malaysia, August 2004.

Neel, R.E., Wooding, C.W. & Padgett, J.H., "Proposed Ocean Shipping Reform Act's likely Effects on Conferences and Rates", 2 *International Advances in Economic Research* 4, November 1996.

Nicolaides, P., "The Problem of Regulation in Traded Services: The Implications for Reciprocal Liberalization", 44: 1 *Aussenwirtschaft* 29, 1989.

Nielsen, J.R., "An Analytical Framework for Studying: Compliance and Legitimacy in Fisheries Management", 27 *Marine Policy*, 2003.

Nijhowne, S., "Classification, the Measurement of Production and International Trade in Services and GATS", Statistics Canada and David Usher, Services Trade Policy, Department of Foreign Affairs and International Trade, Atlanta, Georgia, 1999.

Nordquist, M.H., *United Nations Convention on the Law of the Sea, 1982*, Leiden, 1985.

Northrup, H.R. & Rowan, R.L., "The International Transport Workers' Federation and Flag of Convenience Shipping Industrial Research Unit", Wharton School, University of Pennsylvania, Philadelphia, 1983.

O'Connell, D.P. & Shearer, I.A., "The International Law of the Sea", 78 *American Journal of International Law* 1, January 1984.

Oda, S., "Dispute Settlement Prospects in the Law of the Sea", 44 *International & Comparative Law Quarterly*, 1995.

OECD Working Papers, "Competitive Advantages Obtained by some Shipowners as a Result of Non-Observance of Applicable International Rules and Standards", Volume IV No. 2, Paris, 1996.

OECD Division of Transport, DSTI/DOT/MTC (99) 8, "Discussion Document on Regulatory Reform in International Maritime Transport", 1999.

OECD, Joint MTC/CLP Workshop on Regulatory Reform in Maritime Transport: Submissions, 12 May, 2000 (DSTI/DOT/MTC/(2000) 8 and addendum 1–3).

OECD Working Party of the Trade Committee, "Trade in Services: A Roadmap to GATS MFN Exemptions", TD/TC/WP (2001)25/FINAL, 29 October 2001.

OECD, Working Party of the Trade Committee, the Relationship between Regional Trade Agreement and the Multilateral Trading System, TD/TC/WP(2002)27/FINAL, 09 October 2002.

OECD Division of Transport, DSTI/DOT (2002) 2, "Final Report of Competition Policy in Liner Shipping", 16 April 2002.

OECD Trade Policy Working Paper No. 22, "The Role of Automation in Trade Facilitation", 17 October 2005, TD/TC/WP (2003) 12/FINAL.

OECD Maritime Transport, "UN Hamburg Rules of 1978", available at: <http://www.oecd.org/document>, visited in August 2006.

OECD, "Information Related to the WTO and Maritime Transport Services", available at OECD website: <http://www.oecd.org/document/27/0,2340,en_2649_34367_2087003_1_1_1_1,00.html>, revisited in May 2006.

OECD Secretariat, "Recommendation of the Council concerning Common Principles of Shipping Policy for Member countries", Council Recommendation [(87)11(Final), 13 February 1987] amended on 28 September 2000 – C (2000)124/Final, available at: <http://www.olis.oecd.org/horizontal/oecdacts.nsf>, revisited in July 2006.

OECD Secretariat, "Regulatory Issues in International Maritime Transport", available at: <http://www.oecd.org/dataoecd/0/63/2065436.pdf>, revisited in July 2006.

Oppenheim, L., *International Law (A Treatise)* Vol. I, 8th ed., Lauterpacht, H. (ed.), London, 1955.

Orellana, M., "The Swordfish in Peril: the EU Challenges Chilean Port Access Restrictions at the WTO", BRIDGES, August 2000, available at: <www.ictsd.org>, revisited in August 2006.

Orellana, M., "The EU and Chile Suspended the Swordfish Case Proceedings at the WTO and the International Tribunal of the Law of the Sea", ASIL Insights, February 2001. The paper is available at ASIL website: <www.asil.org>, revisited in August 2006.

Orrego Vicuña, F., *The Exclusive Economic Zone*, Cambridge, 1989.

Orrego Vicuña, F., "Toward an Effective Management of High Sea Fisheries and the Settlement of the Pending Issues of the Law of the Sea" 24 *Ocean Development and International Law*, 1993.

Orrego Vicuña, F., *The Changing International Law of High Seas Fisheries*, Cambridge, 1999.

Oxley, A., *The Challenge of Free Trade*, London, 1990.

Oyejide, T.A., "Interests and Options of Developing Countries and LDCs in a New Round of Multilateral Trade Negotiations", G-24 Discussion Paper No. 2, New York: United Nations, 2000.

Pamborides, G.P., "The Shipping Policy of the EU", *International Journal of Shipping Law*, Part 3, September 1998.

Papavizas, C.G. & Kiern, L.I., "2001–2002 U.S. Maritime Legislative Developments", 34 *Journal of Maritime Law and Commerce*, 2003.

Parameswaran, B., *The Liberalization of Maritime Transport Services, With Special Reference to the WTO/GATS Framework*, Berlin, September 2004.

Pauwelyn, J., "The Role of Public International Law in the WTO: How Far Can We Go?" 95 *The American Journal of International Law*, 2001.

Pauwelyn, J., "The Nature of WTO Obligations", Jean Monnet Working Paper No. 1/02, 2002.

Pauwelyn, J., *Conflict of Norms in Public International Law, How WTO Law Relates to Other Rules of International Law*, Cambridge, 2003.

Pauwelyn, J., "The Jurisdiction of the WTO", in: Proceedings of the 98th Annual Meeting of the American Society of International Law, 2004.

Pauwelyn, J., "WTO Dispute Settlement: Of Sovereign Interests, Private Rights, and Public Goods", in Maskus, K.E. & Reichman J.H. (eds.), *International Public Goods and Transfer of Technology under a Globalized Intellectual Property Regime*, 2005.

Pauwelyn, J., "Expert Advice in WTO Dispute Settlement", in Bermann, G.A. & Mavriodis, P.C. (eds.), *Trade and Human Health and Safety*, 2006.

Perakis, A. & Jaramillo, D., "Fleet Deployment Optimization for Liner Shipping", 18 *Maritime Policy and Management* 3, 1991.

Percy, H.K., Bibliography. "Admiralty and Maritime Law Articles Published in Non-Maritime Law Journals (2002)", 34 *Journal of Maritime Law and Commerce*, 2003.

Pérez-Sánchez, E. & Muir, J.F., "Fishermen Perception on Resources Management and Aquaculture Development in the Mecoacan Estuary, Tabasco, Mexico", 46 *Ocean & Coastal Management*, 2003.

Pergler, C., "Constitutional Recognition of International Law", 30 *Virginia Law Review* 2, March 1944.

Petersmann, E.-U., "Improvements to the Functioning of the GATT System Including Dispute Settlement" A New GATT for the Nineties and Europe '92: international conference held in Tübingen 25–27 July 1990. Baden-Baden, 1991.

Petersmann, E.-U., "GATT Dispute Settlement Proceedings under Article XXIII 1948–1990: Chronological List of Complaints Submitted under GATT Article XXIII to the GATT Contracting Parties or the GATT Council", *Adjudication of International Trade Disputes in International and National Economic Law*, ed. by Petersmann, E.-U. & Jaenicke, G., Fribourg, 1992.

Petersmann, E.-U., "Current Legal Problems in GATT Dispute Settlement Proceedings in the Field of Antidumping Law", *Conflict Resolution in International Trade: a Symposium*, ed. Friedmann, D. & Mestmäcker, E.-J., Baden-Baden, 1993.

Petersmann, E.-U., "Settlement of International Environmental Disputes in GATT and the EC: Comparative Legal Aspects", in: Blokker, N. & Muller, S. (eds.), *Towards More Effective Supervision by International Organizations: Essays in Honor of Henry G. Schermers*, Vol. 1. Dordrecht, 1994.

Petersmann, E.-U., "The GATT Dispute Settlement System as an Instrument of the Foreign Trade Policy of the EC: GATT Article XXIII Dispute Settlement Procedures: Kinds of Complaints and Remedies". *The European Union and World Trade Law: after the GATT Uruguay Round*. Chichester, 1996.

Petersmann, E.-U., *International Trade Law and the GATT/WTO*, Dordrecht, 1997.

Petersmann, E.-U., *The GATT/WTO Dispute Settlement System*, Dordrecht, 1997.

Petersmann, E.-U., "Addressing Institutional Challenges to the WTO in the New Millennium: A Longer-Term Perspective", *Journal of International Economic Law* 8, 2005.

Petronella M. A. & Meilink-Roelofsz, *Asian Trade and European Influence in the Indonesian Archipelago between 1500 and about 1630*, 's-Gravenhage, 1962.

Pickrill, R. A. & Todd, Brian J., "The Multiple Roles of Acoustic Mapping in Integrated Ocean Management, Canadian Atlantic Continental Margin", 46 *Ocean & Coastal Management*, 2003.

Plaza, F., "Port State Control: Towards Global Standardization", *IMO News*, No. 1, 1994.

Pons, J.-F., "Liner Shipping: Market Developments and Government Action – The EU Perspective", EC Competition Directorate-General, Speech given at the 1st International Shipping Convention, London, 18–20 October 2000.

Raghavan, C., "Revised GATS Guidelines Attempt to Mollify Developing World", *Third World Economics* 254, 2001.

Rambusch, L., "The Legal Implications of the ISM Code", Maritime Cyprus 1995 Conference Proceedings, Cyprus, 1995.

Rao, P. S., "Multiple International Judicial Forums: A Reflection of the Growing Strength of International Law or Its Fragmentation?", 25–929 *Michigan Journal of International Law*, 2004.

Rasmussen, H., "The Institutions of the World Trade Law after the WTO Confronted with some of the Legacies of the Past. The Uruguay Round Results: a European Lawyers' Perspective", Brussels, 1995.

Rawlinson, H. G., *Intercourse between India and the Western World: From the Earliest Times to the Fall of Rome*, Cambridge, 1926.

Ready, N., "Port State Control", 2 *International Maritime Law* 6, 1995.

Reeves, J. S., "The Jones Act and the Denunciation of Treaties", 15 *American Journal of International Law* 1, January 1921.

Reid, C., Squires, D., Jeon, Y., Rodwell, L. & Clarke, R., "An Analysis of Fishing Capacity in the Western and Central Pacific Ocean Tuna Fishery and Management Implications", 27 *Marine Policy*, 2003.

Reinhardt, E., "Adjudication without enforcement in GATT disputes", *Journal of Conflict Resolution* 45, 2001.

René, D., "The International Unification of Private Law", 2 *International Encyclopedia of Comparative Law*, Hamburg, 1971.

Reynolds, F., "The Hague Rules, The Hague-Visby Rules, and the Hamburg Rules", 7 *MLAANZ Journal*, 1990.

Richardson, M., "Crimes under Flags of Convenience – in a Depressed Shipping Market, Poor Nations Sell Flags for Criminal Venture" *Maritime Studies* 127, November/December 2002.

Riddle, D.I., *Service-Led Growth: The Role of the Service Sector in World Development*, New York, 1986.

Riphagen, W., "Some Reflections on Functional Sovereignty", 6 *Netherlands Yearbook of International Law* 121, 1975.

Robertson, H.B., "Navigation in the Exclusive Economic Zone", 24 *Virginia Journal of International Law*, 1984.

Rockhill, W.W., "Notes on the Relations and Trade of China with the Eastern Archipelago and the Coast of the Indian Ocean during the Fourteenth Century", 1913, in: Cordier, H., *Ser Marco Polo, Notes and Addenda to Sir Henry Yule's Edition*, Boston, 1920.

Rodrigue, J.-P., Comtois, C. & Slack, B., *The Geography of Transport Systems*, Part I, London, 2006.

Rodrigue, J.-P., "Transportation and Globalization", in: Robertson, R. & Scholte, J.A. (eds.), *Encyclopedia of Globalization*, London, 2007.

Rudolf, J.R. Peritz, *Competition Policy in America, 1888–1892: History, Rhetoric, Law*, New York, 1996.

Ruggiero, R., "Towards GATS 2000 – A European Strategy", address to the Conference on Trade in Services, organized by the European Commission, Brussels, 2 June 1998.

Sacerdoti, G. (book review), "The WTO Dispute Settlement System: 1995–2003" (Studies in Transnational Economic Law, volume 18), edited by Ortino, F. & Petersmann, E.U., The Hague, 2004.

Salas, M. & Jackson, J.H., "Procedural Overview of the WTO EC – banana dispute", *Journal of International Economic Law*, 2000 3 (1).

Sampson, G.P. & Chambers, W.B., *Trade, Environment, and the Millennium*, Tokyo: 1999.

Sapir, A. & Winter, C., "Service Trade" in: Greenaway, D. & Winters, A. (eds.), *Surveys in International Trade*, Oxford, 1994.

Sauvé, P., "Services and the International Contestability of Markets", 5 *Transnational Corporations* 1, 1996.

Sauvé, P. & Wilkie, C., "Investment Liberalization in GATS", in: Sauvé, P. and Stern, R.M. (eds.), *GATS 2000: New Directions in Services Trade Liberalization*, Washington, D.C., 2000.

Schiffman, H., "The Dispute Settlement Mechanism of UNCLOS: A Potentially Important Apparatus for Marine Wildlife Management", *Journal of International Wildlife Law and Policy*, 1998.

Schuyler, R.L., *The Making of English History*, New York, 1952.

Schwarzenberger, G. & Brown, E.D., *A Manual of International Law*, 6th ed., Milton, England, 1975.

Schwarzenberger, G., *The Principles and Standards of International Economic Law*, The Hague, Recueil des Cours – Academie de Droit International (1965/1) 1.

Schwebel, S. M., Wetter, J.G., "Arbitration and the Exhaustion of Local Remedies", 60 *The American Journal of International Law* 3, July 1966.

Sebenius, J.K., *Negotiating the Law of the Sea*, Cambridge, Massachussets, 1984.

Senti, R. & Conlan, P., *WTO Regulation of World Trade after the Uruguay Round*, Zurich, 1997.

Shashikumar, N., "The United States Ocean Shipping Reform Act of 1998: An Analysis of its Economic Impact on Carriers, Shippers and Third Parties", Speech given at the International Association of Maritime Economists Annual Conference "Liner Shipping: What's next?", Halifax, Canada, 13 September, 1999.

Shaw, M.N., "The International Court of Justice: A Practical Perspective", 46 *International & Comparative Law Quarterly*, 1997.

Shiferli, R., "Regional Concepts of Port State Control: A Regional Effort with Global Effects", 11 *Ocean Yearbook*, 1994.

Siebert, H., *Economics of the Environment Theory and Policy*, 5th ed., Heidelberg, 1998.

Sien, C.L., Onyirimba, L.C. & Akpan, G.S., "Liberalization of Maritime Transport Services: Directions and Options for Asia", in: Martin, W. & Pangestu, M. (eds.), *Options for Global Trade Reform, A View from the Asia-Pacific*, Cambridge, 2003.

Sinclair, S., "GATS: How the World Trade Organization's New Services Negotiations Threaten Democracy", Canadian Centre for Policy Alternatives. Ottawa, September 2000.

Sjostrom, W., "Antitrust Immunity for Shipping Conferences: an Empty Core Approach", 38 *Antitrust Bulletin* 2, 1993.

Smith, H.A., *The Law and Custom of the Sea*, 3rd ed., London, 1959.

Smith, G.P., "The Politics of Lawmaking Problems in International Maritime Regulation – Innocent Passage vs. Free Transit", 37 *University of Pittsburgh Law Review* 487, 1976.

Smith, H.D., Editorial, "Emerging Issues in Oceans, Coasts and Islands", 27 *Marine Policy*, 2003.

Sohn, K. & Taek, D.Y., "Does the International Trade Help to Enhance National Security?" available at: <http://www.eastwestcenter.org>, revisited in July 2006.

Song, Y.-H. "The Overall Situation in the South China Sea in the New Millennium: Before and After the September 11 Terrorist Attacks", 34 *Ocean Development & International Law*, 2003.

Sorice, M.G., Shafer, C.S. & Scott, D., "Managing Endangered Species within the Use/Preservation Paradox: Understanding and Defining Harassment of the West Indian Manatee (Trichechus manatus)", 31 *Coastal Management*, 2003.

Southcott, R.F. & Walsh, K.A., "Canadian Maritime Law Update: 2002", 34 *Journal of Maritime Law and Commerce*, 2003.

Srinivasan, T.N., *Developing Countries and the Multilateral Trading System*, New York, 1998.

Staring, G.S., "Admiralty and Maritime Law: Selected Topics" 26 *Tort & Ins. L.J.*, 538, 1991.

Stavrianos, L.S., *The World Since 1500: A Global History*, Englewood, New Jersey, 1966.

Stephenson, C. & Marcham, F.G., (eds.), *Sources of English Constitutional History*, New York, 1937.

Stephenson, S., "Approaches to Services Liberalization by Developing Countries", a Publication of the Organization of American States Trade Unit, February 1999, available at: <http://www.sice.oas.org/tunit/studies>, revisited in July 2006.

Stephenson, S. & Yi, S., "Transparency in Regulation of Services", paper prepared for the APEC Group on Services meeting held on 19–20 February 2002.

Stern, R., "Quantifying Barriers to Trade in Services", in: Hoekman, B., English, P. & Mattoo, A. (eds.), *Development, Trade and the WTO: A Handbook*, Washington, 2002.

Stevenson, D.B., "Tanker Crew Fatigue: Some New Solutions to an Old Problem", 27 *Journal of Maritime Law and Commerce* 3, July 1996.

Stewart, T.P., *Dispute Settlement Mechanisms. The GATT Uruguay Round: a Negotiating History (1986–1992)*, Vol. II, Deventer, 1993.

Stone, F., "Canada, the GATT and the International Trade System", Montreal, 1984.

Stopford, M., *Maritime Economics*, London, 1997.

Streit, M.E. & Voigt, S., "The Economics of Conflict Resolution in International Trade Conflict Resolution in International Trade: a Symposium", Friedmann, D. & Mestmäcker, E.-J. (eds.), *Conflict Resoluation in International Trade*, Munich, 1993.

Sturmey, S.G., "The Open Registry Controversy and the Developing Issue", The Institute of Shipping Economics, Bremen, 1983.

Tetley, W., "Glossary of International Conventions and National Laws of Canada, the United States, the United Kingdom, France and the People's Republic of China on Maritime Law", available at: <http://tetley.law.mcgill.ca>, visited in April 2001 and revisited in August 2005.

Thao, N.H., "The 2002 Declaration on the Conduct of Parties in the South China Sea: A Note", 34 *Ocean Development & International Law*, 2003.

Thompson, C.A., "Shipping Act of 1916: The Effect of Section 15 on the Sherman Anti-trust Law", 22 *Michigan Law Review* 2, December 1923.

Trans-Atlantic Conference Agreement (TACA), "Trans-Atlantic Conference Agreement submission to the OECD Division of Transport Inquiry on Regulatory Reform in Maritime Transport", March 2001.

Transport Canada, Shipping Conferences Exemption Act of 1987: Consultation Paper, Transport Canada, July 1999, available at: <www.tc.gc.ca/pol/en>, viewed in October 2001.

Transport Intermediaries Association, "Transport Intermediaries Association and American International Freight Association Submission to the OECD Division of Transport Inquiry on Regulatory Reform in Maritime Transport", June 2001.

Treves, T., "Conflicts between the International Tribunal for the Law of the Sea and the International Court of Justice", 31: 809 *International Law and Politics*, 2004.

UN Secretary General, "Study of the Question of Free Access to the Sea of Landlocked Countries and of the Special Problems of Landlocked Countries Relating to the Exploration and Exploitation of the Resources of the Seabed and the Ocean Floor beyond the Limits of National Jurisdiction", UN Doc A/AC 138/37, 1971.

UNCTAD report: Economic Co-operation in Merchant Shipping – Treatment of Foreign Merchant Vessels in Ports, UNCTAD/TD/B/C. 4/136, 9 September 1975.

UNCTAD (1998), Review of Maritime Transport 1998, New York and Geneva: United Nations.

UNCTAD (1999), Review of Maritime Transport 1999, New York and Geneva: United Nations.

UNCTAD (2000), Review of Maritime Transport 2000, New York and Geneva: United Nations.

UNCTAD, Duty and Quota Free Market Access for LDCs: An Analysis of Quad Initiatives, Geneva: UNCTAD, 2001.

UNCTAD (2002), Review of Maritime Transport 2002, New York and Geneva: United Nations.

UNCTAD, "Negotiations on Transport and Logistics Services: Issues to Consider", UNCTAD/SDTE/TLB/2005/3.

UNECE "Trade Facilitation: The Challenges for Growth and Development", Geneva: United Nations Commission for Europe, 2003.

United Nations Document LC/G. 2027, Economic Commission for Latin American and the Caribbean, Concentration in Liner Shipping: Its Causes and Impacts for Ports and Shipping Services in Developing Regions, Santiago, Chile, 1998.

United Nations, *The Law of the Sea: Rights of Access of Land-locked States to and from the Sea, and Freedom of Transit – Legislative History of Part X, Articles 124–132 of the United Nations Convention on the Law of the Sea*, New York: United Nations, 1987.

United States Department of Justice, Nannes, J., Free Market Antitrust Immunity Reform Act of 1999: Statement of John Nannes, Deputy Assistant Attorney General, Antitrust Division, US Department of Justice before the House Committee on the Judiciary on H.R. 3138, 22 March 2000.

Valencia, M.J., "Asia, the Law of the Sea and International Relations", 73 *International Affairs (Royal Institute of International Affairs 1944)* 2, Asia and the Pacific, April 1997, New York and Geneva: United Nations.

Valenzuela, M., "IMO: Public International Law and Regulation", in: Johnson, D.M., & Letalic, N.G., *The Law of the Sea and Ocean Industry: New Opportunities and Restraints*, 16th Annual Conference of the Law of the Sea Institute, University of Hawaii, 1983.

Vandenbosch, A. & Willard, N.H., *The United Nations: Background, Organization, Functions, Activities*, New York, 1952.

VanGrasstek, C. & Sauvé, P., "The Consistency of WTO Rules: Can the Single Undertaking Be Squared with Variable Geometry?", 9 Journal of *International Economic Law*, 2006.

Victor, D.G., "Design options for Article 13 of the Framework Convention on Climate Change: lessons from the GATT Dispute Panel system", working paper no. er95001, Laxenburg: International Institute for Applied Systems Analysis, 1995.

Vieira, M.B., "Mare Liberum vs. Mare Clausum: Grotius, Freitas, and Selden's Debate on Dominion over the Seas", 64 *Journal of the History of Ideas* 3, July 2003.

Waesche, D.M., "Choice and Uniformity of Law Generally" Admiralty Law Institute Symposium: Marine Insurance, 66 *Tulane Law Review*, 1991.

Wang, G., "The Nanhai Trade: A Study of the Early History of Chinese Trade in the South China Sea", 31 *Journal of the Royal Asiatic Society Malayan Branch* 2, Kuala Lumpur, 1959.

Wang, Z.K. & Winters, L.A., "Putting 'Humpty' Together Again: Including Developing Countries in a Consensus for the WTO", Discussion Paper no. 2297, London, 2000.

Warren, T. and Findlay, C., "How Significant are the Barriers? Measuring Impediments to Trade in Services," paper presented at the "Services 2000: New Directions in Services Trade Liberalization" Conference at the University Club in Washington DC, 1–2 June 1999.

Watson, A., *Revised English-language Edition of the Digest of Justinian*, Philadelphia, 1997.

Webb, R., "Coastal Shipping: An Overview", Parliament of Australia, Research Paper No. 12, 2003–04, May 2004.

Whiteman, M.M., *Digest of International Law* 4, US Department of State Publication, 1965.

Wilkinson, J., "The First Declaration of the Freedom of the Seas: The Rhodian Sea Laws", Appendix to Chapter XIX of John Wilkinson's paper *A Tentative Program for Simulation of Historical Ecology of the Mediterranean,*

The Mediterranean Marine Environment and Development of Region, Malta.

Wilson, J. S., "Bridging the Standards Divide: Recommendations for Reform from a Development Perspective", World Bank, 2001, available at: <www.worldbank.org/trade>, viewed in August 2002.

Wood, D. P., "The Impossible Dream: Real International Antitrust", University of Chicago Legal Forum, 1992.

World Bank, "Trade Blocs", *Policy Research Report*, Washington D.C., 2000.

WTO, Working Group on the Interaction between Trade and Competition Policy, Communication from the United States, WT/WGTCP/W/35, 1 October, 1997.

WTO Annual Report for 1997, Special Study on Trade and Competition Policy; American Bar Association, Report of the Sections of Antitrust Law and International Law and Practice on the Internationalizing of Competition Law Rules: Coordination and Convergence 17–19, 2000.

WTO Council for Trade in Services, "Maritime Transport Services, Background Note by the Secretariat", S/C/W/62, 16 November 1998.

WTO Council for Trade in Services, "Article VI: 4 of the GATS: Disciplines on Domestic Regulation Applicable to all Services", Note by the Secretariat, S/C/W/96, 1 March 1999.

WTO Draft Final Report of the Working Party on Preshipment Inspection, G/PSI/WP/W/24, 5 March 1999.

WTO Secretariat, "the Fundamental WTO Principles of National Treatment, Most-Favored-Nation Treatment and Transparency", WT/WGTCP/W/114, 1999.

WTO Secretariat, *Guide to the Uruguay Round Agreements*, The Hague/Boston, 1999.

WTO Secretariat, "Recent Developments in Services Trade", 9 February 1999, S/C/W/94, available at: <http://docsonline.wto.org>, quoted in Gould, E., The 2001 GATS Negotiations: The Political Challenge Ahead, The Alliance for Democracy, March 2001, available at: <www.theallianceforDemocracy.org/campaigns/2000>, viewed in September 2002.

WTO, Working Group on the Interaction between Trade and Competition Policy, Communication from Hong Kong, China, Contribution of Competition Policy to Achieving the Objectives of the WTO, WT/WGTCP/W/118, May 26, 1999.

WTO Secretariat, Trade in Services Division, "An Introduction to the GATS", October 1999, available at: <http://www.union-network.org/unisite/regions/africa/pdf/labourissues/gatsintroduction.pdf>, revisited in August 2006.

WTO, Working Group on the Interaction between Trade and Competition Policy, Communication from the United States, Creating a Culture of Competition: Issues Involved in Establishing an Effective Antitrust Agency, WT/WFTCP/W/142, August 2000.

WTO Secretariat, *Guide to the GATS, An Overview of Issues for Further Liberalization of Trade in Services*, The Hague, 2000.

WTO Council for Trade in Services, "Joint Statement from the European Communities and Their Member States; Hong Kong, China; Japan; Republic of Korea; Norway and Singapore, the Negotiations on Maritime Transport Services", S/CSS/W/8, 6 October 2000.

WTO Council for Trade in Services, "Maritime Transport Services, Background Note by the Secretariat", S/CSS/W/106, 4 October 2001.

WTO Dispute Settlement Body Special Session, Negotiations on the Dispute Settlement Understanding, "Proposals on DSU by Cuba, Honduras, India, Indonesia, Malaysia, Pakistan, Sri Lanka, Tanzania and Zimbabwe", TN/DS/W/19, 9 October 2002.

WTO Negotiating Group on Trade Facilitation, "Clarifications and Improvements in the GATT Article VIII, Proposals on Simplification, Reduction and Standardization of Trade Documents", TN/TF/W/36, 29 April 2005, Communication from New Zealand, Norway and Switzerland.

WTO, "The General Agreement on Trade in Services (GATS): objectives, coverage and disciplines", available at: <http://www.wto.org/english/tratop_e/serv_e/gatsqa_e.htm>, revisited in July 2006.

Wyatt, D. & Dashwood, A., *European Community Law*, 3rd ed., London, 1993.

Young, Ch., "Comprehensive Revision of the STCW: An Overview", 26 *Journal of Maritime Law and Commerce* 1, January 1995.

Zanamwe, G. "Trade Facilitation and the WTO: a critical analysis of the proposals on trade facilitation and their implications for African countries", tralac Working Paper, No. 5/2005, September 2005.

Studies in Global Economic Law
Studien zum globalen Wirtschaftsrecht
Études en droit économique mondial

Present and future economic, technological and societal changes and evolutions fundamentally affect traditional legal structures of the territorial state system. They increasingly call for global approaches and solutions, transgressing the tools of classical public international law. This trilingual series publishes monographs, studies and collected papers dedicated to these challenges. The contributions examine existing instruments, in particular within the framework of the international trading system. They explore new approaches and search for innovative solutions within the global process of legal integration. Research efforts are dedicated to different walks of life and areas of regulation, and to the quest for adequate constitutional structures of transnational and democratic processes.

Wirtschaftliche, technologische und gesellschaftliche Entwicklungen der Gegenwart und Zukunft bewirken tiefgreifende Änderungen traditioneller Strukturen des Rechts des Territorialstaats und rufen zunehmend nach globalen Vorgehensweisen und Lösungen, die oftmals über das Instrumentarium des klassischen Völkerrechts hinaus weisen. Die dreisprachige Reihe publiziert Monographien, Studien und Tagungsbände, die sich vertieft mit diesen Herausforderungen auseinandersetzen. Die Beiträge untersuchen das bestehende Instrumentarium namentlich im Rahmen des Welthandelssystems und forschen nach neuen Ansätzen und Lösungen im Rahmen des globalen Integrationsprozesses. Dazu gehören Studien zu den Regelungen einzelner Sach- und Lebensbereiche wie auch zu Fragen adäquater transnationaler demokratischer Verfassungs- und Entscheidungsstrukturen.

Les évolutions actuelles et futures sur le plan technique, économique et social ne cesseront d'influencer profondément les structures traditionnelles du droit de l'état territorial. Par conséquent, des approches et des solutions dépassant les instruments du droit international public classique deviennent de plus en plus nécessaires. Cette collection trilingue publie des monographies, études et actes de colloques qui analysent et font face à ces défis. Les contributions examinent les instruments existants, notamment dans la domaine du système commercial mondiale. Elles cherchent à développer des approches nouvelles et des solutions innovatrices dans le contexte du processus d'intégration globale en incluant des études de droit touchant aux différents secteurs et domaines de vie. De plus, les travaux de recherche seront également destinés à trouver les procédures consti-tutionnelles et décisionnelles les plus adéquates et démocratiques au niveau transnational.

Studies in Global Economic Law
Studien zum globalen Wirtschaftsrecht
Études en droit économique mondial

edited by Thomas Cottier

Vol. 1 Martin A. Girsberger – Biodiversity and the Concept of Farmers' Rights in International Law. Factual Background and Legal Analysis, 1999

Vol. 2 David Wyss – Bankdienstleistungen im Allgemeinen Dienstleistungsabkommen der WTO. Auswirkungen auf das schweizerische Bankenrecht, 1999

Vol. 3 Benoît Merkt – Harmonisation internationale et entraide administrative internationale en droit de la concurrence. Droit du GATT/OMC, droit européen, accords bilatéraux et perspectives pour le droit suisse, 2000

Vol. 4 Ingo Meitinger – Der Schutz von Geschäftsgeheimnissen im globalen und regionalen Wirtschaftsrecht. Stand und mögliche Entwicklungen der internationalen und regionalen Rechtsharmonisierung, 2001

Vol. 5 Joëlle de Sépibus – Die Umweltschutzsubvention im Gemeinschaftsrecht. Eine umweltrechtliche Kritik der europäischen Beihilfekontrolle, 2003

Vol. 6 Bobjoseph Mathew – The WTO Agreements on Telecommunications, 2003

Vol. 7 Lukas Engelberger – Die unmittelbare Anwendbarkeit des WTO-Rechts in der Schweiz. Grundlagen und Perspektiven im Kontext internationaler Rechtsentwicklungen, 2004

Vol. 8 Thomas M. Fischer – Die Entbündelung der letzten Meile in der Schweiz im Lichte des GATS, 2004

Vol. 9 Dae-Won Kim – Non-Violation Complaints in WTO Law. Theory and Practice, 2006

Vol. 10 Qi Zhang – Consultation within WTO Dispute Settlement. A Chinese Perspective, 2007

Vol. 11 FELIX BLOCH – Technologietransfer zum internationalen Umweltschutz. Eine völkerrechtliche Untersuchung unter besonderer Berücksichtigung des Schutzes der Ozonschicht und des Weltklimas, 2007

Vol. 12 BETTINA BECK – Die Regelung von Slots (Zeitnischen) im Luftverkehrsrecht. Vergabe, Übertragung und Anfechtung in der Schweiz und der EG unter rechtsvergleichender Berücksichtigung US-amerikanischer Normen, 2008

Vol. 13 Forthcoming

Vol. 14 CHUYANG LIU – Maritime Transport Services in the Law of the Sea and the World Trade Organization, 2009